THE OFFICIA

MW00719128

A Guide Book of
The Official Red Book
of United States Coins®

Frank J. Colletti

Forewords by Kenneth Bressett
and Q. David Bowers

Whitman
Publishing, LLC
PUBLISHING SINCE 1934

A Guide Book of
The Official Red Book
of United States Coins®

Other books in 🌐 THE OFFICIAL RED BOOK® series include *A Guide Book of Lincoln Cents; A Guide Book of United States Tokens and Medals; A Guide Book of Gold Dollars; A Guide Book of Peace Dollars; A Guide Book of Morgan Silver Dollars; A Guide Book of Double Eagle Gold Coins; A Guide Book of United States Type Coins; A Guide Book of Modern United States Proof Coin Sets; A Guide Book of Shield and Liberty Head Nickels; A Guide Book of Buffalo and Jefferson Nickels; A Guide Book of Flying Eagle and Indian Head Cents; A Guide Book of Washington and State Quarters; A Guide Book of United States Commemorative Coins; A Guide Book of Barber Silver Coins;* and *A Guide Book of Liberty Seated Silver Coins.*

For a complete catalog of numismatic reference books, supplies, and storage products, visit Whitman Publishing online at www.whitman**books**.com.

CONTENTS

ABOUT THE AUTHOR

Frank J. Colletti is a Certified Public Accountant with an interest in coin collecting and metal detecting. His coin collection was started in 1962 when he received a Barber quarter in payment on his paper route. During the subsequent years, with periodic times away from the hobby, his interest in numismatics grew. He has had well over 100 articles published in various metal-detecting publications, including monthly columns on coin collecting ("Money Talk") and the good deeds that metal detectorists perform ("Civic Patrol"). He feels that metal detectorists may be able to locate scarce and unusual coins and should become knowledgeable about  their finds. He encourages them to learn about their finds with the hope that it will kindle an interest in forming a collection, as opposed to an accumulation.

Frank is married to Ilene and has two children, Ariel and Alex, who have come to accept his strange obsessions.

CREDITS AND ACKNOWLEDGMENTS

I would like to thank Rich Schemmer, Fred Weinberg, and Richard J. Thomson Jr. for their contributions to this book. I would also like to thank all of the *Guide Book* contributors and others who took the time to describe their experiences for me.

A special thank-you to Dave Bowers and Ken Bressett for writing the forewords to this book.

Most importantly, I would like to thank my family. Thanks to my wife Ilene and my son Alex for their patience with this project. A special thank-you to my daughter Ariel for editing my manuscript and finding my errors.

This book is dedicated to my family, for their patience and help, and to Charlie, who patiently listened to me read many of these pages.

The following people and organizations graciously provided assistance. The author and publisher would like to thank them for their contributions.

American Numismatic Association Archives
Q. David Bowers
Kenneth Bressett
Coin World Archives
David Crenshaw
Charles Davis
Estate of Abe Kosoff
George F. Kolbe
David W. Lange
Tom Mulvaney
Bill Spencer
University of Wisconsin-Madison Archives

FOREWORD

by Kenneth Bressett

When R.S. Yeoman published the first edition of his now-famous *Guide Book of United States Coins* in 1946, he could hardly have guessed that a day would come when another book would be written recounting the history of his effort. Nor could he have envisioned his book becoming a collectible in its own right. Yet that is just what has happened to this unique coin reference. It is probably every author's dream that their published work will pass the test of time, but few books have ever achieved the longevity of what has turned out to be the world's most popular coin price guide.

The genesis and development of what has become known simply as the "Red Book" are ably narrated by author Frank Colletti in the fascinating account given in this book. The numerous editions of *A Guide Book of United States Coins* that have been issued annually since its inception have, over the years, become a mainstay of the coin hobby, and a challenge to collectors to save as sets for a permanent reference to track the price performance of their coins. A complete set of Red Books can now be assembled only through a combination of chance and persistence. The result of such effort, however, provides the collector with a wealth of information about U.S. numismatics, an excellent insight into coin values and price trends, and an important asset that continues to grow each year.

It was my pleasure to have known R.S. Yeoman from my early days in numismatics, in 1948, to the time of his death 40 years later. My respect for him never wavered. He was a man of the highest integrity, gentle, thoughtful of others, and a keen businessman. His understanding of coin collectors kept him always in tune with their needs and wishes. It was his desire to provide collectors with products that were as precise as possible, sparing no effort to give unbiased pricing information and up-to-date numismatic information.

Dick Yeoman's involvement in the hobby was ubiquitous. He traveled extensively and was a keynote speaker throughout the country at local and national coin shows. He was always available to converse with young and old alike about their involvement in numismatics. As a keen observer of trends and events, he instinctively knew what was missing from the marketplace and set to work developing products that would satisfy collectors' needs. Not content with producing the first and only book dedicated to giving factual, unbiased pricing information for people who had coins to sell (the *Handbook of United States Coins*), he immediately set about designing the *Guide Book*, as a companion piece that would give even more information and list current retail prices for all U.S. coins. Later he expanded the Whitman line of coin collectors' products into the most extensive ever produced. The coverage included books on many areas of numismatics, coin folders and holders of all kinds, and a broad array of related accessories.

The legacy that Yeoman left to the hobby lives on in annual editions of the Red Book. Over time, countless numismatists, students, collectors, and dealers have contributed to the vast amount of information contained in "their" book. The work has become something of a community effort, as users have assumed ownership and share in making it as useful and accurate as possible through their ever-watchful eyes. No typographical errors ever go unnoticed, and no erroneous prices go unchallenged; the numismatic community demands that each edition be as accurate as possible.

Orchestrating the efforts of numerous contributions each year is the mission of the book's editor, and I have been blessed with that responsibility for many years. After working directly under the guidance of Dick Yeoman for over 15 years as co-coordinating editor for all Whitman products, I assumed full editorship of the *Guide Book* in 1975.

Throughout the years it has been my privilege to work with many of the leading numismatic dealers and scholars. Among the hundreds of experts who have contributed to the content of the book is my son Philip Bressett, a keen numismatist and companion, who has assisted in the pricing compilations since 1980. My involvement has been a richly rewarding experience, for which I will be eternally grateful to my friend Dick Yeoman.

The story of *A Guide Book of United States Coins* as told by Frank Colletti in this fascinating account is not merely a story about those who produced it, but a tribute to the thousands of individual contributors who have honed its contents to the point that it has become a numismatic standard and a valuable collectible in its own right. It is a success story that remains unparalleled by any other similar book.

Kenneth Bressett worked with R.S. Yeoman for more than 20 years. "My respect for him never wavered," says Bressett. Here they are joined by Western Publishing president Gerald Slade as they celebrate another edition of the *Guide Book*.

FOREWORD

by Q. David Bowers

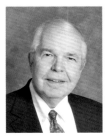

In 1952, when I first discovered numismatics by way of looking for Lincoln cents to fill the spaces in a blue Whitman folder, there was one and only one source on pricing information: *A Guide Book of United States Coins.* This gave the approximate retail price of everything from colonials to commemoratives, including Lincoln cents. My first use was to check the values of the rarities I hoped to find in pocket change, such as the 1909-S V.D.B., 1914-D, and 1931-S. I never was lucky enough to find them on my own, and later did as most collectors do—bought them from a dealer.

Now in the early 21st century there are more price information sources than can be imagined—ranging from the Internet to supplements in magazines plus any number of books and booklets. However, among all of this competition, the *Guide Book* stands supreme, as *the* source for authoritative information. In recent years I have been the research editor, working with editor Ken Bressett, a very pleasurable experience. Each year I and others within Whitman exchange ideas, consider the addition or dropping of certain varieties, and seek improvements. Every year in every way the *Guide Book* continues to get better. Skeptical? Just compare the current edition with one of 10 or 20 years ago.

Along the way the *Guide Book* has become a collectible in its own right, with the focal point being the first edition, bearing the cover date of 1947, but issued in 1946. R.S. Yeoman, the author, was not a technical numismatist at the time. He drew upon the talents of Stuart Mosher to do most of the legwork in assembling the *Guide Book*, later presenting him with the very first copy of the first edition. Mosher donated this to the Library of Congress, which in its infinite wisdom decided to deaccession it a few years ago. One way or another it ended up in an auction conducted by our company, where a frantic bidding frenzy ensued, and it sold for $4,180.

In time, Ken Bressett, who was the numismatic expert at Whitman Publishing Company, then located in Racine, Wisconsin, became the main editor of the *Guide Book*, working under Yeoman. After the latter's passing in 1988, Ken was full editor, a position that he enjoys today.

Back in about 1956 Ken and I, and a number of other numismatists interested in writing and research, formed the Rittenhouse Society. This met informally until 1960, when we decided to make it official, setting up some rules to admit new members. Since that time it has grown to include several dozen members by invitation. Since the 1950s, and before my association with Whitman, Ken and I have continued to be close friends and collaborators and consultants on certain research projects.

Every once in a while I would tease Ken—this being when he was out in Racine—by giving him improbable ideas. The *Guide Book*, as I call it to this day, became known as the "Red Book" to many. Ken decided to make this official and put this as a subtitle on the first page, or publicized it, or whatever. I wrote him a mock-serious letter stating that this was an unfortunate step, as, first of all, there might have been some editions that had covers other than red, and, second, what if the *Guide Book* wanted to use a different hue? Ken thereupon made up a special copy bound in gray, with all of the proper stamping on it, and sent it to me as the only one known.

One of Dick Yeoman's favorite stories involved someone coming up to him at a convention and showing him a *Guide Book* that had been bound with the cover upside down. Immediately, Dick apologized and said, "I'll replace it!"

This wasn't what the collector wanted. He was very proud of this misprint, considering it to have great value, and would not have parted with it for the world!

Longtime friends and colleagues on the *Guide Book*, Q. David Bowers and Kenneth Bressett have a custom of exchanging one-of-a-kind versions of the venerable reference. This unique fur-covered 30th edition was presented by Bowers to Bressett.

Bowers and Bressett autograph the year's new Red Book at the June 2004 Whitman Coin and Collectibles Atlanta Expo. Behind them are life-size likenesses of themselves and of other Whitman numismatic authors.

PREFACE

Throughout the 1970s, I acquired quite a number of different editions of the *Guide Book*, but not in a systematic manner. Instead, I accumulated them randomly as I methodically expanded my coin collection. Sometimes, intrigued, I would flip through them. Other times, my interest waned. During one of these down times, I traded them to an antique book dealer in exchange for bindings for my old book collection. Now, I occasionally wonder about the editions that were given away that day. I can only hope they weren't particularly scarce or early editions.

I attended the 2001 ANA convention, held in New York City, to search for Barber dimes and quarters. There I had the pleasure of meeting Remy Bourne, a prominent numismatic bookseller. Our enlightening discussion convinced me to immediately purchase one of his special-edition Red Books. I returned home and started my search for other special editions. I was hooked. My collection of Red Books gradually grew and changed.

Everywhere I looked—old auction catalogs, Internet auction lots, other collectors, and dealers—there were different opinions and ideas regarding what was available in the realm of *Guide Book* collecting. I knew about the two different printings of the first edition, but what other special or authorized editions were available? I found the *Coin World* 1970 premium edition, and then the 1985 *Coin World* edition. But how much should I pay for them? Were they rare? Scarce? Valuable? Or common? Were there any others?

Starting in the 1995 edition of the *Guide Book*, Ken Bressett added a section discussing the Red Book as a collectible. Although this section offered tremendous guidance as far as regular editions—and even some special editions—were concerned, I needed to know about the authorized editions and the error printings. I felt the need to document the extra value attached to presentation and editing copies.

And thus, this book was born out of necessity. More Red Books are described in the pages of this book than anywhere else.

Of course, there are still more unanswered questions and other varieties that may not be listed here. For that reason, I ask you, the reader of this book, to contribute any information that you deem necessary for the next edition of this reference. Please feel free to forward any additional comments, corrections, and new information that may be available to you.

Frank J. Colletti
East Meadow, New York

HOW TO USE THIS BOOK

The question of organizing a book so that the maximum number of readers will be able to easily locate the information they need is one that has dogged the makers of the Red Book throughout its publication. Similarly, in a book *about* the Red Book, one faces the dilemma of whether, for example, readers will expect to see leather Limited Editions discussed alongside regular hardbacks. Are they like Proof coins, which the *Guide Book* groups with standard circulation-strike issues? Or are they more akin to commemorative issues, and deserving of their own section of the book?

We have chosen to operate on the latter basis, so the reader will find separate chapters for limited and special editions (chapter 5), authorized editions (chapter 6), and varieties such as editing copies and error books (chapter 7). Unique Red Books created for special circumstances and never intended for distribution are discussed in chapter 8 along with collectibles related to the Red Book—both official Whitman products and curiosities not meant for circulation.

For convenience, value listings for all official Red Book issues of a given edition are grouped under the standard edition's listing in chapter 4. Readers who would like detailed information on a particular special edition, Limited Edition, or authorized edition can consult the pertinent chapter, which is cross-referenced within the entry. Values for items in chapters 7 and 8 are given in the text.

The dating system of the Red Book gives each edition a cover date a year ahead of its publication date. For the individual listings in chapter 4 of all standard Red Book editions, each issue is identified by its edition number, with the cover date—*not* the publication year—following in parentheses. The actual year of publication is discussed in each listing's "The year was . . ." feature, which should help to orient the reader by placing each edition in its context. Similarly, in chapters 5 through 7, listings give the year of the cover date on the edition in question, not the actual year in which the book was printed and distributed. Chapter 8 follows a different pattern because for the most part it covers nonbook items. Where this chapter gives a date in a heading, it is the actual year that the item was produced. The appendix, which discusses several editions of the Blue Book, follows the conventions of chapter 4.

As numismatists through the years have noted, previous editions of the *Guide Book* are an invaluable resource for studying price changes over time. To illustrate this, and to put each Red Book into the context of its time, each listing contains a chart giving the values for two coins according to that edition of the Red Book: the 1895 Philadelphia (P) dollar and the 1903 New Orleans (O) Morgan dollar. To quote the advertisements of many financial institutions, "Past performance is no guarantee of future results"—but the historical study of price performance is both enjoyable and educational for the hobbyist.

Finally, appearing throughout the book are "Red Book Recollections," narratives written by Red Book contributors, collectors, or cognoscenti. These personal reflections offer different perspectives on the long-lived reference work.

EARLY COIN-PRICING REFERENCES

Reference books for determining the value of U.S. coins are modern tools rather than historical ones. When coin collecting caught on in America in the mid-19th century, available information for pricing coins was very limited. Most collectors seeking coin values had to make do with what they could derive by studying auction catalogs or dealers' price lists. Although auction records could provide a fair representation of cost, dealers' price lists were influenced more by their desire to make money than by any inclination to provide a fair market value. In 1859 a collector could consult the new reference work by Montroville W. Dickeson, the sweepingly titled *American Numismatical Manual of the Currency or Money of the Aborigines, and Colonial, State and United States Coins*, but its contents mixed fact with "legends and downright fairy tales," in the words of numismatic author David T. Alexander.[1] Only after decades of influential works on coin values would the Red Book become possible.

J.W. SCOTT

Although known today as the "father of American philately," John Walter Scott was an important figure in numismatic history as well. Born in England in 1845, Scott moved to America while still in his teens, and after a brief stint seeking California gold he settled in New York. There, in 1867, he founded J.W. Scott & Co., which would become one of the largest stamp and coin businesses in the world. He would ultimately, in fact, found *two* businesses under his own name—a wrinkle that led to a bizarre court case in which he found himself defending his right to use his own name!

As early as 1871 Scott published a price catalog for American coins, and in 1875 he founded the *Coin Collector's Journal*, a magazine that would continue publication through 1888. (It would be revived nearly half a century later by an even more important figure in numismatics, Wayte Raymond.) A shorter-lived publication, his *American Journal of Philately and Coin Advertiser*, lasted only from 1879 to 1886. Perhaps his greatest contribution to the development of the coin-pricing reference was his 1906 catalog, *Standard Coin Catalogue No. 1: The Silver Coins of the World, to Which Is Added U.S. National and Territorial Gold*. It was reprinted in 1913, and by R.S. Yeoman's reckoning the collecting community then had to face a void of nearly 20 years before an equally useful resource came on the scene—Raymond's *Standard Catalogue*.

In 1884 Scott sold his original business, which had become known as the Scott Stamp & Coin Co., but financial reverses led him to launch another stamp company five years later under the J.W. Scott moniker. After successfully defending a lawsuit brought by the purchasers of the first Scott company, he settled into a(nother) thriving career as a stamp dealer. In 1906, the same year that the influential *Standard Coin Catalogue* first appeared, he joined what was then known as the American Numismatic and Archaeological Society. (The next year it would revert to its original name, by which it is still known today: the American Numismatic Society, or ANS.) When Scott died in 1919, however, he was most famous for his contributions to the field of stamp collecting. Through his "Scott catalogs" of stamp values, he essentially became to the field of philately what R.S. Yeoman would be to numismatics.

WILLIAM VON BERGEN

In the late 19th century, Boston coin dealer William von Bergen released the first of two influential references on contemporary coin pricing. *The Rare Coins of America, England, Ireland, Scotland, France, Germany, and Spain*, which was first published around 1885 and would go through numerous editions, is a fascinating look at the coin market of this time. It sold for $1.00 in hardcover and was, according to von Bergen's note, "bound in cloth and gold, gilt edge." Von Bergen's focus was clearly commercial, as can be seen in his "Terms to Agents and Collectors":

> In order to meet the constantly increasing demand for rare coins, a few intelligent and respectable persons (ladies or gentlemen) can have profitable employment in collecting them, and by following the instruction given here can make at least $7 per day, and some day an agent might make $100 or $1000 if he is lucky enough to come across a lot of rare coins of which the owner does not know the value. . . . [But] a collector ought not to depend upon buying coins to make his pay, but upon selling the Coin Books.

Here von Bergen manages to make his book doubly desirable: not only could it show the collector how to profit from collecting (if necessary, through others' ignorance), but

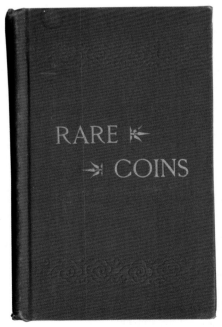
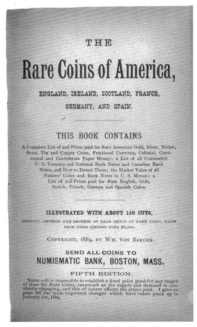

This fifth-edition copy of William von Bergen's *Rare Coins* dates to 1889 and measures a compact 4 by 6-3/8 inches.

it would practically sell itself to the collector's like-minded friends. A pyramid scheme like this would be right at home in today's infomercials!

As a reference to coin values, *Rare Coins* is far from objective: the prices given are what von Bergen was willing to pay for the coins listed, and his own collecting preferences serve as the arbiter of value. To read this book is to take a fascinating trip through time and into the mind of this collector. Von Bergen describes Civil War tokens, for example, this way: "Issued by different parties during the late war of the Rebellion. There are about 500 different patterns. None are very valuable, and average not over 5 cents apiece. I have no use for them and do not buy them at present." These days, of course, Civil War tokens are quite popular, with some specimens worth thousands of dollars.

Other listings also reveal interesting idiosyncrasies. For the silver three-cent piece, von Bergen makes it clear that "positively uncirculated ones or proof only [are] wanted. 1851 to 1863 I do not want." Regarding two-cent pieces, he states, "only those coined in 1872 and 1873 are wanted, and they must be strictly proofs or uncirculated." Under the heading "One-Cent Piece, Nickel" he asserts that "I only buy those coined in 1856, for which I pay—proofs, $5.00; uncirculated, $2.00. Positively no other dates wanted." Although these strict limitations on date may startle today's collectors, von Bergen deserves a place in numismatic history for popularizing various scarce dates. It should also be remembered that at the time this book was published, some dates that are now much sought after were fairly common; even the 1877 Indian Head cent was readily available in pocket change.

Notice also that there is no mention in von Bergen's text of the various mintmarks. Not until the 1893 publication of A.G. Heaton's *Treatise on the Coinage of the United States Branch Mints* would collecting by date *and* mintmark become popular. Now popularly known simply as *Mint Marks*, the treatise pointed out that coins issued by branch mints were often far scarcer, and thus more valuable, than those struck at the Philadelphia mint. Heaton's book would launch a new development in the collecting of coins and the development of numismatics—one that was unknown even four years earlier. Augustus Goodyear Heaton, an artist as well as numismatist, would go on to be the third president of the American Numismatic Association (ANA).

Von Bergen followed up *Rare Coins* with *The Rare Coin Encyclopedia (Universal Coin Dealers Directory)*, which also went through numerous editions; the last was published in 1907. Both books were widely read, and the *Rare Coin Encyclopedia* seems to have been an important influence on the next major figure in coin-pricing references: the legendary B. Max Mehl.

B. MAX MEHL

One of the most famous, influential, and downright colorful figures in 20th-century numismatics, Benjamin Max Mehl was born in Lithuania in 1884 but settled in Fort Worth, Texas. At just 11 years old, he began a home coin business, and he was not yet 20 when he joined the ANA and placed his first ad, which appeared in the December 1903 issue of *The Numismatist*. A few months later in 1904, he issued his first catalog: *Catalogue of Fine Selections of Choice United States Gold, Silver, and Copper Coins, Private and Territorial Gold, United States Fractional Currency*. By 1916, Mehl's Star Rare Coin Company had prospered to the extent that he was able to pay $25,000 for the construction of his own office building, which he later depicted on the cover of his catalogs (see illustrations).

Thanks to his talent for publicity and showmanship, Mehl's numismatic venture was incredibly successful. It is estimated that at one time more than half the mail received at the Fort Worth post office was addressed to him. By the mid-1920s, he was spending $50,000 annually on advertising—a small fortune by the standards of the day. Mehl was also the first coin dealer to use the new medium of radio to reach the public. In what was probably his most famous advertising venture, during the Great Depression he spent millions of dollars on ads that offered a then-substantial $50 for a 1913 Liberty Head nickel. Mehl must have known that his offer was hollow—only five pieces were known to exist, and these were already held by a collector. However, his campaign prompted countless people to search for the elusive treasure, eager for the distraction from everyday life and hopeful for sudden riches. Succeeding generations continued to search for these coins (none of which Mehl ever owned). The expensive promotion was a huge success for the brilliant marketer, creating countless new coin collectors—and therefore customers. Throughout his career, the man Q. David Bowers has called "the numismatic equivalent of P.T. Barnum"[2] did more to popularize the hobby of coin collecting than anyone before him. Not until the advent of R.S. Yeoman would one man be so influential in popularizing coin collecting among the general public.

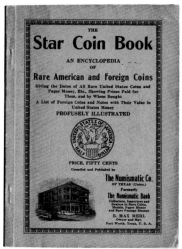

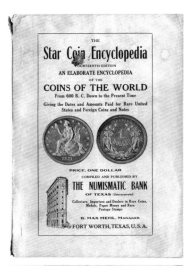

The B. Max Mehl Building, depicted here on the cover of the 31st edition of the *Star Coin Book* (circa 1937), publicized its owner's name and served to impress potential customers with his prosperity. After falling into disrepair following Mehl's death in 1957, it was recently restored to its former glory. Also shown are the 14th edition of the *Star Coin Encyclopedia* (1916) and the 51st edition of the *Star Rare Coin Encyclopedia* (1944).

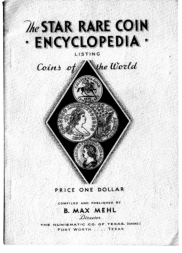

The work Mehl is best remembered for, today generally referred to as the *Star Rare Coin Encyclopedia*, was published in different forms and under different names. In format it was clearly influenced by von Bergen's *Rare Coin Encyclopedia*, and recent research also shows some overlapping of content between Mehl's and von Bergen's coin-pricing books. It is still unclear whether Mehl purchased the rights to von Bergen's work, chose to imitate his predecessor, or worked in concert with him.[3] The first incarnation of Mehl's best-selling reference, *The Star Coin Book: An Encyclopedia of Rare American and Foreign Coins*, cost 50¢ and was issued through the Mehl-owned Numismatic Bank of Texas. Most editions of this book—including the 31st, shown here—were 112 pages long, with much of that length devoted to American coins. Yet of the 44 pages of photographs in the catalog, 27 illustrated ancient coins, for which no values were noted. The practice of including pictures of ancient coins would continue throughout Mehl's publication of *The Star Coin Book*.

Like his predecessor von Bergen, Mehl did not usually reference mintmarks. In most instances, he simply listed the year of production and the price he was willing to pay. He would include the mintmark information if it applied to a specific coin he wanted, but collecting by mintmarks had not yet become common practice.

Eventually *The Star Coin Book* gave place to a longer reference, *The Star Coin Encyclopedia: An Elaborate Encyclopedia of the Coins of the World*. At 208 pages, it included illustrations and values of many foreign coins, as well as a number of essays. Although it carried a price tag of $1, for many readers it was well worth the cost.

The *Encyclopedia* continued the pattern set by the *Book* in that it disregarded most mintmarks. In the 14th edition's section on dimes, for example, mintmarks were listed for only four dates. Among these was the 1894-S Barber dime, valued at between $50 and $100. In the quarter dollar section, which contained listings through 1893, mintmarks were included for only two dates. A brief section of the book entitled "Mint Marks That Command a Premium" supplemented (and occasionally repeated) the standard type listings with specific values for particular dates and mintmarks, but at the equivalent of about two text pages, this list could hardly be called exhaustive.

Another idiosyncrasy of the *Encyclopedia* listings was its organization. Even by the time the 51st edition was released in 1944, some coins were listed as a group rather than by individual date. In the section on Barber dimes, for example, appears a listing for 1892 to 1905-O issues as a single entity, with values of between 20¢ and $1.00. Today no reference work would dare insinuate that an 1895-O is worth the same as a 1905-O!

Mehl's books and promotional ventures have landed him a place in numismatic history as one of the premier architects of 20th-century coin collecting. By telling the public that they could start collecting simply by glancing through their loose change, Mehl introduced the idea that numismatics was a pastime for everyone, not just the elite. He was instrumental in popularizing coin collecting and brought unprecedented numbers of people into the hobby. In the words of former ANA vice president Scott A. Travers, "Mehl did more than anyone else to increase awareness of coins among the general populace."[4]

Ever the innovative marketer, Mehl introduced this token (shown here at actual size) as another promotion for his books and coin sales. The number produced is unknown, and pieces in average condition usually sell at auction for between $15 and $30.

WAYTE RAYMOND

New York coin dealer Wayte Raymond is not as widely known today as some of his numismatic brethren, but he brought distinction to the hobby—and many new collectors—by creating high-quality coin-pricing guides. After his death in 1956, John J. Ford Jr. wrote an obituary that provides most of the information available today on this private man. The only obituary ever to win the ANA's Heath Literary Award, it tells us that Raymond, who was born in Connecticut in 1886, started his numismatic career as a vest-pocket dealer. In 1912, a $500 loan from his parents enabled him to leave his position as a bank teller and become a full-time coin dealer. Although a quiet, unassuming man who avoided the spotlight craved by so many other dealers, Raymond was well regarded by his contemporaries for the thorough research and desire for accuracy that he brought to his publications. He also designed and sold the popular National Coin Albums. Today he is acknowledged by numismatic scholars like David T. Alexander as being the 20th century's "godfather of quality numismatic publishing," producing reference works that did not make their author rich but hugely stimulated numismatic interest and activity.[5] As Q. David Bowers observes in his essay "Inside the Red Book," "any survey of pivotal figures in American numismatics during the [20th] century must have Raymond near the top of the list."

His most famous reference work debuted in 1934, four years after he went to work for the Scott Stamp and Coin Company. Originally this book was titled *Standard Catalogue of United States Coins and Tokens;* later, tokens would be dropped from both title and contents. The *Standard Catalogue* soon became the leading numismatic reference of its day. David Alexander calls it "the first truly objective pricing guide covering the broad field of U.S. coinage,"[6] and as an annual publication (at least initially) it was also the first coin-pricing guide to be regularly updated. The early editions are notable in part for their invaluable information relating to U.S. tokens. In the first edition, the section on Hard Times tokens spanned a then-unusual 10 pages and included illustrations. Raymond's listings included both hand-drawn illustrations and photographs of early merchants' tokens, and a section on Civil War tokens and cards. By listing these tokens, Raymond greatly furthered the hobby of collecting them.

Yet, at the same time, the catalog was awkwardly organized in certain ways. The minor coinage (that which is struck without silver or gold, such as the cent and nickel coins) is clearly listed by date and mintmark within each coin's type. Inexplicably, however, a different method was used in the silver and gold coinage sections. These coins, rather than being arranged by series, were listed by the mint at which they were produced. This unwieldy system required users to search by mint—and to be aware of which mint produced which dates. Each edition after the first was also dated a year ahead of its publication date, a convention that would also be used in Yeoman's *Guide Book* and that has perplexed some modern collectors.

The *Standard Catalogue of United States Coins and Tokens* continued to be released annually through 1942. In 1943, Raymond published a supplement that contained values for minor, silver, and commemorative coinage. This 16-page pamphlet was priced at 25¢—rather expensive if you consider that the full clothbound 1942 edition was $2.50, and the 1940 edition was then available for a discounted price of $1.00.

When the book reappeared in 1944, its name had been shortened to *Standard Catalogue of United States Coins,* and the 60 pages devoted to tokens had been removed. The remaining listings were completely reworked so that all dates and mints were listed within their appropriate headings, rather than being organized by mint. The decision to reorganize the listings may have been influenced by the release in 1942 of the user-friendly *Handbook of United States Coins With Premium List* by R.S. Yeoman (see chapter 2).

Although the *Standard Catalogue* would no longer appear on a regular annual basis, Raymond continued publishing his popular reference even after a potential competitor emerged in 1946 in the form of Yeoman's *Guide Book of United States Coins.* (Chapter 2 discusses in more detail the position these two works occupied with respect to each other.) Interestingly, while the 14th edition (1950) of the *Standard Catalogue* listed 32 contributors, the 15th edition (1951) listed only the editor, Wayte Raymond. When the 16th edition was published in 1953, however, John J. Ford Jr. was credited as associate editor and Walter Breen as researcher. Raymond had taken the innovative approach of

Raymond's *Standard Catalogue* is fascinating to many collectors of today, yet this book is often difficult to find. Copies complete with original dust jacket, like the 18th (1957) edition shown here, are especially scarce. A word of caution to collectors: every edition of the *Standard Catalogue* was released in a different-color cover, and red was chosen for the 1947 edition. As a result, books from this year are often mistaken for first-edition Red Books and sold for exorbitant amounts.

sending Breen to the National Archives in Washington, D.C., to investigate original historical documents relating to the U.S. coinage. The research Breen carried out at Raymond's behest broke new ground in numismatic scholarship and further helped to establish the *Standard Catalogue* as a landmark reference.

In 1953, the catalog's title was changed to include "The," and it was released as *The Standard Catalogue of United States Coins*. Most likely, this was an attempt by Raymond to establish his publication as *the* definitive research material on U.S. coins. But the 1953 *Standard Catalogue* ended up being the second-to-last edition issued. The final edition was released in 1957, after Raymond's death; his widow, Olga (as O.E. Raymond), was credited as editor of this edition. For the first time, mintages were given in an easy-to-read format—at least, those from 1936 to 1956. Mintage quantities for earlier years, on the other hand, were still presented as they had been previously: copied from the report of the director of the Mint, which was more difficult to comprehend quickly.

Raymond's achievements in the field did not end with the *Standard Catalogue*. During its publication, he revived J.W. Scott's *Coin Collector's Journal*, and under his direction it enjoyed a successful run from 1934 to 1954. Raymond also produced numerous other books, such as *The Standard Paper Money Catalogue*, in 1940, and *Coins of the World: Twentieth Century Issues*. This popular title saw five editions, the last of which appeared in 1955, and a counterpart publication, *Coins of the World: Nineteenth Century Issues*. Published in 1947, this book too was later succeeded by another edition.

In honor of Raymond's contributions to numismatic literature, the Wayte and Olga Raymond Memorial Award for literature was established. It is awarded to authors of articles in *The Numismatist*, the ANA journal, that display "original and comprehensive research in U.S. numismatics."

RED BOOK RECOLLECTIONS
David T. Alexander

My recollections of the *Guide Book of United States Coins*, the slim volume that everybody has long called the "Red Book," are somewhat conflicted. As young numismatists in Miami, Florida, during the early 1950s, my late brother John and I did not successfully collect U.S. coins, but we were already well aware of the "Red Book." Our family lived in what the Victorians used to call "genteel poverty," with essentially no money for hobbies. Rent, school tuition, and basic diet were barely covered by severely limited family funds each month.

Newspaper routes and corner sales brought in some spending money in the day when the *Miami Daily News* cost a nickel, an evening paper bringing our readers "today's news today!" Neither of us showed any skill at saving and such good coins as the customers gave us were generally spent on such "staffs of life" as chocolate. What were then called "foreign coins" were far easier to keep since they usually couldn't be spent, though with Canadian coins and the omnipresent Cuban coins you had at least a chance.

Young collectors in that long-ago Miami had two things going for them that many other American cities did not: a really outstanding public library and a vibrant, welcoming coin club. We made good use of both. The Miami Coin Club had been founded in 1948, and the dapper founder, Otto

T. Sghia, formerly of The Bronx, New York, was still active. He had organized the Miami group and endowed it with the constitution of the New York Numismatic Club, emphasizing fellowship, speakers, and member exhibits while forbidding excessive commercialism.

In the early 1950s the club was in its heyday. Local members rubbed elbows with visitors and what were called "winter residents," including the venerable Abraham Heppner, who carried what he confidently asserted was a genuine 1804 silver dollar. One especially elderly club officer member was James Pollard of Indianapolis, who was said to have collected U.S. half cents from circulation! There were far more down-to-earth members, older men wearing overalls and drawling, "Well, ah save quarters 'n half dollars. . . ."

Then there was Lee A. Hervey Jr., who gave us his 1955 "Red Book" at the May 1957 meeting. We had already encountered the "Red Book" at the downtown library, the great white marble structure built in 1952 to block off Miami's view of Biscayne Bay at the foot of Flagler Street. This library was unusual in that it had several running feet of shelves in the *circulation* section with all sorts of coin books ready and waiting. Among these titles were the widely respected *Standard Catalogue of United States Coins* and several "Red Books" of varying ages. I came to know both, and was especially impressed by the "Red Book's" in-detail descriptions of U.S. commemorative coins. The *Standard Catalogue* offered each a single line, often followed by a somewhat disapproving value in italics for issues Raymond regarded as "speculative."

In the 11 years I devoted to the Historical Museum of Southern Florida (1963 to 1974), I always kept current "Red Books" next to the two telephones, upstairs and down. Inevitably, often on weekends and (we suspected) from parties, would come the calls: "Hey, I gotta old penny. . . ." The "Red Book" made many friends for the museum because it ensured that we always had an answer!

In the spring of 1974 I found myself in a new career and town, as a staff writer for *Coin World* in Sidney, Ohio, where I came to know much more about the "Red Book." The observant reader will have noticed that as an ex–*Coin World* writer, force of habit still demands quotation marks around the *Guide Book*'s nickname!

Whitman was one of the few rival publishers with whom Amos Press Inc. had fraternal relations. I learned that the great success of the "Red Book" was the result not just of content but of distribution. The then owners of Whitman Publishing in Racine, Wisconsin, had a nationwide distribution network already in existence to serve such other products as Little Golden Books and the Whitman "penny boards" of an earlier generation. This network included five-and-10-cent stores, such as Woolworth's, that were found everywhere. Wayte Raymond, on the other hand, limited distribution of his otherwise excellent titles to a very small network of what he called "established coin dealers." Availability spelled success. Then there was the unchanging appearance. Stability was absolute for decades in number of pages, continued use of the same black-and-white halftone illustrations, and standardized descriptions.

Coin World brought home to me that many thrifty main-line collectors often failed to buy a new "Red Book" each year. This was made clear in the unfolding of a subscription-building promotion of 1970 that promised new *Coin World* subscribers a brand-new "Red Book" autographed by the newspaper's whole editorial staff. The inrush was amazing: scores of subscriptions were taken out by readers who had been relying on "Red Books" eight to 10 years out of date but still in loyal and tattered use.

As a younger collector, I tried to keep up with succeeding editions, and today my own collection is extensive, though not complete. Yes, I have the 1947 edition, in a heavily used condition which a coin grader might optimistically call About Very Fine. My fourth edition of 1950 is virtually new, as are most of my "Red Books" since that time. Among my special editions is a 1974 with the cover gold-stamped, "Miami Beach International Coin Convention, January 3, 4, 5, 6, 1974, Deauville Hotel," and a deep-maroon-cover volume distributed at the 1997 Denver ANA convention. Most imposing is the spectacular oversize, genuine leather, gold-leaved 2008 Limited Edition distributed at the Numismatic Literary Guild bash during the 2007 ANA convention in Milwaukee, Wisconsin.

The "Red Book" (sorry for the quote marks) and I go back a long way, and each copy on my shelf recalls wonderful times, places, and above all, people. Few collectibles bring with them not only an implicit history of U.S. coin collecting, but also such a wealth of warm recollection!

LEE F. HEWITT

At around the same time that Raymond was revolutionizing the coin-pricing guide, printer and coin collector Lee Hewitt launched his own highly influential work. Hewitt was reportedly inspired by the flood of commemorative coins emerging at the time, and in 1935 he began production of the *Numismatic Scrapbook Magazine* at the Chicago printing shop he owned with his brother. Published monthly, the *Scrapbook* became a respected and popular periodical, praised by R.S. Yeoman in particular for being "no-nonsense, non-technical" and "down-to-earth."[7] Q. David Bowers recalls that in the 1950s it was "the be-all and end-all in monthly coin market spirit and information."[8] Hewitt continued as editor until 1968, when he sold the magazine to Amos Press. As popular as it was, however, Hewitt's magazine did not regularly provide comprehensive coin-pricing information—leaving a void that R.S. Yeoman would fill.

R.S. Yeoman felt that "coin collecting . . . came alive in the modern sense" when Lee F. Hewitt launched the *Numismatic Scrapbook Magazine* (shown here is the January 1940 issue). Hewitt was also the prime mover in the birth of the Central States Numismatic Society in 1939.

2

THE EVOLUTION OF THE RED BOOK

I have been asked a number of times what led to the Guide Book. *Of course, the Whitman marketing group did not confer one day to say "Let's get into the numismatic market." —R.S. Yeoman, "The Red Book Story"*

The story of the Red Book is to a great extent the story of its creator, the man known to generations of coin collectors as R.S. Yeoman. But it is also the story of a company, Whitman Publishing, and of radical changes in the pastime of coin collecting. As many Red Book collectors have already discovered, behind this seemingly straightforward coin-pricing guide is a capsule history of American numismatics in the 20th century. Here we will look at the Red Book's origins, its development, and its context in the larger culture of coin-collecting history.

RICHARD YEO

Richard Sperry ("Dick") Yeo was born in Milwaukee, Wisconsin, on August 15, 1904. The Yeos were of English stock: Richard's paternal grandparents, William and Katie, had come to the United States from Devonshire, England, in 1871. A few years later, Richard's future father, Frederick, was born in Elgin, Illinois. Frederick would take an Illinois-born bride, Jennie, although he settled his family in Wisconsin, where he worked as a clerk.

Richard Yeo was the middle child of three brothers: Stewart was born in 1901, William in 1907. (Another brother, Frank, died in 1903.) He grew up in Milwaukee's East Side, but the family kept close ties to Illinois, and Yeo would later join the Chicago Coin Club. In 1985 he reminisced, "As far back as I can remember, Chicago was an attractive, exciting locality down the road. The family changed trains there for my parents' native Elgin, where most of my cousins live. Quite naturally the Windy City skyline became an early impression and later a familiar haunt."[9]

His interest in coins was already evident by 1915, when he was 11 years old and working as a paperboy. On the first day that he collected payments from the customers on his route, he was given an Indian Head cent for change. The coin was even more common then than it is today, but he went home, cut a hole in a piece of cardboard, and placed the coin in this improvised holder. Although the display never grew to include more than the single one-cent piece, it was Yeo's first coin board. It maintained a place of honor in his home for years. Also among the first coins in his collection was a commemorative Columbian half dollar that his father had brought back from a visit to the World's Columbian Exposition.

Richard Yeo's application for admission to the University of Wisconsin-Madison indicates that his intended field of study was applied arts.

After attending Riverside High School, Yeo was admitted to the University of Wisconsin–Madison in 1923. There he majored in applied arts, but he was also active in numerous organizations: the school literary magazine, where he worked in "art publicity"; the Arts and Crafts Club, of which he was president; and Sigma Phi Sigma fraternity, where among his fraternity brothers was his older brother Stewart. (Stewart had followed Yeo's example and entered UWM in 1924, which actually put him in the class behind his little brother.) In 1925, Yeo left the university and married Leila Marion Junkermann. Two years his senior, Marion was also the grandchild of an emigré, as her paternal grandfather had come from Germany. By 1910 the Junkermanns had settled in Milwaukee, where Marion's father worked as a dentist.

K. Godfrey   J. Bailes   **R. Yeo**   G. Jones   L. Mrkvicka   O. Riegel   V. Beardsley   W. Wittenberg   K. Butler
A. Moorhead   Dorothy Burns   Marguerite Widmann   Agnes Zeimet   Edna Walter   Ruth Hewitt   Doris Gormley   Dorothy Strauss   Mary Husving   S. Hetland
E. Gigssel   M. Klefeker   J. Weimer   Rosanna Kudschi   Katherine Kennedy   Florence Kilidex   C. Hanson   W. Rietsen   W. Boethe

Top Row—E. Keir, E. Kreimann, G. Abendroth, W. Treichel.
2nd Row—M. Rick, E. Abendroth, M. Teska, J. Trapp, F. Renner, S. Yeo,
Niedercorn.
3rd Row—H. G. Holmes, W. Laut, H. Wagenknecht, H. H. Naujoks, R. R. Smith,
N. Rick, C. R. Dale, **R. Yeo.**
Bottom Row—V. Scott, A. H. Reinert, E. R. Summers, E. V. Hicks, V. A. Otto,
P. F. Murphy, W. H. Taylor, Wolff.

Sigma Phi Sigma

Founded at University of Pennsylvania, 1908
Number of chapters, 13
Local chapter, Mu   Date established, 1922

A young Yeo at college: top, in his 1925 yearbook photograph; below, pictured in the 1926 yearbook with the other members of the Sigma Phi Sigma fraternity, including his older brother Stewart, who appears in the row above.

After their marriage, Yeo worked as a greeting-card distributor for the Milprint Company in Milwaukee, and for a time the young couple lived with Marion's aunt. That changed in the year 1932, however, when Yeo was hired by Whitman Publishing Company in Racine, Wisconsin. His new position drew on both his training in commercial design and his experience in sales and distribution—and soon would encompass a new product that would change the course of his life.

WHITMAN PUBLISHING COMPANY

When young salesman Richard Yeo joined the staff of Whitman Publishing in 1932, it was a subsidiary of the Western Printing Company. Western began as West Side Printing Company, which by 1907 was sinking into debt and probably would have vanished into oblivion if not for the enterprise shown by its part-time bookkeeper, Edward H. Wadewitz. The son of German immigrants, Wadewitz had moved to Racine at age 17, leaving only to attend Potts Shorthand College in Pennsylvania. By 1907, when he was 29, he had held a number of jobs, at one time working at his cousins' trunk factory. Now, seeing the opportunity to go into business for himself, he formed a partnership with his brother Al and bought the foundering print shop. Joined by their brother Bill and a respected journalist named Roy A. Spencer, they reversed the fortunes of the West Side Printing Company and quickly earned a reputation among Racine's rising manufacturing companies for reliability and fair dealing.

By 1910 the company was prospering enough to justify investment in a new lithographic offset press, which was reflected in the business's new name: Western Printing & Lithographing Company. The growing company relocated to the six-story Shoop Building, named for a patent-medicine entrepreneur who became one of Western's clients.

Also among Western's customers was a Chicago publishing company, Hamming-Whitman (sometimes given as Hammerung-Whitman), which specialized in children's books. This business relationship soon turned into a liability, however: after printing thousands of books for Hamming-Whitman, Western discovered that the publisher was verging on bankruptcy and unable to pay for the job. Western took ownership of the stock, and Wadewitz, inexperienced as he was in sales, set about trying to sell the books to recoup his company's losses.

His unexpected success in finding buyers led him to decide to acquire the bankrupt company in 1916 as a subsidiary. Now named simply Whitman Publishing Company, it was relocated in Racine and staffed with two salesmen—one of whom, a former social worker named Samuel E. Lowe, would prove instrumental to Whitman's success with children's books.

It was Lowe who in 1918 landed the company's first book order from a retailer: S.S. Kresge, then a major chain of five-and-ten-cent stores. But the Kresge order was misread, and a confusion between "dozens" and "gross" led to a print run of 12 times as

Humble beginnings: in 1907, West Side Printing Company operated out of a basement. From left to right are Roy Spencer, Catherine Bongarts Rutledge, E.H. Wadewitz, W.R. Wadewitz, and William Bell.

E.H. Wadewitz in 1910.

Roy Spencer in 1910.

In 1910 the Shoop Building became the home of the newly renamed Western Printing & Lithographing Co., and was featured on the company's letterhead. The building was placed on the National Register of Historic Places in 1978.

many books as had been requested. This potential disaster turned Western's fortunes in a positive new direction, thanks to Lowe's innovative thinking. Not only did he persuade rival chains such as F.W. Woolworth's to stock the surplus, but he convinced them that they should display the books year round, even though at that time booksellers sold children's titles only during the Christmas-shopping season. The enthusiastic response of parents showed that the market for children's books held enormous untapped potential. In this way a single clerical blunder revolutionized the children's book industry, and set the stage for the long-term success of Whitman Publishing.

Over the next five years, Western's product line expanded to embrace not only the popular Whitman children's books but puzzles and board games as well. In 1925, the company took on the challenge of manufacturing playing cards, which demanded particularly high precision in color alignment and die cutting; by acquiring the specialized equipment and expertise this product required, Western soon positioned itself as an industry leader. By 1928 the company had a staff of 300, necessitating a move to new quarters: the "Main Plant" on Mound Avenue, a cutting-edge facility (complete with air conditioning) that was designed and built to meet Western's needs. Also in 1928, Western established a smaller plant in Chicago to more conveniently handle printing jobs for that area.

The "Main Plant" in Racine, which became Western's headquarters in 1928, was constructed in accordance with the specific needs of a graphic-arts business. One of the first completely climate- and humidity-controlled printing facilities in America, the building is still standing today.

The coming of the Great Depression, rather than handicapping Western, actually served to increase demand for its products. Inexpensive activities like jigsaw puzzles and board games became more popular than ever among families who could no longer afford more costly forms of entertainment, and Western was operating round the clock to meet demand. Their specialized die-cutting equipment would also be put to use on a new paper-based product that would have an unimaginable impact on the company's fortunes—and the face of American coin collecting.

THE COIN BOARD REVOLUTION

In 1934, a Wisconsin engineer and coin collector named Joseph Kent Post was feeling the economic crunch of the Depression. To supplement his straitened income, he started a sideline business making a new hobby product: cardboard coin boards for minor-denomination coins. Before Post's innovation, collectors had few options for housing their coins: cabinets and albums were expensive, and storing coins in envelopes, the thrifty alternative, kept them hidden from view. At only 25¢ each, Post's coin boards provided an affordable and attractive way to store coins. Post and his family initially made the boards themselves, and later arranged with two separate companies to do the printing and hole punching. Western Printing could carry out both steps, however, and it made sense for Post to transfer the manufacture of the boards to this company—and later the marketing as well. Post was finding it increasingly difficult to juggle the demands of his home business with his engineering job, and Whitman Publishing's network of distributors and clients made it the logical party to take over the marketing of the boards.

Thus, Whitman Publishing took over the rights to Post's invention, although according to David W. Lange's engrossing account in *Coin Collecting Boards of the 1930s and 1940s*, the exact nature of the legal arrangement is impossible now to determine. The traditional story is that Post, overwhelmed by the demands of juggling his two careers, simply sold his invention to Whitman. Other accounts cast the publisher in an opportunistic light, suggesting that Post did not receive all the royalties due him for his product. In still another version of the story, which Yeo reportedly confided to friends, Whitman was forced to assume the rights to Post's product when he was unable to pay the company's bills—much as Whitman was acquired by Western. What is clear is that Post dropped out of the picture at this point, and the "game" he had invented became the germ of a numismatic revolution.

Richard Yeo was assigned to market the company's new product, and he soon discovered that it was poised for success. It demanded no great investment of money or time; anyone could go through their pocket change and extract a penny or nickel here and there without feeling a financial pinch, and the satisfaction of filling a board was not limited by age or educational level. Whitman employees were even taking the boards home to fill. The extraordinary popularity of the new boards had an enormous impact on coin collecting, creating massive numbers of new collectors, boosting the collectible values of 20th-century minor coins, and changing the face of the numismatic community. As David Lange observes, "In 1930 nearly all American numismatists were well-off, male and of middle-age or older," and with "little interest in current or recent coins."[10] Yeo himself would later point out, "up until this time, numismatics had been almost exclusively the pursuit of intellectuals . . . researchers, historians, museum curators and the like."[11] The coin board transformed all this. Now the hobby saw an influx of young, working-class collectors, and their collecting zeal focused on modern coins, not antique rarities. Many of the new collectors held jobs in which they handled small change often during the course of their work: waiters, cashiers, streetcar conductors—and paperboys like the young Richard Yeo. Coin collecting was no longer reserved for the elite; it was everyone's hobby.

In 1940 Whitman launched its coin folders, an offshoot of the original coin board that offered greater storage capacity, protection, and convenience. As developer and promoter of the folders, Yeo saw that the line was expanded to include many new coin series, both American and foreign. Although coin folders had been introduced in 1939 by the Daniel Stamp Company (Dansco), Whitman was the first company to effectively market and publicize them. As a result, says Lange, the Whitman folders "quickly became the industry standard for decades afterward." Through Yeo's efforts, coin-collecting supplies shed their earlier association with children's games and took on a more serious, intellectual cast.

Yeo's involvement with the marketing of the boards and folders steered his professional life firmly in the direction of numismatics. In his own words, he "somewhat timidly broke into the national numismatic scene," attending such events as the ANA convention in Detroit and meetings of the Chicago Coin Club, and he represented Whitman at the 1940 Hobby Show in Chicago. "When we came along with the coin boards things started to really come alive," he remembered. "The show provided their first formal public appearance."[12] Because he was there only to display the boards, not to sell them, would-be buyers "were referred across the aisle, to an enterprising young coin dealer, Ben Dreiske." Dreiske would go on to be of great help in producing the Red Book; this was just one of many important friendships Yeo formed in the numismatic community around that time.

Events like these did far more than introduce the neophyte numismatist to new connections in the hobby: they literally brought him the idea for the *Handbook of United States Coins*—the Blue Book.

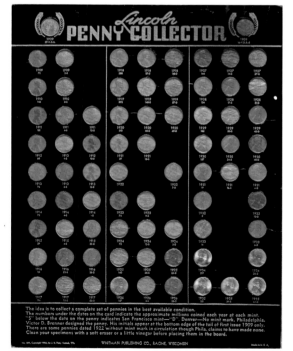

Whitman coin boards, such as this "Lincoln Penny Collector" from 1935, helped to revolutionize numismatics. This board instructs collectors to "clean [their] specimens with a soft eraser or a little vinegar before placing them in the board"—standard advice at the time, but not recommended by today's collectors.

In a whimsical bit of recycling, old Whitman coin folders were used as menu covers at the Racine Numismatic Society's 1943 banquet. R.S. Yeoman is listed in the program as the society's secretary.

This advertisement in the January 1942 *Numismatist* announced the debut of the *Handbook*. No false modesty here: the new reference is touted as "the outstanding coin book of a generation"!

THE BLUE BOOK

Before the advent of the Blue Book, according to a 1969 issue of the Whitman *Merchandiser*, "buying and selling coins had been very much a secretive, almost mysterious process." Yeo now discovered that many of those involved in the business wanted a disinterested party to dispel that mystery. He described the book's genesis this way:

> Several coin dealers, consulted at those gatherings, came forward with offers of assistance and encouragement to publish a premium (wholesale) catalog. Their rationale for pushing the idea with our particular publishing house was, simply, that established dealers had long sought an unbiased publisher with nationwide distribution, outside the numismatic domain of buying and selling coins. I was made aware that all coin catalogs then on the market were published by certain dealers, and other dealers felt uncomfortable dealing in the shadow of a competitor's "price list."[13]

A completely unbiased catalog of wholesale prices would be a new prospect for the hobby, and no small task to assemble; but with the help of leading numismatists, most notably Charles Green and Lee Hewitt—who would be listed as his coauthors—Yeo took on the challenge and began compiling data.

The first *Handbook of United States Coins With Premium List* appeared in 1942, with a cover date of the same year. It made its debut at the ANA Convention in Cincinnati, Ohio. Due to the color of the cover, it would soon come to be known as the "Blue Book." Priced at 50¢, the new reference provided collectors with averages of the prices dealers across the country would pay for regular-issue U.S. coins, plus additional comments on varieties of note. It also established a new identity for Yeo as "R.S. Yeoman," the name that would appear on all his numismatic publications. It has been said that he adopted the now-famous pen name because it was more memorable than his own, but he may also have been motivated, as longtime friend Lincoln Higgie has suggested, by a desire to preserve his privacy. If this was the case, it was certainly not the first time—or the last—that an author would take on an alias to keep his personal and authorial lives separate.

The *Handbook* differed from previously published coin books in that it included, in the words of the title page, "mint records and prices paid by dealers for all U.S. coins—how coins are produced—mints and mint marks—conditions of coins—[and] locations of mint marks." At that time, mintage figures were not readily available, and even the records of the U.S. Mint itself weren't always reliable. As a Western Publishing press release pointed out, "Attempting to list all of the U.S. issues, with mintage figures, was a major challenge for R.S. Yeoman at a time when such information was just not available . . . and every piece of 'traditional fact' had to be questioned."[14] In addition, the Blue Book included a 12-page primer on coin collecting, in which coin grading and handling (with an illustration of proper and improper techniques) were explained.

However, the listings were the meat and potatoes of the *Handbook*. Each coin type was illustrated and featured a short narrative that described the coin's design and offered other relevant information. On page 36 was a section of particular interest: "Die-Cracks and Other Varieties of Lincoln Cents." The discussion includes comments and descriptions of collectible varieties. The authors noted, for example, that a 1913-D cent with "mint letter off center" was worth 30¢ in Good condition, while the regular issue was only worth face value. On the other hand, the 1922 "Without D" cent was assigned a value of 25¢ in Good and annotated with the statement, "According to Mint records [there are] no cents from Philadelphia so those without Mint letter are evidently freaks from Denver." Surely readers who purchased the 1913-D variety instead of the 1922 No D regretted their choice in the years to come!

The first edition of the *Handbook* must have been a good seller, because later that same year Whitman released the second edition. This edition, however, bore a date of 1943.

Except for two gaps—in 1944 and 1950—the Blue Book has been published annually ever since. Each edition after the fifth has carried the date of the year following publication.[15]

Although it is frequently overshadowed by its crimson counterpart, the Blue Book was a groundbreaking publication for its day, educating consumers and forcing unscrupulous dealers (which, sadly, exist in every market) to act with honesty and accountability. It was instrumental in the process of democratizing the hobby of coin collecting—a transformation begun by the coin boards and folders, and most powerfully effected by the publication of the Red Book.

1942
HANDBOOK
OF
UNITED STATES
COINS

With Premium List

★

By
R. S. YEOMAN • LEE F. HEWITT
CHARLES E. GREEN

Containing mint record and prices paid by dealers for all U. S. coins. Information on collecting coins — how coins are produced—mints and mint marks—condition of coins—location of mint marks—preserving and cleaning coins—starting a collection—coin club directory—what to buy—history of mints and interesting descriptions of all U.S. copper, nickel, silver and gold coins. Fully illustrated.

Copyright MCMXLII by
WHITMAN PUBLISHING COMPANY
RACINE, WISCONSIN

9050   Printed in U. S. A.

The first edition of the *Handbook of United States Coins*, soon to be known as the Blue Book, was published in 1942. (See appendix for details on this and other editions of the Blue Book.)

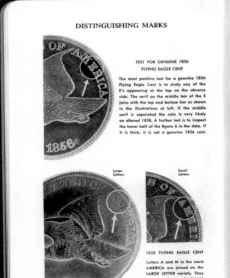

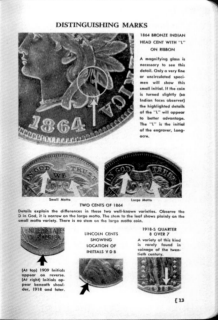

THE COMING OF THE RED BOOK

A counterpart to the Blue Book that would list retail values of U.S. coins was already in the works, but it would be years before it actually saw the light of day. As Yeoman recounted later, "The Guide Book was in the planning stage when Adolf Hitler went berserk, and we put the project in cold storage for the duration." The wartime paper shortage brought new publishing restrictions, so that starting in 1943 paper supplies were allotted to publishers according to their previous year's paper use. In practice, this meant that although a successful volume like the Blue Book could (and did) continue its annual publication, going forward with the planned companion volume would have eaten into the paper allotment for other, established books. As a consequence, the Red Book would not debut until 1946. Yeoman would later observe that the postponement "was not all bad, for it gave me time to meet some key people and discuss details and features with them." Among these key people were coin dealers Aubrey Bebee and Hubert Polzer, who assisted Yeoman in the intensive research that he carried out during the enforced delay.

A Guide Book of United States Coins was published in November 1946, with a cover date of 1947. The system of postdating each edition has confused later generations of readers, but at the time it was not unusual; Wayte Raymond's *Standard Catalogue* also carried a cover date one year ahead of its publication date, which may even have influenced the decision to date the *Guide Book* this way.[16] The distinctive color of the cover, which would give the book its enduring nickname, was Yeoman's choice because it was a "good, bright, attention-getting color." In fact, the early editions of what would later come to be known as the Red Book are closer to maroon than red, and not until the 10th edition would the now-standard red shade appear.

The *Guide Book* contained even more material than its predecessor, with the most prominent content being, of course, the retail values in the listings. To assemble those values, Yeoman drew on a distinguished panel of contributors in the coin field, a list that grew over the years to include some of the first names in numismatics. Because the Red Book was created to provide *unbiased* values for coins, all of the values were averaged from multiple contributors' input—no small feat, particularly as the panel of contributors grew in number. The list of 14 contributors in the first edition (see illustration on next page) reads like a who's who of numismatics of the day.

R.S. Yeoman with his most famous creation: in the proof stage (left) and as a finished product (right). The photograph on the right appeared in the July 1970 *Merchandiser*, with the caption "R.S. Yeoman working on the charts featured for the first time in the new Red Book. These compare coin values listed in the last twenty-three editions."

CONTRIBUTORS

A. E. Bebee	Abner Kreisberg
Malcolm O. E. Chell-Frost	Edmund E. Lamb
William L. Clark	Stuart Mosher
Damon G. Douglas	Hubert L. Polzer
Charles E. Green	Lewis M. Reagan
Ted R. Hammer	Max M. Schwartz
A. Kosoff	Farran Zerbe

Several of these panelists—Aubrey Bebee, Charles E. Green, Abe Kosoff, and Stuart Mosher—were also listed as contributors to Raymond's *Standard Catalogue of United States Coins* (although Raymond spelled Bebee's name "Beebee"). We can only wonder how Raymond felt about these contributors' helping his competition! As David Bowers put it, Yeoman sought out "the brightest and the best" for his contributors. (See the boxed section "Architects of the Red Book" for more information on the original panel of contributors.) The number would increase steadily in the years and decades to come, and the esteem of the Red Book and its creator could be gauged by the distinguished names that they attracted. David Alexander sums up the trend: "The notation 'Red Book contributor' became a badge of honor worn by succeeding generations of numismatists."

RED BOOK RECOLLECTIONS
Lincoln W. Higgie III

In October 1938, Richard S. Yeo approached my father, Lincoln W. Higgie Sr., with questions concerning numismatics and coin collecting in general. Yeo had come to Racine from his native Milwaukee to work for Whitman Publishing Co. and was given the "penny boards" section of the children's games department to develop and expand.

My father was a founder of the Racine Numismatic Society, and he invited Yeo to accompany him and my mother to a coin convention being held in Des Moines, Iowa. A few weeks after that convention I was born. In later years, with so very many coin conventions behind all of us, there were numerous stories about the destiny of those people driving off to Iowa together in the autumn of 1938.

My parents' birthdays were August 24 and 25, just about a week after Yeoman's. Every year they exchanged birthday cards and letters. In his last birthday letter to my parents in 1987, Yeoman fondly recalled that trip to Iowa and their friendship during the years that followed.

How excited my father was when the first *Guide Book of United States Coins* appeared! Yeoman had brought copies to the Racine Numismatic Society meeting, and the results were electrifying. Over the years, how many times Daddy would be reading that book and say, "I still can't believe that this man came to ask me about numismatics and coin collecting. Look at what he has accomplished!"

Yeoman remained faithful to the Racine Numismatic Society and to the many friendships he made there. He encouraged young people like me and the sons of other members to attend meetings, picnics, banquets, and other club events. Usually he had a "story coin" to show us. It could have been a widow's mite, piece of eight, or his wonderful 1848 CAL. quarter eagle, whose story he would relate. Thus he would lead us to higher levels of intellectual study and collecting pleasure well beyond the completion of a penny board. His tastefully mounted exhibitions of story coins at major coin club functions were fascinating to collectors and non-collectors alike.

Although Yeoman himself never collected any coins in a Whitman coin album, he realized that there was a large audience for that product. He edited and produced a wide variety of coin albums for collectors. He would bring the latest album to a coin club meeting and suddenly some of the "wise eyes" collectors would rush out to get the key dates for whatever new series was going to be collected in this way. Clever pressmen and type-setters in the plant liked being able to "get in early" on a series of coins as well. Yeoman enjoyed creating a collecting frenzy every so often, and it would perk up the sales of Whitman albums or books.

Growing up as I did with collectors as family members and Yeoman as a mentor, I was hopelessly hooked on numismatics. My brain filled up with coins and their stories from Croesus to the Franklin half dollars. Ties of friendship were nurtured to other collectors, dealers, and experts which proved to be among the most rewarding of our lifetimes.

High school and university studies in Wisconsin and Germany were always enhanced by the added historical and art-historical knowledge I had gained through numismatics. After my graduation from the University of Wisconsin, Yeoman asked me to work for him as an editor and writer. My dreams had come true! Happily, I have a gift for writing, and with Yeoman's coaching I learned a great deal more. By the end of 1961 I had written and edited several books, and it was time for me to return to Europe. Yeoman helped me to get a position as foreign correspondent for *Numismatic News* with our good friend Chet Krause, and off I went.

As I visited numerous royal and national coin collections in Europe and the Near East as a newspaper man, I was always well received because I was a protegé of R.S. Yeoman. The finest European numismatic scholars openly admired Yeoman as a pioneer with a gift for organizing and presenting not only American but also world coins in such a lucid fashion. They saw that he was the best working example for future generations to follow in promoting our hobby.

By virtue of his intelligence and interest in numismatics, he taught millions of people an appreciation of history, art history, and economics via numismatics. No assemblage of professors could claim to have educated so many people in this way.

Yeoman understood that the history of every nation is reflected by its money. Price guides had been printed before he came along, but he understood how to explain in very precise language the story of the coins. He told you where the coins fit into the picture puzzle of the nation's history, to the delight of the scholar and common man alike. He also told you what to pay for a coin and got you looking for a rare date or mintmark in your change. He had created the basic formula for the success of a coin book in modern times.

However, as important as it is to appreciate Yeoman as an author who was a pioneer in his literary style, we must also admire his talents as a businessman and manufacturer. He had to learn about the printing trade and the functions of the typesetter, pressman, binder, and shipper. He had to know how much and what kind of paper, ink, bindery materials, and glue to order, and when to schedule new press runs. Then he would go to coin conventions to find reliable people to wholesale and retail his books and coin supplies. These people often profited greatly from Yeoman's favors. Likewise, they frequently had good suggestions from which Yeoman would prosper.

Yeoman learned to do a lot of jobs, and he had to do them all right. As his success grew and the responsibilities multiplied, he needed full-time professionals to shoulder various responsibilities. For him it was a lucky day when he found Ken Bressett.

Ken had grown up as a printer in Keene, New Hampshire. At an early age he had fallen in love with numismatics. Add to this the gift of an expressive writing style as sharp as Yeoman's. He understood how to work with collectors and dealers as well as typesetters, pressmen, and binders to deliver a quality product. To this list of qualifications add a lovely wife who helped entertain collectors and dealers at coin shows where Whitman was represented.

For many decades Bressett has maintained the integrity of Yeoman's *Guide Book* and has expanded its scope with changing times. Thanks to both these scholars, it remains the most trusted and widely read collector reference book ever written. Its formula for coin-book text and layout is the accepted standard of excellence, not only for Whitman books but also for the outstanding works of Yeoman's old friend Chet Krause.

My collection of Yeoman books continues to be a source of happiness. Like revisiting an old friend, I'll read them over again from time to time. The memories come back, and I can see Yeoman at his desk, deep in thought with one of his workbooks, polishing a sentence to define and immortalize a coin for his readers. I also see us with a typesetter who has pulled the individual lead letters out of a type case, has put them on his "stick," and is assembling a page of cold lead type. These typesetters were all prima donnas, but Yeoman and Bressett knew how to flatter them to get a nice job. Some typesetters were coin club members and would later point with pride to various pages of the Red Book which they had set with Yeoman's approval. A lot of people in Racine, Wisconsin, also took pride in their part of the success story of Yeoman and his wonderful books.

So I thank Dick Yeo and Ken Bressett for the many good things they did for me personally and for illuminating the lives of other people who love numismatics.

ARCHITECTS OF THE RED BOOK

No study of the *Guide Book of United States Coins* can be complete without the understanding that the book is not the work of one individual. Starting with the first edition, which named 14 contributors—many still household names among coin collectors—R.S. Yeoman surrounded himself with many of the most knowledgeable and distinguished numismatists of his day. In 1971, Yeoman described the contributors this way:

> Contributors to the *Guide Book* were then and still are volunteers who come to us with price projections annually, and with full knowledge that their data will be merged with that of their fellow experts and averaged for listing in the catalog. This dedicated group represents every geographical region, age group, and degree of knowledge and experience. They are truly a cross-section of our American numismatic community.

Since taking the editorial helm in 1965, Kenneth Bressett has carried on the tradition of bringing the finest numismatic minds to the creation of the Red Book. Here we will take a closer look at the 14 original contributors, as well as two other important men who worked behind the scenes to bring it to fruition.

Of course, far more people than can be listed here were crucial to the Red Book's continued production over the years. The contributions of all these people to the Red Book's continuing success cannot be overstated.

A.E. (Aubrey) Bebee. Aubrey Bebee and his wife, Adeline, were a successful team as direct-sale retailers of coins and currency. Based in Omaha, Nebraska, they were prominent advertisers in the *Numismatic Scrapbook Magazine* and *The Numismatist*. Their coin specialties were commemoratives, silver dollars, and Proof sets, although it was their paper money collection that would become one of their most impressive legacies when they donated it to the ANA in 1988. David Bowers particularly recalls the duo's gift for recognizing quality. Bebee was awarded the ANA Medal of Merit in 1968 and was appointed by President Nixon to the Assay Commission in 1971. In 1988, the couple was jointly awarded the Farran Zerbe Memorial Award. The Bebee name is still attached to one of the legendary 1913 Liberty Head nickels, which the Bebees purchased at auction in 1967.

Malcolm O.E. Chell-Frost. Boston coin dealer Chell-Frost was, in Yeoman's estimation, "one of the most prominent numismatic authorities in New England" and an unofficial ambassador for the hobby over many decades. Most of his business was conducted through mail order, but he also had a small brick-and-mortar store in downtown Boston, which David Bowers recalls visiting in the late 1950s. His particular interest was the 1939 Jefferson nickel with doubled MONTICELLO, which he felt was an underappreciated variety. According to Yeoman, Chell-Frost was instrumental in forming the coin collection of Francis Cardinal Spellman.

William L. Clark. Of all the listed contributors to the first-edition Red Book, Clark may well be the most obscure today. *The American Numismatic Society: 1858–1958*, by Howard Adelson, tells us that in 1937 Clark was appointed to succeed Robert Robertson as assistant curator of the ANS when Robertson died suddenly. To this point, we are told, "Clark's interest in numismatics had been almost purely from the standpoint of the collector"; by 1937, he had become a member of the ANA and the ANS as well as regional coin clubs. Evidently Clark's numismatic background was broad, and he was particularly helpful to curator Howland Wood in the field of modern coins. We can only surmise that he was helpful to Yeoman in this regard as well.

Damon G. Douglas. At the time of the Red Book's creation, New Jersey–based Douglas was already an established numismatic researcher and author. He received the ANA Medal of Merit in 1948, and served on that organization's board of governors; he also held the now-defunct position of third vice president with the ANS for six years. His area of specialization was colonial coins, particularly New Jersey coppers, and for decades his unpublished manuscript on the subject was held in the ANS archives, where it was frequently sought by researchers. In 2004, the ANS published Douglas's manuscript—now annotated and updated—to make it more accessible to other numismatists.

Charles E. Green. Due to an injury in World War I, Green found walking difficult, but he nevertheless played an active role in the creation of the Blue Book, which credited him as coauthor through the 13th edition. In addition to being one of the first contributors to the Red Book, he also contributed to Wayte Raymond's *Standard Catalogue*. His Chicago-based coin business was named "R. Green" after his wife, Ruth, who conducted many of the responsibilities that her husband was unable to carry out after a 1950 accident confined him to a wheelchair. From the mid-1930s to his death in 1955 he conducted a thriving rare-coin business, which Ruth carried on for some time after his death. During the 1940s and into the 1950s he worked closely with Charles Frederick Childs in acquiring gold coins for the Childs collection.

Ted R. Hammer. Theodore Hammer, known as Ted, started a coin business in Burlington, Iowa, in the late 1930s. In 1938 he became the first president of the Iowa Numismatic Society, and through the 1940s he served as ANA librarian and (through 1948) curator of the ANA's collection. By 1947 he had been appointed to the U.S. Assay Commission and had relocated to Marinette, Wisconsin. A frequent contributor to *The Numismatist*, he received the ANA Medal of Merit in 1950.

A. (Abe) Kosoff. Kosoff was one half of the powerhouse business Numismatic Gallery, together with the contributor listed next, Abner Kreisberg. From 1944 to 1954, their company "conducted its business with a *joie de vivre* unique in its time," David Bowers says.[17] In 1947 he became one of the founding members of the Professional Numismatists Guild (PNG), and its first president. In 1976 he and Kenneth Bressett formulated a system of coin-grading standards, which they outlined in *The Official ANA Grading*

Abe Kosoff (left), one of the first Red Book contributors, makes a presentation to R.S. Yeoman at the PNG banquet during the 1981 ANA convention in New Orleans. (Photo courtesy of the estate of Abe Kosoff)

Guide. Also in this decade, he was one of the founders of the American Numismatic Association Certification Service (ANACS). Kosoff died in 1983, a year after he was elected to the ANA Hall of Fame.

Abner Kreisberg. As Kosoff's partner in the Numismatic Gallery, Kreisberg was involved in some of the highest-profile coin auctions of the mid-1940s to mid-1950s. Kreisberg and Kosoff also helped King Farouk of Egypt form his now-legendary coin collection. Around 1950 Kreisberg gained a new appreciation for life when he spontaneously opted to discontinue a plane trip during a layover, and the plane then crashed on takeoff. After the Numismatic Gallery dissolved, Kreisberg adopted the business name of Coin Gallery and took a new partner, Jerry Cohen; their business partnership lasted from 1958 to 1984. Kreisberg died in 1997 at the age of 93.

Edmund E. Lamb. Lamb may be tied with William Clark as the most elusive of the first-edition Red Book contributors. What little information we do have comes from the Chicago Coin Club, which he joined in 1936. An employee of the Columbian National Life Insurance company in Chicago, he listed U.S. coins as his collecting specialty. In 1939 Lamb became vice president of the club, and two years later he was elected president. His wife was also active in this organization, leading the women's social group. In 1943, in the normal course of succession of club officers, he stepped down and was replaced in this position. It is likely that he and Yeoman met through the Chicago Coin Club, since Yeoman was a member as well, and that their professional relationship grew from there.

Stuart Mosher. Yeoman's primary advisor during the creation of the Red Book, Mosher had worked for Wayte Raymond before becoming editor of *The Numismatist*, a position he held from 1945 until poor health forced him to step down in 1954. During the same period he worked as curator for the Smithsonian Institution's Division of Numismatics. In 1954 he received the ANA Medal of Merit, and in 1972 he was elected to their Hall of Fame. Yeoman credited Mosher with having been "a particularly supportive friend" when the Red Book "was little more than a dream." In appreciation of the guidance and counsel he had offered during the book's creation, Yeoman presented him with the very first Red Book to come off the press, inscribed to him by the grateful author.

Hubert L. Polzer. Owner of a coin shop in Milwaukee, Polzer was close friends with fellow Wisconsiner Yeoman, and contributed to the Red Book for decades—only ceasing about the time of Yeoman's retirement. A member of the Central States Numismatic Society (CSNS), he served as its president in 1941. Polzer's son-in-law, Pete Foerster, went to work for Western Printing in the late 1950s, first as production manager, then as director of sales. Ken Bressett notes that Polzer's greatest claim to fame was discovering a rare 1849-O quarter that was not listed in the official Mint report and had not been listed in any coin catalog. Not surprisingly, once he made this discovery, it was quickly added to the Red Book!

Lewis M. Reagan. Born in Indianapolis in 1904, "Lew" Reagan became the backbone of the ANA, serving as its secretary from 1944 until his sudden death in December 1961. A mathematician by profession, he moved his family to Wichita,

Kansas, in 1946 upon being granted an assistant professorship at Wichita University. He was a fellow of the ANS and the Royal Numismatic Society; altogether, his obituary noted, he was "a member, honorary member, or officer of more local clubs and regional associations than any other person." In 1954 he received the Farran Zerbe Memorial Award as well as a special ANA award. Genial, popular, and devoted to establishing a sense of fraternity among numismatists, he became for many, in the words of *The Numismatist*, "the ANA itself." A year after his death, the Lewis M. Reagan Memorial Foundation was founded in Cincinnati, Ohio, in his honor.

Max M. Schwartz. By the time the Red Book came to be, Schwartz was already on his way to a distinguished career as a numismatic author. An attorney by profession, he would go on to serve as the ANA's legal counsel and later the general secretary of the PNG. In 1945 he became a member of the U.S. Assay Commission, and two years later he received the ANA Medal of Merit. In 1990 Krause Publications honored him with its Numismatic Ambassador Award.

Farran Zerbe. The namesake of the ANA's highest honor, the Farran Zerbe Memorial Award, served as the association's president for two terms, from 1907 to 1909. In 1908, on the death of *Numismatist* founder George Heath, Zerbe purchased the publication and served as editor until 1910, when it was bought by W.C. Wilson and given to the ANA. One of the greatest promoters and showmen in 20th-century numismatics, Zerbe popularized coin collecting through his Money of the World exhibit, which he displayed throughout the United States at fairs, expositions, and banks. Zerbe wrote numerous articles, many of which were published in *The Numismatist*, most notably his 1926 study "Bryan Money." Zerbe died in 1949 at the age of 78, and when the ANA created its Hall of Fame two decades later, he was among the first honorees.

Also playing a vital role in the launching of the Red Book, although not listed among the contributors to the first edition, were the following:

Ben Dreiske. As recounted by Yeoman, Dreiske was an up-and-coming young coin dealer at the time that Yeoman took his first baby steps into the convention world. He was also a contributor to Wayte Raymond's *Standard Catalogue*. His Chicago-based business began in the 1940s as Ben's Stamp and Coin company; later he renamed it Rare Coin Co. of America, and in early 1960 it took the abbreviated name of Rarcoa. Ken Bressett credits Dreiske with having been a "major helper in the early Red Book days" and remembers him as a charming person with a sharp sense of humor. Among his strengths as a member of the Red Book team were his strong grasp of price trends and his ability to quickly compute mental averages of the prices that were submitted from the various contributors. For many years he was one of the "inner circle" of consultants who determined final Red Book values. He was a member of the CSNS and the Chicago Coin Club, and served as vice president of the PNG. Dreiske ultimately sold Rarcoa to Ed Milas and started a new coin business in Florida, where he died in 1978 at the age of 65.

Lee F. Hewitt. Hewitt was integral to the creation of the Blue Book, without which the Red Book would never have come to pass. Starting with the first edi-

THE 1960S AND 1970S: RED BOOK RAMPANT

The 1960s saw a coin-collecting boom in America unlike any before or since, and the Red Book's fortunes went hand in hand with the trend. By the middle of the decade, the Red Book was a best seller, ranking fifth among modern nonfiction titles—right after *Betty Crocker's Picture Cook Book* and just before Dale Carnegie's *How to Win Friends and Influence People.* The Blue Book, no slouch itself, ranked number 12 on the same list. Perhaps even more impressive, the Red Book was ranked ninth in the top 10 all-time best sellers, tabulated through 1965—just behind Margaret Mitchell's *Gone With the Wind!*

It was also at this time that the Red Book set a record for copies printed and sold: the 1965 or 18th edition went into multiple printings to satisfy the high demand, and the final count came to a staggering 1.2 million copies. Although the exact print runs and sales figures of the following years are unknown, this undoubtedly remains the high-water mark of Red Book sales.

The triumph of the Red Book was all the more notable in that serious competition had begun to emerge. Before 1960, periodicals like *The Numismatist* and Lee Hewitt's *Numismatic Scrapbook* posed little threat because they did not regularly include comprehensive coin pricing. *Numismatic News* was founded in 1952 by Chester "Chet" Krause, who would become a good friend of Yeoman's, but it would be a number of years before this modest weekly newsletter developed into a major publication. The emergence in 1960 of *Coin World*, the first successful weekly numismatic newspaper, presented more of a challenge. In 1963, the *Coin Dealer Newsletter*, popularly known as the "Greysheet," appeared.

The 1960s also saw some reconfiguring behind the scenes. In 1959 Kenneth Bressett had joined the Red Book staff, and in 1965 he began inheriting Red Book editorial duties from Yeoman, whose position was shifting more toward managerial responsibilities as the staff expanded. Just two years later the company was restructured: a line of stamp-collecting books and supplies was added, and Whitman Publishing became the Whitman Hobby Division of Western Publishing.

During this decade the Red Book was also supplemented, for a short time, by the *Whitman Numismatic Journal* (subtitled "A Monthly Magazine Devoted to All Phases of Numismatics"). This monthly publication, whose staff included R.S. Yeoman as editor in chief and Kenneth Bressett as managing editor, was published from January 1964 to December 1968. According to a 1968 advertisement, the *Journal* "will keep your copy of the *Guide Book of United States Coins* always up-to-date." (See chapter 8 for more information on the *Whitman Numismatic Journal.*) Retailers who stocked Whitman coin products also received a newsletter that kept them informed of the latest news about the Red Book, the Blue Book, and other Whitman coin titles. This newsletter was published as the *Whitman Coin Supply Merchandiser* from 1960 to 1966, then resumed in 1969 as the *Stamp and Coin Supply Merchandiser*, reflecting the company's acquisition of the stamp division over the interim. By 1971 this new line had been cancelled, however, and the newsletter was discontinued. The next year it was revived as the *Coin Supply Merchandiser*, and it ran under that name through the end of 1974. In its various incarnations, the *Merchandiser* offers a wealth of inside information on the evolution of the Red Book, some of which is excerpted in the individual listings for each Red Book edition in chapter 4.

BEHIND THE SCENES OF RED BOOK PRODUCTION IN THE 1960s

Examining a Red Book press sheet with Yeoman in 1960 are then–assistant editor Kenneth Bressett (center) and production manager Pete Foerster (left). In the background, pressman Al Rivers keeps an eye on production.

Neil Shafer was the newest member of the Whitman editorial staff when this photograph was taken in 1962. He and Bressett are shown in consultation with typesetter Wil Winters. (See Neil Shafer's Red Book Recollection on page 38.)

Carried by conveyor belt, Red Books are individually inspected before shipment in 1963. Books found to be defective were repaired or destroyed—although some did elude inspectors, resulting in the sought-after error copies known today.

In 1964, new equipment enhanced the Red Book casing-in process. The *Merchandiser* reported, "the entire mechanics of adding covers to the GUIDE BOOK has been speeded up this year through the use of a complex series of new machines."

In this 1965 photograph, Yeoman (far left) explains Red Book printing procedures to two guests, who are being led on a tour of the facilities by Foerster (far right), now director of sales.

Orders for the 1970 Red Books were so large that this entire truckload was destined for just one vendor.

Meanwhile, of course, Yeoman did not merely sit back and admire the success of his two popular series. Expanding into other areas of collecting, he continued to introduce important reference books to the market. Yeoman scored another hit with *A Catalogue of Modern World Coins* (1957), which listed thousands of coins from the period of 1850 to 1955. It was later updated with a second volume, *Current Coins of the World*, which began at the point that *A Catalogue of Modern World Coins* had concluded. Working together, he and Bressett produced more than 300 hobby-related titles and products.

But Yeoman's contributions to the hobby included more than these important books. He participated in numerous coin organizations, and served on the board of governors of the American Numismatic Association (ANA) from 1946 to 1951. That organization honored him with its highest honor, the Farran Zerbe Memorial Award, in 1956. In 1964, President Lyndon Johnson appointed Yeoman chairman of the U.S. Assay Commission, the distinguished organization founded in 1797 to verify the metal content of U.S. coins.

"Yeoman was always helpful to the young numismatists," recalls coin dealer Bill Spencer, who was only 13 when he met R.S. Yeoman through the Racine Numismatic Society in 1951. Here the two attend the club's 1968 coin show in Kenosha, Wisconsin. From left to right are Leroy Jakubowski, Bill Spencer, Roy Miller, and Yeoman.

By the start of the 1970s, Red Books were becoming collectible themselves. The 1971 Red Book introduced a new feature, "Old Red Books Never Die," which demonstrated the usefulness of the fund of historical price data furnished by a collection of old Red Books. The chapter observed that Red Books were already becoming collectibles, and offered some observations on what made them attractive and interesting to collect:

The growing popularity of the Red Book led to autograph sessions, where fans like this one would line up to get Yeoman's signature on their new Red Books.

Reports reach us more and more that many collectors are assembling yearly editions of this catalog and occasionally we hear from proud owners who have complete sets. These individuals are truly fortunate, for they have a generation of coin values to check, to study, and to give them an understanding of what makes our American coin market what it is today. . . For the most part, a search through old editions proves exciting and rewarding, and in some few instances, a little disappointing. . . .

In 1971, the Red Book reached a mile-stone with the printing of its 10 millionth copy. Gathered to observe the event are (from left to right) Kenneth Bressett, Neil Shafer, R.S. Yeoman, Ed Metzger, and Holland Wallace.

Those collectors who have told us of their partly formed or completed sets have empha-sized how fascinating and help-ful early-year Red Books have been to them.

Western Publishing president Gerald Slade presents Yeoman (accompanied by Kenneth Bressett) with a plaque to commemorate the landmark printing.

Bill Whaley, manager of activity and hobby products, offers congratulations to Yeoman and Bressett.

The chapter shows that, as early as 1970, the Red Book creators were aware that their product was "both a needed tool and a permanent record of market performance for the American collecting fraternity." Ken Bressett discussed the reasoning behind this spe-cial feature in the July-August 1970 *Merchandiser:*

> The basic premise of this innovation [the price performance history] is that a given coin's potential value can only be determined if the investor knows something about its past. Up to now this information was usually available only to those col-lectors who were fortunate enough to own a complete set of all editions of the Red Book. Unfortunately, we know that very few people own all of these books. It has only been in recent years that a number of collectors have attempted to save each edition. . . . No doubt the added feature in the 1971 Red Book will encourage many others to do the same.

It is interesting to speculate whether this prediction was correct, and whether this use-ful feature did increase the number of *Guide Book* collectors. In another testament to the value of a Red Book collection, Yeoman related that an accountant once told him that he kept a complete set of Red Books to appraise coin values for estate taxes. When he had only the date of purchase to go by, he looked up the coin's value in the appropriate edition of the Red Book, and the IRS accepted the source.

In 1977, Dick and Marion Yeoman were honored on the cover of the *Centinel*, the publication of the Central States Numismatic Society.

In 1971, Whitman prepared a special silver anniversary edition of the Red Book, and during this book's press run, another milestone was reached when the 10 millionth Red Book was printed. Yeoman had retired in 1970, but he was present to accept a plaque from Gerald Slade, then president of the Whitman Hobby Division, commemorating the landmark event.

Yeoman's departure foreshadowed some upheavals in the Red Book world. Later in the 1970s further company restructuring resulted in the reduction of the line of coin products, and by 1980 several valuable members of the coin department had left. Among these was editor Kenneth Bressett, although he continued to serve as an independent consultant for the numismatic publications.

RED BOOK RECOLLECTIONS
Neil Shafer

All the years I was at Whitman (1962 to 1981), the Red Book was always the product of primary importance. This fact was well supported by sales, which as I recall topped one million in 1964 alone. The collecting of Red Books was well underway and had been an ongoing activity for many collectors, and of course this aspect has continued unabated into present times.

My participation in the preparation of this book was somewhat limited, as my particular fields of activity centered more on world numismatics. Yet each year around April, when the next edition was in earnest preparation, I was called upon to work alongside Dick Yeo and Ken Bressett in entering values and doing anything else there was to be done editorially in order to get the book ready for publication.

In order for us to be able to work uninterruptedly and in a peaceful atmosphere, we always went to stay for a few days at Lake Lawn Lodge in Delavan, Wisconsin. As needed, we had guest assistants to provide some degree of guidance with respect to what the coin market had done the past year, and to help with a value structure that would accurately mirror and in some ways predict market activity. Individuals including Ben Dreiske and Art Kagin were such participants, each acting individually, as only one such assistant would work with us during any given session. Remember that in those years the activities of the market were not nearly so frenetic, and the Red Book was the absolute bellwether of all market trends. Its July release date was always very eagerly anticipated by the hobby. In fact, there was so much attention given to what the new Red Book would say that security measures had to be imposed in order to make sure no new information or books leaked out before July!

As an aside, Lake Lawn Lodge had a decoration on each outer door of every room consisting of a little Indian with several feathers, the exact number of which varied slightly from door to door. As we walked the hall to the dining room or to our work room we would often take notice of these feathers, likening them in a joking way to the tail feather varieties on Morgan dollars!

We had a number of specially prepared books to help with our compilation of data and values.

R.S. Yeoman and Neil Shafer consulting together in 1969.

Chief among them were the interleaved editions, now considered to be prime Red Book rarities. How I wish I had thought of saving them when they were so available to me!

My work on the Red Book remained pretty much the same through Dick Yeo's retirement in 1969 and Ken Bressett's 1980 departure; at that time, and for only a single year, I became the coordinating editor. Ken then resumed that position and has maintained it admirably well ever since.

THE SECOND "MR. RED BOOK": KENNETH BRESSETT

New Hampshire native Kenneth Bressett had been seriously collecting coins since 1943, when he was working as a grocery store clerk. Through high school, business school, and college, his interest never waned. In the late 1940s he took a position as printer-compositor with the Sentinel Publishing Company in Keene, New Hampshire, but continued to pursue his avocation, joining the ANA in 1947 and the ANS in 1954.

When he first met R.S. Yeoman at a coin convention in the mid-1950s, the two hobbyists discussed the latest edition of the *Guide Book of United States Coins.* Bressett mentioned a number of errors he had found in the volume. At Yeoman's request, he later sent a list of them to the Whitman office. Yeoman welcomed his observations, and in 1956 asked Bressett to become a freelance editor for the book. He has been a member of the Red Book editorial staff ever since.

A photograph from the mid-1960s finds Kenneth Bressett at work on the Red Book with Pete Foerster and R.S. Yeoman.

Bressett was first mentioned in the *Guide Book* in the 11th edition (1958), where he was listed as a member of the panel of contributors. For the following two editions, Bressett was part of the group to whom "credit for counsel and advice is due." In 1959, he moved to Racine and took a full-time editorial position with Whitman. By the 14th edition (published in 1960 with a cover date of 1961), he was listed as editorial assistant. Two years later, in the 1963 edition, he was promoted to coordinating editor, and was credited in this fashion for nearly a decade, even as he took over editing duties from Yeoman, whose role was becoming more managerial. In the 27th (1974) edition, in belated recognition of Bressett's pivotal role, the title page added the declaration "Edited by Kenneth Bressett." By the 2000 edition, in a show of appreciation by the publisher, this was added to the Red Book's cover.

Like Yeoman, Bressett continued to play a significant role in the hobby through means other than his Whitman achievements. Starting in 1962, he served as consultant on the Childs Collection, an impressive collection of nearly every half cent through $5 gold coin dated from 1793 through the dates it was assembled (the 1870s through the mid-1900s). He helped research and catalog this remarkable collection until its sale in 1999. Bressett was appointed to the U.S. Assay Commission by President Lyndon Johnson in 1966. Thirty years later, he was made a member of the Citizens Commemorative Coin Advisory Committee (CCCAC). In that capacity, he was instrumental in the launch of the tremendously successful 50 State Quarters® Program, and in selecting many of the designs that were used.

During the more than 60 years that Bressett has been involved in numismatics, he has actively promoted the hobby. He has worked as editor of numerous books and products. He has written on many topics, including ancient coins, paper money, and both U.S. and world coins. He has also taught the subject of numismatics and coin collecting to hundreds of college students, at Colorado College and elsewhere. From 1983 to 1988, he served the ANA as director of the coin authentication and educational programs. Subsequently, he was elected to the organization's board of governors, and later served as vice president and president. He is a life member of that organization and a fellow of the American Numismatic Society.

He has received numerous awards in recognition of his service and dedication to numismatics, including the ANA Medal of Merit, the Farran Zerbe Memorial Award (awarded jointly to him and his wife, "Bert"), and the Numismatic Literary Guild's Clemy Award. In 1996, he was inducted into the Numismatic Hall of Fame.

Bressett remains active in the numismatic community today. In 2005, the first edition of his *Money of the Bible* was released; in 2007, *Milestone Coins: A Pageant of the World's Most Significant and Popular Money* was published. Among his other books are *Money of the American Civil War,* the *Guide Book of United*

By 1980, Kenneth Bressett's son Phil (left) had joined him on the Red Book staff. (See Phil Bressett's Red Book Recollection on page 149.)

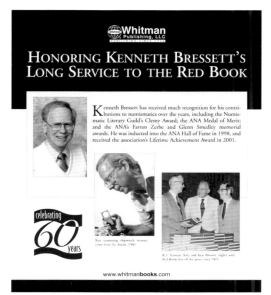

In 2007 Whitman Publishing celebrated the Red Book's 60th anniversary—and its long association with Kenneth Bressett.

Longtime colleagues Kenneth Bressett and Neil Shafer pause for a photo at the August 2008 ANA show in Baltimore, Maryland. Shafer joined the Whitman staff in 1962 and remained for almost two decades.

States Currency, and the *Handbook of Ancient Greek and Roman Coins* (editor). Somehow, among all his other activities, he continues to produce the annual Red Book and Blue Book. Both still display R.S. Yeoman's name on the cover, but they have truly become Bressett's projects.

Fittingly, Bressett has accumulated an extensive collection of *Guide Book*s. In 1947 he received the first edition as a gift from his future wife, Bertha "Bert" Britton, and he has added each successive edition as it was released. Among the more unusual Red Books that have belonged to his collection are the joke books prepared for him by long-time friend and Red Book contributor Q. David Bowers, including a fur-covered 30th edition (see the foreword by Bowers). "I still have that treasure," Bressett comments, "and it still tickles me!"

THE 1980S: NOSTALGIA AND NEGOTIATION

By the 1980s, the Red Book had become such a firmly established institution that nostalgia was gathering around it. Articles about collecting Red Books begin to proliferate: in 1983, David Bowers's column "The Guide Book Revisited" appeared in *The Numismatist;* in 1983 through 1986, *Coin World* ran a series of articles by Red Book collector and dealer Ed Lesniak, who offered collecting advice and published accounts of newly discovered error copies. The 1984 edition of the Red Book also contained an essay by R.S. Yeoman himself, "The Red Book Story," in which we find more evidence that past editions—including error copies—had already become collectible: "There are increasing signs that more and more collectors are assembling sets of back editions," he wrote, adding that "printing and binding discrepancies have taken on a special interest for a growing number of Red Book owners." (Chapter 7 discusses collectible error copies of the Red Book.)

The appeal of the Red Book was not merely sentimental, however, as many fans were quick to point out. In 1987, noted numismatist Col. Bill Murray wrote an appreciative essay that appeared under the title "'Red Book' Still an Informative Guide" in the October 21 issue of *Coin World*. As the title indicates, he stressed the continuing relevance of the venerable guide book, and urged the novice coin collector, or "new-mismatist," to explore it:

> If you want to determine the greatest value of the "Red Book" for a New-Mismatist, take time to read the words in paragraphs, not just the numbers and column introductions and headings. You'll learn. In fact, I firmly believe that if you know all that is in the "Red Book," truly know it, you'll know more about United States coinage than many, not to say most, dealers. . . . Purchase it, and immerse yourself in the material therein. You'll be a better numismatist as a result. Besides, it's fun.

Although Murray warned readers that "prices in the coin market change too often and too rapidly for an annual publication to keep pace," he asserted that the price listings in the Red Book "still have utility." As proof, he offered the intriguing information that "a small survey conducted a few years ago disclosed that virtually all dealers in United States coins not only owned the 'Red Book' but purchased one each year. Primarily these dealers use the 'Red Book' to determine relative values of coins, especially some of the more esoteric varieties not usually listed in the various weekly price guides." It seems that coin dealers as well as collectors were recognizing the usefulness of a library of Red Books!

In a similar vein, Q. David Bowers's essay in the November 1987 *Numismatist* discussed the perspective that could be gleaned from examining older editions of the guide. Entitled "The Red Book: Great Value for the Money," his discussion also provided an insightful look at the history and development of the Red Book, and mused on some of the changes the famous volume had undergone through the years:

> Though many products deteriorate once they achieve a measure of success, the opposite has happened to the Red Book. Over the years it has improved, and this year's edition contains much more information than its predecessor of some 30 years ago. Of course, things were simpler back then—grading was not nearly as complicated—and it can be argued that not as much information was necessary. . . . Back then a coin was either uncirculated or it wasn't; likewise, a Proof was a Proof— not a Proof-60, Proof-61, etc.

He went on to provide the reader with a sense of how the Red Book had fit into the numismatic community during its early years: "in the 1950s, the Red Book was all things to all people," he pointed out. "With this guide in hand, you didn't need any other price references, except perhaps lists of prices realized from auction sales if you wanted to track down the selling price of some landmark rarity. The hobby was slower back then."

The same year, Yeoman himself was present at the ANA convention that year as part of the celebration of the Red Book's 40th anniversary.

The September 1988 *Numismatist* celebrated the Red Book with a nostalgic cover and an article by Ginger Rapsus. (See her Red Book Recollection on page 151.)

The following year, in 1988, the Red Book appeared on the cover of the September issue of *The Numismatist*, in recognition of that issue's article "The Red Book Story" by Ginger Rapsus. The 42nd-edition Red Book even received a two-part review from David Bowers, which spanned the December 1988 and January 1989 issues of *The Numismatist.*

Meanwhile, however, the situation at the book's parent company remained unsettled. In 1982 Western Publishing was bought by Mattel Company, which made no attempt to restore the coin-collecting line to its former glory. Two years later Western changed hands again, when Richard A. Bernstein bought out Mattel's interest in the company. Again, no improvements came about under the new management. The next time the company was put up for sale, in 1992, it would be several years before it found a buyer.

The Red Book itself also came in for some backlash. In November 1988 *The Numismatist* printed this letter to the editor, under the heading "Red Book Overrated," by ANA member Daniel Byrns:

> I am writing to say that I am very tired of reading articles in the numismatic press that glorify the Red Book (*A Guide Book of United States Coins*). I'm sure it was a very good book when it was originally written in 1946, but the fact is that it is largely obsolete today and of only limited utility.
>
> It was created for a generation of date and mintmark collectors and does not reflect the needs and interests of the broad mass of today's numismatists. The Red Book does not contain the most up-to-date numismatic research and presents many areas, especially early American coins, in a misleading or even incoherent fashion.
>
> If the publishers and editors of *A Guide Book of United States Coins* want their product to continue to be a useful tool, it will need radical changes in format, content and scope.

Byrns's letter brought rapid responses from the Red Book faithful. The following January, *The Numismatist* printed two of these under the title "Forty-Two Editions of Red Book Bespeak Its Value." One read, in part, "What [Byrns] needs is not a guide book but an atlas of coins. The Red Book is great as a guide—long may it survive." The other implied that Byrns's criticism was born of snobbishness:

> I find it extremely interesting that a relatively new member of the ANA can find so much fault with a book that has been through 42 editions, and then pick as an organ to express his displeasure a magazine with less circulation than the annual sales of the book in question.
>
> I believe this strongly indicates that the ANA has lost the average numismatist, or that maybe coin collecting and numismatics are no longer compatible, let alone synonymous.

Clearly, although the advent of the Red Book had done much to unite the scholarly numismatic interests with the hobbyists, there was still the sense of a rift. In response to this thrust, Byrns came back in the April 1989 issue with a long letter, in which he specified some of his grounds for criticizing the *Guide Book:*

> Many old-time collectors seem to be emotionally attached to the Red Book, so I suppose I should have expected to be condemned for having the audacity to suggest that R.S. Yeoman's *A Guide Book of United States Coins* is in need of revision. . . . It is true that I am an ordinary collector and a relative newcomer to the hobby, but, because the Red Book is the primary (and often the only) reference book used by beginning collectors, I believe I have a perfect right to complain.

. . . The reader is confronted with a commemorative coin section in which issues inexplicably are listed alphabetically rather than chronologically. Gold [commemorative] coins are separated from their companion silver coins so that you have to flip back and forth constantly to find related issues. A whole class of officially minted gold coins—the "ingots" of the United States Assay Office—are buried in a listing of private-issue coins.

. . . *A Guide Book of United States Coins* was a landmark numismatic publication. It is a truism among coin dealers that coins listed in the Red Book are avidly collected, while those ignored by the reference are not. I cannot believe that the late author of the Guide Book would want his most popular and influential work to become obsolete because no one saw fit to bring it up to date.

Since the Red Book has throughout its history undergone constant evolution and revision in an effort to stay current, it should be no surprise that future editions of the Red Book would address some of the concerns that Byrns voices here. Starting with the 59th edition, for example, the commemorative section has been organized in chronological order and no longer separates the gold classic commemoratives from their silver fellows. It is amusing to note that Byrns posits the very popularity of the book as a rationale for airing his grievances, implying that the book is practically mandatory for new collectors!

Sadly, as the final sally in this epistolary dust-up acknowledges, the creator of the Red Book was no longer alive to defend it, had he wished to. Richard Yeo died in November 1988 at the age of 84. Ed Metzger, the manager of Whitman Coin Division, wrote this moving eulogy for the January 1989 *Numismatist:*

The recent death of Richard S. Yeo, who wrote under the pen name "R.S. Yeoman," leaves the numismatic hobby with a heartfelt sense of loss. Considered by many to be the father of modern-day coin collecting, Yeo's considerable contributions to the hobby have made it what it is today.

Once called a "20th-century coin genius," Yeo helped to create the basic tools and framework of coin collecting reference materials. His efforts came as a result of a keen skill in determining and fulfilling the needs of the collector.

Yeo served his hobby in a number of capacities: as author of *A Guide Book of United States Coins* ("Red Book") and the *Handbook of United States Coins* ("Blue Book"); inventor of the coin folder; speaker; exhibit judge; and noted authority on American and world coins. He took none of these roles less seriously than the others. His total commitment to the hobby was reflected in everything he did.

Among the riches Yeo gave to the coin collecting community was his constant personal goal to "do what is best for the hobby." The highest tribute coin collecting can pay to this great man would be to never lose sight of that goal.

Upon his retirement, R.S. Yeoman and his wife moved to Arizona. There he sketched this colorful view of a local landmark as a gift for the Bressetts. The inscription reads, "Gunsight Pass from 'Ghost' Helvetia sketched especially for Bert and Ken Bressett by Dick Yeo."

RED BOOK RECOLLECTIONS

Richard Schwary

Everyone who has considered coins most probably used the Red Book at one time or another. It has been part of my "carry-around" library for so long that I can't remember when I did not have a copy. It was of course Richard Yeoman's magnum opus and it provides order and reason to a numismatic world in which general information and pricing was needed to educate the public and conduct business. Over the years the name "Red Book" became so comfortable that even today I pause a moment to recall the actual title of *A Guide Book of United States Coins* when recommending it to the public. Like today, it was an absolute necessity when I was in grade school. But in those early years pricing was rather flat so a new copy each year was considered a luxury. I taped and numbered my most popular sections, those being silver dollars and Lincoln cents, for easy access. And when constant use broke down the binder I repaired it with more tape and reinforcements. There were, of course, other good sources of information but these insights were simply noted in the margins of my current Red Book and the back cover used to note questions or other things of interest.

Years later it was these fond memories that made being a price contributor to this fine book a particular honor. But the really fortunate part of this numismatic fun happened at the 1987 ANA convention. Concurrently each year the Professional Numismatists Guild held its annual banquet. After a round of drinks and the usual conversation we all settled down to a table for dinner and the usual festivities. The seat next to me was vacant and soon a dignified older fellow sat down and began a polite conversation. His dress was a conservative suit and tie and we talked quietly about the banquet and the number of people attending. After a few minutes it dawned on me that this was Richard S. Yeoman. I excused myself and said, "You must be Richard Yeoman, of Red Book fame." I had never met him in person so I introduced myself.

He shook my hand and quietly said, "Why, yes I am, it is nice to meet you." That was it, not an ounce of pretense in this man who helped form the complete structure of my early coin career. At any ANA convention the amount of bravado most dealers are exposed to amounts to something like going to the Super Bowl. But here, by complete chance I talked with an icon whose book will always be quoted. Yet he was so unassuming that it caught me quite off guard. Our entire conversation had nothing to do with his accomplishments but focused on the coin industry. To say that such a touch is rare today has to be an understatement.

As the night drew to a close we all prepared to leave, and I could not help but wonder: how many people recognized this conservatively dressed gentleman? This banquet room was filled with noted dealers, numismatic scholars, the coin press, fascinating writers, and interesting coin people of every stripe. Yet how many of these notables could claim to have touched everyone in the room? Surely such a list would be short, but R.S. Yeoman and *A Guide Book of United States Coins* would be a contender for first place.

THE 1990S TO THE PRESENT: THE ENDURING RED BOOK

The 50th anniversary of the Red Book in 1996 was a major milestone. A special anniversary cover and a new spiralbound edition marked the occasion, and Q. David Bowers launched a five-part series called "Inside the Red Book" in *The Numismatist.*

In the same year, Western Publishing was finally sold after four years on the market. The new owner, Richard E. Snyder, changed the company name to Golden Books Family Entertainment—a reflection of his vision for the company, which was to focus on children's publishing. Whitman Publishing was renamed "Whitman Coin Products," and it was now just a part of Golden's relatively small adult publishing division. Whitman brought steady profits to the division, but, as David Crenshaw observes, "little was done to reverse the continuing slump in the numismatic line," and the low product inventories allowed other numismatic publishers to take a bigger bite of the market. Yet another change of hands, in 1999, had a more positive outcome: St. Martin's Press, the new owner, gave the coin division a much-needed boost by overhauling the company's sales strategy and launching products related to the 50 State Quarters® Program.

The 1990s also saw the emergence of a potentially serious threat to the Red Book: the Internet. As the possibilities offered by the new technology grew, more and more numismatists felt obliged to address the question of whether the Red Book would be rendered obsolete by online coin-pricing references, which could offer up-to-the-minute data updates. In a review, ANA member Susan Headley explained that she prized the book because it was "inexpensive and portable," and pointed out that up-to-the-minute pricing wasn't necessarily a major consideration for the average collector:

> Although the Internet has more up-to-date pricing than the book, this type of information is only useful for high-grade and rare coins. The vast majority of buying and selling is done in collector-grade material, which doesn't change much in value in the short term. Internet price listings are a great source of extra information, but until somebody invents a $15 real-time-pricing coins-based handheld computer, online price lists will not be replacing my Red Book![19]

Likewise, Bowers noted that "the Red Book is convenient, portable and offers a very large database of price and mintage information. You don't have to charge its batteries or plug it in, nor does it cost $2,000 or arbitrarily decide to stop working!"

Nevertheless, doubts as to the venerable book's continued relevance would occasionally arise. In a 2002 essay in *COINage*, for example, Mike Thorne wrote, "in the early 1950s, determining a coin's value was easy for many dealers: If you were selling, the coin was worth full Red Book. . . . Today, the situation is drastically different." At the same time, however, Thorne was enthusiastic about the changes that the Red Book had undergone during its long life. (See chapter 4 for more excerpts from his essay.) Just three years later, reviewing the 2006 edition, he would assert that "the current Red Book is much more than just a list of coins and prices," and observe that the presence of competing coin guides had evidently been beneficial to the book.[20]

Further changes were still in store for the Red Book. In 2003 St. Martin's Press in New York City sold Whitman Coin Products to H.E. Harris & Company, the noted stamp- and coin-collecting supply firm. Harris and Whitman were combined under the name of Whitman Publishing, with the new company's base of operations in Atlanta, Georgia. This alliance of the two leading numismatic and philatelic supply firms reinvigorated the Whitman coin-collecting line of books and supplemented it with a line of licensed U.S. Mint products.

In spite of the competition posed by new technology and other coin-pricing guides, the Red Book endured, as did its popularity. Different readers cite different reasons for their loyalty. Q. David Bowers wrote in 1997, "Despite the abundance of timely numismatic references . . . I rely most on the familiar, red-covered *Guide Book*. It is not that it has more pricing information, but rather because it is so easy to use. It is small enough to tuck into a coat pocket, yet big enough to provide mintage figures, general price indications and a wealth of information."

David Alexander, in his 2005 article "The 'Red Book' of U.S. Coins," also cites its ease of use, as well as its familiarity and long history—which carry both the appeal of nostalgia and the sense of stability that may be absent from other areas of coin collecting (and life in general). "In some ways," he concludes, "the public affection that is lavished on the Red Book recalls baseball fans' devotion to some of the more lop-eared home teams in places such as Brooklyn or Chicago over the years. Sure, there are things to affectionately criticize, 'but they're our guys, and we're gonna love 'em even if we lambaste 'em!'"

INTO THE FUTURE

A Guide Book of United States Coins is constantly changing. From its first publication in 1946 to the current edition, the Red Book has been a work in progress. Coin varieties are discovered, new coins are issued, the coin market fluctuates, coin collecting evolves as a hobby—and the *Guide Book* has recorded and responded to it all.

As coin collecting has changed, the Red Book has grown and evolved from a simple listing of two different grades of coins to an elaborate listing that reflects the refinement in grading that later developed. The first issue contained listings for approximately 3,400 different coins. Today, the *Guide Book* has expanded to list more than 6,000 pieces. The original volume listed two condition grades; now there are as many as nine grades and values. The first edition was a compilation of the knowledge of the author, R.S. Yeoman, and 14 contributors. Today, editor Ken Bressett utilizes the skills and experience of more than 100 contributors plus several special consultants. Rather than being a collection of information from a select few, the book is now composed from the knowledge and research of many contributors, each of whom works in a specialized niche of the market.

What follows is a look back through time that will view coin collecting and the *Guide Book* as they have changed and developed over the course of more than six decades. As Thomas Wolfe wrote, "You can't go home again," and neither can we return to the days when a coin was simply either circulated or uncirculated. Yet we can look through the window of the past that the early editions of the Red Book represent to gain from our predecessors a clearer picture of the hobby, not only as it was but as it may become.

Kenneth Bressett autographed copies of the 2008 American Numismatic Association special edition Red Book at the ANA banquet in Milwaukee, Saturday evening, August 11, 2007. Here he visits with another hobby legend, Clifford Mishler.

3

HOW TO BE A
SMART COLLECTOR

This chapter will cover some basic information that every Red Book collector should consider before starting—or expanding—a collection.

Those who collect the *Guide Book* are very often coin collectors. Although it is perfectly logical to progress from coins to the coin guide, the two pursuits differ in some important ways, and numismatists who are new to collecting books may find that a different mind-set is required. In order to familiarize the reader with some of the major considerations in forming a book collection, the first part of this chapter will discuss how to approach book collecting.

The section that follows explains the grading system used in this book to describe collectible Red Books. Most coin collectors are familiar with the grading process because they have been evaluating coins for some time. There are, however, different terms and qualifications for grading books. The first half of this chapter will focus on grading Red Books, so that you can evaluate both your own copies and copies you may come across at different venues.

Finally, you will learn how to properly care for your collection so that the books remain in the condition in which you bought them. The goal of a *Guide Book* collector is not only to acquire one of each title; you should also strive to find books in the best possible condition. Yet buying a book in new condition is meaningless if you then take it home and fail to take care of it. For that reason, "Caring for Your Collection" is one of the most important sections in this book.

HOW—AND WHY—TO COLLECT
RED BOOKS

Whereas many people collect coins more for their value as investments than for the pleasure and historical insight they provide, collecting books with an eye solely on their financial return can be a dicey proposition. Needless to say, coins don't come with any guarantee of resale value—as a quick perusal through past Red Books will prove!—but in many ways books present even less certainty. In the excellent discussion of collecting numismatic books in Q. David Bowers's *Expert's Guide to Collecting and Investing in Rare Coins*, Bowers makes this point. To the question "Are books a good *financial* investment on their own, without regard to any other consideration?" he responds "usually not." He goes on to consult noted numismatic book dealer George F. Kolbe, who warns that some numismatic publications have actually depreciated in value over the years.

Likewise, in his *Coin World* articles about collecting Red Books, dealer-collector Ed Lesniak urges readers, in the words of one article title, to "Collect 'Red Books' for

Enjoyment First."[21] He too poses the question "Should 'Red Books' be collected as an investment?" and responds, "I feel that they should be, but I won't recommend them because there are far better investments to be found." Rather, he asserts, Red Books "should be purchased for two reasons. First as an enjoyment and secondly as a necessary part of a coin library."

Of course, different collectors will take pleasure in their collections for different reasons. Some will enjoy the thrill of the hunt and find their satisfaction in the mere act of owning the books. Some may not ever read the books they collect—but here they deprive themselves of one of the chief benefits of their trophies. George Kolbe makes a key point when he comments, "I have always thought of numismatic literature as an investment in *knowledge*." Bowers adds, "Knowledge is also the *key to profit*, and in that way books can be a superb financial investment in the long run." One of the chief advantages to owning Red Books spanning many years is the insight they provide into a coin's performance over time. Without such knowledge, it is all the more difficult to determine whether to invest in the coin. As long ago as 1970, the Whitman *Merchandiser* noted that "a coin's potential value can only be determined if the investor knows something about its past. . . . Collectors who buy a new [Red] book each year and save it will eventually own a good set of records to use for price trend comparison." Since there is no other numismatic retail reference that has been continuously produced for more than 60 years, a Red Book collection is an invaluable tool.

Vintage Red Books also offer an unequaled window into the development of coin collecting. As each edition is succeeded by the next, you will see varieties appear and disappear, descriptive text change to reflect new research, new types come into being, and changing coin values reflect the state of the coin market. Many of these changes and insights are recorded in chapter 4 in the listings for individual Red Book editions, but the books themselves have even more stories to tell.

Now that you've decided to build (or build on) a Red Book library, where do you find the books? Twenty years ago, the task was easier, and stories of lucky finds proliferated. Lesniak recounted the tales of a woman who came away from a yard sale with a run of Red Books from the second edition through the 22nd; of a man who found a first edition on a bookstore's bargain table and purchased it for 50¢; and of another collector whose local bookseller had more than 40 pre-1956 Red Books, and was so glad to get rid of them that he even carried them out to the buyer's car!

Collecting is both easier and more difficult for today's collector than his counterpart in the past: easier, because the Internet provides more outlets for finding rare books; and more difficult, because the growth of online sales and auctions means that fewer copies will be languishing at yard sales or in the stockroom of your neighborhood bookstore, just waiting for you to unearth them! Moreover, the wider availability of information means that fewer sellers will be ignorant of the real value of their wares, and bargains may be scarce.

Nevertheless, such discoveries, while uncommon, are still possible. Collectors should certainly not neglect the possibilities offered by flea markets, used bookstores, and library sales. Bowers recommends the ANA Library sales, where ANA members can pay nominal prices for books donated by numismatists who are cleaning house.

For many collectors, the most convenient options are online book dealers and Internet auction sites such as eBay. However, the same standards of common sense that apply to any online purchase of a vintage item are all the more important when buying collectible books. Try to deal with established, reputable sellers, such as members of the Antiquarian

Booksellers Association of America. Familiarize yourself with sellers' customer feedback, if it is posted, to learn whether they are generally reliable and trustworthy.

Feedback can also alert you to a novice seller who may not know enough about the item being sold to give you an accurate description of it. Whenever you are unable to examine the book in person, it is crucial to find out all you can about its condition before bidding or buying, particularly since not all sellers accept returns. You may wish to open the discussion with a general request that the seller tell you as much as possible about the book's appearance and condition. Ask for a description of the copyright page as well, since a seller inexperienced in Red Books may not understand the distinction between cover date and publication date, which may make the difference between finding a long-sought prize and duplicating a common edition! Other questions are suggested by Bowers in his *Expert's Guide*, which offers a useful list of specific issues to raise before making a purchase from an unfamiliar vendor. Bowers recommends queries such as these:

> Describe the condition of the binding. Is it tight or is it loose?
>
> Describe the cover and binding imprints—lettered and sharp, faded, or—?
>
> Any water staining?
>
> Are any pages torn or incomplete?
>
> If there are markings in the book, what are they?
>
> Is there a return privilege?

The question of marks in the book is one that may be of greater or lesser importance depending on the individual collector. The effect of markings on a book's value is discussed in the section on grading, later in this chapter, but (as with many areas of grading a book's condition) this is not a cut-and-dried issue. If you are less concerned with the resale value of your collection than its personal value, your own preferences will be your guide. Remember, though, that if you will accept only pristine copies, you may have a difficult (and costly) search ahead of you. In this case, too, it is all the more crucial that you ask plenty of questions about a book's condition before purchasing it sight unseen.

Another useful tip offered by Lesniak is to seek out the rarer editions first. "Don't make the mistake that many coin collectors make," he advises. "Concentrate on the key books and leave the common ones for another day. . . . [T]he keys will cost you more a year from now. The common editions will always be common and their prices won't rise much."

With the continued release of annual Red Books and variant editions, special editions, and Limited Editions, the number of collectors seeking to complete their *Guide Book* collections will only increase—as will the prices that sellers demand. When you find yourself buying Red Books, the advice that is given for coin collecting is applicable: buy the best that you can afford. If you do, you will probably never be sorry.

GRADING RED BOOKS

To evaluate your collection, or a potential addition to it, you have to grade each book individually and carefully. The process is similar to that of grading coins, but the terminology is different, and there are no universally agreed-upon standards. In this book we will use five general grades for describing the condition of books: New, Very Fine, Very Good, Good, and Fair. Normally book grades are limited to New, Fine, Very Good, and Good. In recent years some numismatic book dealers have added the grade of Very Fine, which describes a book that is not quite in New condition but is very close.

In this discussion we have added the grade of Fair, which describes a book that has damage (e.g., water damage) or has been abused in some manner. The only Red Book editions that have any value in this grade are the first (both printings) through the fifth. Normally one would only purchase a book in this condition for reading or research—so that a more valuable copy need not be subjected to further wear—or as a "filler" for a collection, to stand in until a better-condition copy can take its place. The price to pay for Fair books is a matter of the individual collector's discretion, but be aware that these books are unlikely to increase in value.

George Kolbe, whose expert opinion has already been cited, offers some valuable counsel for the collector of Red Books. His advice should be kept in mind particularly while seeking and grading early editions.

> A cautionary note to collectors may apply: books are books and coins are coins. Books are often termed indestructible, but that is due to their proliferation rather than their fabric. Bindings and paper discolor with time; few remain unopened or never read; after half a century virtually none are exactly the same as when they were made. *I have never seen an early edition of the Red Book that I would describe as being* new, *i.e.,* Uncirculated *or* Mint State *in numismatic terms.* A few have come close, I admit, and I yearn for the day when I will hold one in my hands. Rare-book dealers and book collectors often describe *Very Fine* as "near new, minimal signs of use." I believe it is incumbent on a condition-conscious collector to understand that *Very Fine* is about the best condition in which any of the first 5 or 10 editions are obtainable. The opportunity to acquire a truly new, MS-60 early-edition Red Book is perhaps analogous to the acquisition of an MS-70 coin of the same era.

It is also important to remember that almost any edition that is signed by either R.S. Yeoman or Kenneth Bressett is valued over the cost of a regular, unsigned copy. The amount of the premium depends upon the scarcity of the particular edition. Generally, of course, earlier editions are less common and more desirable. See chapter 7 for further discussion of autographed and presentation copies of the Red Book.

New Books

A book in pristine condition is called New. The book hasn't even been opened yet. When you pull apart the covers on a new book, you will feel the strain. If you pull too hard, there will be a cracking sound. If you place the book directly on its spine and gently release, it will remain closed. The only blemishes, on both the cover and inside, should be from the printing and binding process. The editions that are particularly susceptible to this type of damage are well known, and covered in chapter 7. The first 10 editions of the Red Book are rarely, if ever, found in New condition.

Very Fine / Near Mint Books

A Very Fine or Near Mint book may appear new at first glance. The binding will be tight. Although the cover may not remain closed if you place the spine down on a table and release, most pages should still have that "new feel" when the book is gently opened—a sense that the pages have never before been turned. They look crisp, and the front flyleaf may even stick to the cover from the pressure of having been packed in a box with other books. The pages also sound crisp, as they are being separated from each other for the first time.

Upon further examination, the book may show evidence of use. Yet these signs should be slight, and there should be no wear or rubs on either the cover or inside pages.

Both the front and back cover should be clean and without marks, stains, or water stains. The corners should be even and squared off. The gilt on the cover and spine should be full and strong. Although there are times when a new book will not have full gilt because of the printing process, this is clearly distinguishable from a book that is missing gilt because of wear to its cover. Unless evidently the result of an error in the printing, missing gilt will detract from its value.

Next, examine the inside of the book, beginning with the end pages. There should be no evidence of paper stains or toning (turning color). The rest of the pages should also be clean and free of stains. Throughout the book, there should be no markings from any previous owners, with the frequent exception of the original seller's stamped company name. Unless it is particularly unsightly, such a mark should detract only slightly from the book's appearance and value. Of course, if the markings were made by a famous person, they could actually *enhance* the book's value. Chapter 7 discusses autographed and presentation copies of the Red Book.

Fine Books

A book in Fine condition is attractive, with little obvious wear. The entire volume is essentially clean. A few minor problems or defects are evident, but not without close inspection.

There should not be any bad stains or writing on the cover. It should have strong gilt, but it may be faded in spots. It should not have any tears. The corners may exhibit some rounding from being bumped but are still intact and not abused. Similarly, the edges may show some wear, but this should be light and the cover should not be worn through. There will be no fraying of the edges.

The book may have some very minor discoloration of the end pages. These pages are also likely to have either a stamp of the original selling company or an inscription. Any such markings should be written (or stamped) neatly. The pages should be clean, although they may be starting to tone. There should not be stains but a few minor light marks are generally acceptable. However, stains on the ends of the pages will detract from the book's quality to a greater degree.

Very Good Books

Preferably, your collection will be of books in excellent condition. Recent, easy-to-find books should be sought in Very Fine or New condition. Earlier editions, however, may be difficult to find in these grades. Very Good early editions are still considered collectibles.

The gilt on the cover and spine will be faded in some places. There will probably be some evident rubbing of the gilt. There may be some soiling, but it should not be extreme. In addition, the binding should be complete, but it may have some looseness. This is easily determined: hold the book with the spine in your left palm, fingers around the back, thumb in front. Lightly hold the pages with your right hand and lift. You will see the cover separate from the pages and the book open if the spine is loose.

Corners should be complete, but some evidence of bumping is expected. Also, the edges may show some wear from being removed from the shelf.

Generally, the pages are still whitish and clean, although some discoloration of the pages is expected and acceptable. There may be some notations within the body of the book, but they should be minor and not distracting. There may be some dog-eared pages, but they should be minimal.

RED BOOK RECOLLECTIONS

P. Scott Rubin

The first coin book I ever owned was a Red Book. The year was probably 1955, and I bought a used copy from a neighbor named Jimmy Fritz. Jimmy was about two years older than me (I was seven), and he sold me his sixth edition because he had just bought a new Red Book. Jimmy collected both stamps and coins, as did I, and told me that his great-uncle was big in the stamp business. Years later I found out that his great-uncle was in fact Mekeel of *Mekeel's Weekly Stamp News*.

By the time the 1960s rolled around I had started to collect coin auction catalogs to quench my thirst for information about coins that I could never afford. In the mid-'60s I was regularly receiving auction catalogs from Kagin's and shortly thereafter from Stack's. I decided to keep track of some rare U.S. coins when they appeared at auction, but the question was which coins I should track. I decided to use the Red Book to help me, so I went through the then-current edition and made a list of all regular-issue coins that had sold for $1,000 or more. Over the next few years, a few coins were dropped from the list and a few were added. The ones that I added were newly listed rare Red Book varieties. Today the list totals over 65 thousand auction appearances of over 200 coins. Over the years I have been called upon to supply collectors, dealers, and auction houses with information from the data I have been compiling since the 1960s. I was also honored to be able to assist Kenneth Bressett on the Red Book.

I have all 62 editions of the Red Book. Years ago I decided to complete my collection of Red Books by buying the editions I did not have. At the time most were readily available, but the first edition was harder to get. Luckily for me, my first coin dealer, Ed Hipps, had helped me find not only many coins but also many old auction catalogs and books. So when I asked Ed if he had a copy of the first edition of the Red Book to sell me, he led me to some bookshelves in the back of his store and told me to pick the one I wanted—he had four or five to choose from. I looked them over and found one in almost mint condition. I am so glad I bought it at that time, since its value has risen steadily since Ed sold it to me.

I had decided to put together a complete set of Red Books when I tried to create a list comparing the past selling prices of certain rare coins to their current values. Since there was no reliable weekly, monthly, or yearly price guide for coins outside of the Red Book, I found that I needed a complete set. After completing my Red Book collection I decided that I might as well complete my set of Blue Books, which I did.

By the 1970s, a few collectors and dealers realized there was a profit to be made from selling numismatic books and auction catalogs as collectibles. There were already a handful of numismatic book dealers selling these items to collectors: Aaron Feldman, James Brown, Frank and Laurese Katen, and George Kolbe (originally as G. Frederick Kolbe). These dealers were specializing almost exclusively in numismatic books by 1970. The hobby that had once been transacted almost entirely on a collector-to-collector basis was now starting to see dealers advertising and holding auctions of coin books.

> It was also about this time that people started paying attention to various editions of catalogs and books. I learned that there were two printings of the first edition of the Red Book, and that one of the 1960s editions contained a printing error. I checked my first edition and was happy to discover that it was a first printing. I was not so happy about the error edition, since I had cut out the error page years before. Stupid me!

Good Books

A book with extensive wear and slight damage to its cover and interior may be considered to be in Good condition. The gilt on the cover and spine is barely evident. The cover exhibits extensive use by the owner, and may even have a stain or two. The binding should be complete, but there may be some chipping of the spine, especially near the top and bottom. After all, chipping can occur when an owner simply pulls a book from its shelf incorrectly. (Proper handling of books is discussed later in this chapter.)

There may be stains on the interior, with the end pages particularly discolored. The book may include extensive notations or inscriptions in both pencil and pen. There may even be a tear or two on some pages. The spine may be loose, and a small tear may be evident where the cover attaches to the interior pages.

There is no reason to pass up a copy in Good condition if it completes a collection, but it is generally only kept until a copy is found in better condition.

Fair Books

A Fair book has been used and abused. The gilt on its cover is virtually gone. Stains are to be expected. There may even be pen notations on the cover.

The spine shows clear evidence of wear, along with damage to its top and bottom. It may be worn to the threads. Generally, this book is not easily (or cheaply) repairable.

There are usually extensive notations on the end pages and interior. In addition, some pages may be loose, although they should still be attached to the spine. The interior may even be separating from the cover. Tears to the end pages, where they attach to the interior of the book, are evident. Ex-library copies frequently fall into the category of Fair books. These usually have stickers, markings, and other library notations—in addition to signs of use—and are only rarely collectible.

As noted earlier, a Red Book in Fair condition is generally only worth purchasing as a place filler for an otherwise complete set, or for use as a reference. The advantage of a book in such poor condition is that the owner may use it without needing to worry about reducing its value.

CARING FOR YOUR COLLECTION

A *Guide Book* collection is a considerable investment, and should be cared for with the same tenacity as any of the coins in your collection. Yet there are many factors—from sunlight to humidity—that can and will affect the condition of your books. Consideration of these factors is crucial. After all, the condition of your books directly affects their value, as well as their lifespan.

It is also important to remember that it is unwise to attempt to erase markings made by a previous owner. This is likely to damage the book, as Ed Lesniak stresses:

The [question] that is commonly asked is "How can I remove all the writing and check marks in my older issues to make them more valuable?"

Our first and only answer to this is don't. This is the same as cleaning a coin. It simply should not be done. . . . [C]heck marks do take away from the value of the older books but collectors should not ruin them further by trying to remove the marks.[22]

Check marks are frequently found in older Red Books that were used as purchasing checklists by their owners. Rather than trying to obliterate these signs of the book's past "life," Lesniak urges, readers should enjoy them for the insight they offer into the collecting habits of their former owner. The presence of a collector's name on the inside cover will have a less detrimental impact on value: "If the book has been well taken care of," Lesniak explains, "this name doesn't matter all that much."

Never store books where they are exposed to sunlight—either direct or reflected. Such exposure can dry out the book. This can cause it to become brittle and possibly crack open, causing the spine to split. (See the illustrated example.) At other times, excessive heat exposure on the book's glue can cause the first page to tear. This consigns the book to a much lower grade and greatly reduces its value.

Sunlight can also cause your books to fade in color. The red dyes used for the Red Book cover are very sensitive to sunlight, especially those used in the early—and more valuable—editions. The first eight editions are particularly susceptible to the effects of the sun.

However, it is not just sunlight that will wreak havoc on your books: fluorescent light will damage them as well. Regular incandescent light will cause less harm than most other forms of light, but even this exposure should be kept to a minimum.

Ideally, your books should be stored in a room that is kept at an average of about 70 degrees Fahrenheit with no more than 50 percent humidity. High temperatures will dry out the books, causing them to become brittle. Damp, humid conditions, on the other hand, encourage the growth of mold. You may have seen descriptions of auction lots that mention a "musty smell." If you must purchase these editions, keep them away from the rest of your collection to prevent the mold from spreading to non-infected volumes.

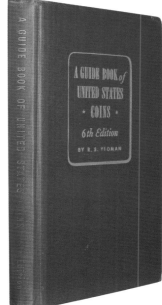

Examples of damage that can take place to Red Books that are improperly stored: left, a split spine; right, sun damage.

Books should always be stored vertically. Laying down a book for any extended period of time can cause it to warp, often permanently. If you must store the book horizontally for a short period of time, rotate the box periodically; this will even out the effects and reduce the damage. However, the books should be removed and properly stored as soon as possible. Storing your book at an angle can be equally damaging. It places a great deal of stress on the binding and can warp the entire book.

Store your books on a bookshelf, leaving enough space in the front and rear for proper air flow. Although the copies should be supported so that they cannot open, do not pack them too tightly. If you do, they will rub against each other whenever one is removed, causing wear on the covers. It is easier to avoid damaging a book's spine as you remove it from the shelf if the books are not tightly packed. Also, compact storage can generate additional and damaging heat.

You may want to purchase plastic covers for your collection. They should be archival-quality plastic and purchased from a reputable dealer. After all, the same polyvinyl chloride (PVC) that can damage your coin collection can affect your *Guide Book* collection if you are not careful. Plastic covers are a worthwhile investment. First, the oils from your hands—which can be very damaging—will not get on the covers of the books. You will also not have to worry about the deterioration that can be caused when covers rub against each other.

If you choose not to buy book covers, always wash your hands before touching the books. This will remove the excess oils and dirt, which can be transferred to the books' covers. You may even want to consider using protective gloves when handling early and valuable editions.

Even with all these restrictions, it *is* possible to read and enjoy your Red Books. To remove the book from the shelf, grasp it with your thumb against the front and your other fingers against the rear cover (see illustration). *Never* pull a book from the shelf by the top of its spine. This is particularly vital for the ninth edition; as chapter 4 discusses, this edition's cover is made from a different material than the other Red Books, one far more fragile and susceptible to chipping—especially on the spine. Always remember to handle it by placing your fingers on its front and rear covers. When stocking your shelves, leave extra space for this.

To read the book, place it so that the spine is in your left palm. When you open the book, it should be supported by your palm. This will prevent the book from falling, while also providing the spine with support so that it will not be damaged. Always hold your book firmly to prevent inadvertent damage.

It only takes a short amount of time to permanently damage your carefully accumulated collection, but proper care can help ensure that its value is maintained. Whether we collect coins or books, we are merely temporary custodians of our collections until they are passed on to the next generation of collectors. When your books ultimately leave your possession, their new owner should be able to tell that they came from a collector who truly appreciated the importance of the *Guide Book*. The next owner of your books should be proud to have acquired your collection.

The right and wrong ways of removing a book from a shelf. The correct way (left) avoids potential damage; the incorrect way (right) puts strain on the book's spine.

RED BOOK RECOLLECTIONS

David W. Lange

I received my first Red Book, the 22nd edition, for Christmas in 1968. Until that time I'd been using the Blue Book as my one-volume numismatic library. At the age of 10, I was only just becoming aware of the difference between the two. I had already begun to memorize the mintages and values for my favorite coins, such as Lincoln cents and Buffalo nickels, and my acquisition of this new and more powerful tool only added to my hobby enjoyment.

About 15 years later, I began to assemble a complete set of Red Books, a project which took me two years or so. The fifth edition was the toughest one, then as now, and I had to buy this and the first edition from numismatic literature dealers. I managed to find most of the others from a variety of sources, such as used book stores and coin club book sales, and putting the set together cost me much less than it ultimately was worth.

I've been present to receive nearly all of the special commemorative editions of the Red Book distributed during ANA conventions, though sadly I missed out on the first one, at the 1986 Milwaukee gathering, because of a work-related commitment. At the 1987 ANA convention in Atlanta, I had R.S. Yeoman sign my first edition, as well as the then-current 41st edition. The following year, at the ANA Summer Seminar in Colorado Springs, I again asked Mr. Yeoman to sign my new Red Book, released that very day, and I snapped a photo of him signing a copy for the person ahead of me in line (see illustration). Little did I know that this would be among the last occasions that he would perform this satisfying ritual, for Dick Yeo (as I later learned his real name was) passed away not long afterward.

As a serious collector of the United States coinage for the Philippines, I was frustrated by the fact that these historic issues were not included in the Red Book. Having come to know editor Ken Bressett fairly well, I repeatedly asked him when these could be added to the lineup, and he assured me that they would whenever the page count permitted a new signature to be added to the book. This time came in 1998, and it was my honor to write the introduction to this series, which has appeared ever since. Coins from my own collection were the plate pieces for this chapter, though a few images have been replaced with sharper ones since then.

I've continued on as a contributor to the Red Book in a number of small capacities since that time, and I'm very pleased to see how the book has been expanded and greatly improved in recent years. It goes to show how a good thing can indeed continue to get better with age.

Red Book collector and contributor David Lange took this snapshot of R.S. Yeoman at a June 1988 book signing, one of the last such events Yeoman attended.

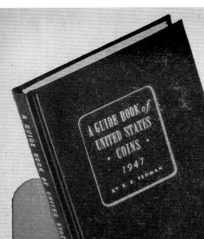
From the December 1946 *Numismatist.* The new *Guide Book* was "not to be confused with any other coin book," declares the ad.

ANALYSIS AND MARKET GUIDE TO THE RED BOOK

THE FIRST EDITION (1947)

The Year Was 1946, and . . .

The design of the dime was changed to portray recently deceased president Franklin D. Roosevelt, the denomination having been chosen to honor his role in the creation of the March of Dimes. Legislation was passed authorizing the coinage of half dollars to commemorate Booker T. Washington.

Inside the Red Book

First Printing

The first printing of the first edition numbered 9,000 copies, which were released in November 1946. A copy from this printing of the first edition is an integral part of any *Guide Book* collection. With a total printing of only 9,000 copies, it is truly scarce, especially in good condition. After all, at the time of its release it was a simple reference

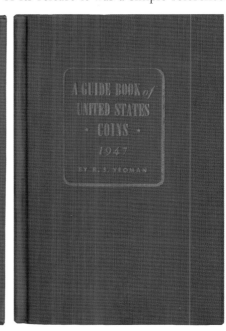

Values of the First Edition

	Issue Price	VG	F	VF
1st Printing	$1.50	$325	$600	$1,250
2nd Printing	$1.50	$275	$500	$1,100

Dollar Price Performance

Year	Uncirculated	Proof
1895-P	$6	$35
1903-O	110	Not applicable

Note: Here and in subsequent tables, Uncirculated is the condition of a coin that shows no evidence of wear, and Proof refers to a coin that has been specially prepared and struck by the Mint for collectors. "Not applicable" means that the 1903-O is not listed as a Proof coin because, until recently, all Proof coins (with rare exceptions) were struck only in Philadelphia.

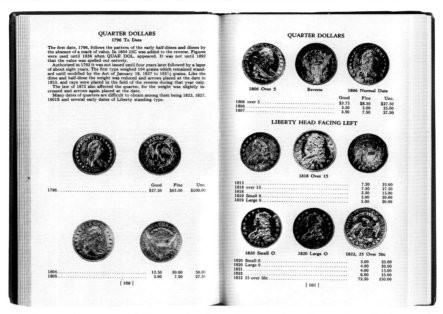

The listings for quarter dollars in the first-edition Red Book contain only three coin grades—Good, Fine, and Uncirculated. The values for dates like 1805 and 1806 are calculated down to fifty-cent increments, when today they carry into five figures!

book. No one could imagine the future value of that printing, or the importance of keeping a nice copy.

The review by Stuart Mosher in the December 1946 *Numismatist* (see chapter 2) praised the new reference work, noting that although "the word 'guide' . . . often suggests a synoptic treatment that leaves no room for details," the *Guide Book* was "much more than the title indicates." Of course, Mosher was not exactly an unbiased critic, despite the neutrality he strives for in his review. As noted in chapter 2, he was not only one of the listed contributors; he had been so vital to the book's creation that Yeoman had presented him with the first copy! Despite—or perhaps because of—Mosher's close involvement with the new reference work, as reviewer he consciously attempts a neutral stance, saying (in the editorial plural), "Lest we appear too enthusiastic over this handy encyclopedia we should remark that we do not subscribe to all the information in it."

Studies of auction listings and book sales show that copies of the 1947 edition sell for strong prices, even when in poor condition. Books that have been separated at the spine, water stained, or otherwise abused often sell for in excess of $100. Books in Very Fine condition can sell for well over $1,000. (See chapter 3 for an explanation of book grading.) In 2007, one Near Mint copy sold on eBay for more than $1,500 despite a clear scratch on its cover. High-grade examples are highly prized and only rarely come on the market.

Second Printing

Due to the instant popularity of the new *Guide Book* the first printing sold out, necessitating a second printing in February 1947. However, first a correction had to be made. On page 135 of the first printing, a discussion of Morgan silver dollar contains this passage: "270,232,722 silver dollars were melted under the Pittman Act of April, 1918. 259 121,554 for export to India, and 11,111,168 for domestic subsidiary coins, which probably accounts for the scarcity of this date." In this edition, there is no way for anyone but the psychic reader to know that "this date" refers to 1903. To correct this, the second printing was amended to read "which probably accounts for the scarcity of 1903 O." Strangely, no one yet thought to correct "259 121,554" by adding the missing comma.

Collectors of the *Guide Book* have to be grateful for Yeoman's thoroughness in his work, without which it would be impossible to differentiate between the first edition's two printings. Although Yeoman noted that other revisions were made before the second printing, this is the only one that has been identified. The alteration expands the number of collectible Red Books by one, increasing the challenge of completing a set.

The second printing was produced in the same quantity (9,000) as the first. However, the first printing sells for more than the second printing, and will probably continue to do so. At the same time, most collectors feel that they need a copy of both printings. The second printing is just as difficult to obtain in high grade as the first, adding to the challenge.

Internet auctions, as we have noted, are a great source for finding copies of the *Guide Book*. However, sellers often do not differentiate between the two printings of the first edition, and most bidders do not ask for clarification. Perhaps the majority of bidders are unaware of the difference, or perhaps they do not want to risk losing potential bidders. In either case, a listing that specifies that the book is from the first printing will usually realize a substantially higher sale price.

In 2006, to commemorate the Red Book's 60th anniversary, Whitman Publishing released a replica of the first edition. See chapter 5 for details on this Tribute Edition.

1891CC	3.75		190?	2.50	20
1892	3.00	10.00	19040	11.00	
18920	7.50		1904S	4.00	

270,232,722 silver dollars were melted under the Pittman Act of April, 1918. 259 121,554 for export to India, and 11,111,168 for domestic subsidiary coins, which probably accounts for the scarcity of this date.

1921		$2.00	$65.00
1921D		2.50	
1921S		2.50	

BIBLIOGRAPHY

Hazeltine, J. W., Type Table of U. S. Dollars, Half and Quarter Dollars. 1881. Reprint 1933.

McIlvaine, A. D. The Silver Dollars of the U. S. A. 1941.

[135]

1891CC	3.75		1904		20.00
1892	3.00	10.00	19040	11.00	
18920	7.50		1904S	4.00	

270,232,722 silver dollars were melted under the Pittman Act of April, 1918. 259 121,554 for export to India, and 11,111,168 for domestic subsidiary coins, which probably accounts for the scarcity of 1903 O.

1921		$2.00	$65.00
1921D		2.50	
1921S		2.50	

BIBLIOGRAPHY

Hazeltine, J. W., Type Table of U. S. Dollars, Half and Quarter Dollars. 1881. Reprint 1933.

McIlvaine, A. D. The Silver Dollars of the U. S. A. 1941.

[135]

From the December 1947 *Numismatist*.

THE SECOND EDITION (1948)

The Year Was 1947, and . . .

For the first time since before World War II, the U.S. Mint sold Mint sets to collectors. An estimated 5,000 sets were sold at $4.87 each. Today these sets are valued at more than $1,000. This was the final year of the Walking Liberty half dollar, which had been issued since 1916. Chief engraver John R. Sinnock died, and President Harry Truman chose Gilroy Roberts as his successor. The Smithsonian Institution established a Section of Numismatics within its Division of History.

Inside the Red Book

The second edition, published in 1947 with a cover date of 1948, maintained the same number of pages as the first edition: 256. The book would remain this length until the 40th edition (1987), when it would be increased to 272 pages.

The major change to this edition was the new section "Condition of Coins." For the first time, the editors listed five grades of coins, with short descriptions, plus Proofs. Although vastly improved from the first edition, when no grade descriptions were given, and probably sufficient for collectors of the day, these descriptions would be extremely lacking today. Good condition was simply described as "a coin that has had considerable wear. Every important part of the design is still plain." Other notable differences in the second edition are the price changes of some coins and an addition of six new names to the list of contributors: F.H. Hiskin, Paul and Arthur Kagin, Herbert E. Rowald, F.K. Saab, and Norman Schultz.

In every edition, Yeoman included a preface that summarized the changes to the current edition and discussed the current state of the coin market. This little section would provide valuable information in subsequent editions. Here Yeoman states that "during the latter part of 1947 prices became temporarily stabilized and in some cases were

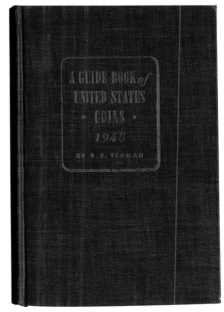

Values of the Second Edition

Year/Edition	Issue Price	VG	F	VF
1948 (2nd ed.)	$1.50	$80	$160	$225

Dollar Price Performance

Year	Uncirculated	Proof
1895-P	$15	$75
1903-O	110	Not applicable

reduced, particularly in the gold classification. It is the considered opinion of experienced authorities, nevertheless, that prices will advance during 1948." This prognostication provides readers—both now and then—with a fascinating look at the market, although this may actually be Yeoman's way of encouraging readers to purchase the next year's edition!

There are a few major content changes to the listings, including the addition of a value to the 1804 large cent (restrike) of $20 in uncirculated condition. The coin was described but unpriced in the first edition. Also, the Lincoln cent section had the addition of the 1922-D (broken D) and 1922 Plain (No D), and included values in Good and Very Good conditions. These are but a few of the interesting changes to the data provided.

As can be seen in the chart on dollar values, a dramatic change in valuation had taken place for the 1895-P Morgan dollar. In the first edition, the value in Uncirculated condition is listed as $6, while Proof coins are listed as $35. The second edition shows an amazing increase in Uncirculated condition to $15 (for an increase of 150 percent) and in Proof condition to $75 (for an increase of 114 percent), which is more than twice the cost of the nearest Proof dollar from 1878 to 1904. It would certainly be interesting to see the reasoning behind these price increases—especially since collectors now agree that this coin does not actually exist in Uncirculated condition. It may have been wishful thinking, resulting from a listed mintage of 12,880 pieces (including Proofs). However, none of these coins have ever surfaced.

Stuart Mosher reviewed the second edition in the February 1948 issue of *The Numismatist*, giving a glowing endorsement of this still-new resource:

> The collector who wants a compact encyclopedia of United States coins, who likes to keep up with the current values of all obtainable pieces, and who prefers this information in a form that is readily accessible, should own this book. It leaves little to be desired and contains far more information than the title suggests. . . . The author has taken great care to explain small details that so often confuse the collector in the early stages of his pursuit.

Mosher also anticipated the sentiments of numismatic author Q. David Bowers in urging readers to peruse the book's overview section: "'An Introduction to United States Coins' takes up eight pages, and we strongly advise not skipping it," he wrote. "Rarely will there be found so much information in so little space."

Today, the value for the second edition averages only 20 percent of the value of the first edition (first printing). Compared to the total 18,000-book run for the first edition, there were 22,000 second-edition books printed. Yet 22,000 is still a very low quantity when considered in terms of availability for today's collectors. At one time, the second edition was considered more common than the third edition, and therefore less valuable, but current pricing shows that their relative values are not clear-cut. In Fine condition the second edition brings a $30 (or higher) premium over the third edition, but in Very Fine the third edition boasts a higher value (by about $50). In any case, current market values for this edition are very reasonable.

From the program of the 1949 CSNS convention, held May 13 through 15 in Detroit, Michigan. This is the only known vintage Red Book advertisement actually printed in red. Notice that although the Red Book was only in its third edition, it had already become "the biggest selling book in its field."

THE THIRD EDITION (1949)

The Year Was 1948, and . . .

The Benjamin Franklin half dollar saw its first year of circulation. It was the first regular circulating U.S. coin to feature a man other than a president (not counting allegorical figures). Although the eagle on the reverse was not replaced with Franklin's candidate for the national bird—the turkey—it was at least relegated to a minor position in the design. With this half dollar design, the figure of Liberty was entirely displaced from circulating coins. Mint Director Nellie Tayloe Ross, the first woman to hold this position, began an unprecedented fourth term. This former governor of Wyoming would retain the office of director of the Mint for a still-unmatched 20 years. The Smithsonian granted divisional status to the former Section of Numismatics, and Red Book contributor Stuart Mosher became its associate curator.

Inside the Red Book

In the third edition, the list of contributors leapt to 25 individuals and included such notable dealers as Robert Friedberg, Joseph Stack, Harold Whiteneck, and Charles Wormser. The preface continued to provide a neat recap of changes in the *Guide Book* and market conditions. Yeoman discussed the decline of some prices, but emphasized that they were "still well in advance of prices quoted two or three years ago." Then he proceeded to state, "The long range investment possibilities of selected coins are as sound as at any time in the past, and can be equal to that of any comparable commodity." Yeoman also pointed out the Red Book's addition of "new illustrations, descriptions, and additional columns of prices." As we will see, there were some interesting changes.

Searching the time capsule that the third edition provides for us, the first fascinating item is the addition of the 1937-D 3-Legged variety to the section on Indian Head or Buffalo nickels. Its first listing shows values of $0.90 in Good, $1.50 in Fine, and $6.50 in

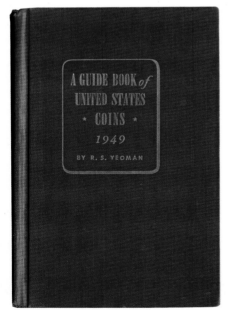

Values of the Third Edition

Year/Edition	Issue Price	VG	F	VF	VF W/Full Gilt
1949 (3rd ed.)	$1.50	$80	$130	$275	$375

Dollar Price Performance

Year	Uncirculated	Proof
1895-P	$50	$80
1903-O	150	Not applicable

Uncirculated. Next, for the first time, there is a listing for the 1892-O Medium O and 1892-O Microscopic O under Barber—or Liberty Head Type—half dollars. The 1892-O Micro O is valued at $20 in Fine and $50 in Uncirculated. To today's collectors, the listing of the 1894-S High S and Low S Barber half dollars may come as a surprise, but they were accepted varieties at the time, and there was no difference in value. (They were distinguished by the positioning of the S mintmark on the reverse.) The addition of these "new" varieties makes for a wonderful way of noting the time when they first became acceptable to the collecting community.

Another interesting change to the listings was the addition of an explanation of the separation of mintages for the 1861-O half dollar (page 120). Yeoman divided the totals by producer: 330,000 from the U.S. government, 1,240,000 from Louisiana, and 962,633 from the Confederacy. He also noted that it was impossible to distinguish one from the other—although professional graders of today would disagree.

Our comparison of the 1895-P and 1903-O Morgan dollars continues. The 1895 Philadelphia dollar increased from $15 to $50 in one year! That is a price growth of 333 percent.

The 1949 edition of the Red Book received another favorable review from *Numismatist* editor and Red Book contributor Stuart Mosher, who commented in the April 1949 issue that it "represents a sincere attempt to present collectors with an up-to-date and accurate survey of the United States coin market." He went on to praise it as being "packed with authentic information, beautiful halftone illustrations, and up-to-the-minute market values." Amusingly, however, Mosher called this the *second* edition, stating that the first edition "of this useful catalogue was published about a year ago." Since Mosher had both contributed to *and* reviewed all editions of the Red Book to date, he should have been well aware that this was the third edition. Perhaps, like some readers after him, he had become momentarily confused by the discrepancy between the cover date and the publication date!

Copies of the third edition in Fine or Very Fine condition are truly scarce. This edition is notorious for the poor survivability of the gilt on its front and spine. The gilt is rarely found full and bright; it is usually subdued even on little-used copies. Books with 50 percent or more gilt remaining are worth a premium of 50 percent over the listed values. In all conditions, this edition garners high prices, and is one of the most difficult to find of Red Books; it is considered by many collectors to be the third-scarcest edition, after the first (both printings) and the fifth. However, as discussed earlier, the second edition and this one vie closely in value.

256 pages packed with helpful information!

4th EDITION
WHITMAN GUIDE BOOK
OF UNITED STATES COINS

No wonder the Whitman Guide Book is the biggest selling book in its field—it is the recognized authority on United States coins. Coin collectors turn to its 256 pages for helpful, illustrated information about individual U. S., Early American and private gold coins. Standard prices and historical references (1616 to date) are included. Cloth bound, with gold stamped cover. Size 5⅛x7¾ inches. Get your copy at your hobby dealer for only $1.50.

$1.50

WHITMAN PUBLISHING CO.
RACINE, WISCONSIN

From the December 1950 *Numismatist.*

THE FOURTH EDITION (1951–1952)

The Year Was 1950, and . . .

Proof coins were struck again for the first time since 1942. The first Proof Roosevelt dime and Franklin half dollar were issued. The issue price of the Proof sets increased modestly from the prewar cost of $1.89 to $2.10 per set. Only 51,386 sets were sold, but this was a 143% increase in sales over the 1942 figure of 21,120 sets. The key date for the Jefferson nickel series was produced by the Denver mint. With a total mintage of 2,630,030, this issue was instantly recognized as a scarcity and was greatly hoarded by collectors and dealers. Even today it is more available in uncirculated than circulated condition. No official Uncirculated Mint sets were produced for collectors this year. The Canadian Numismatic Association was founded. The previous year (1949) had seen the appointment of the first female treasurer of the United States, Georgia Neese Clark.

Inside the Red Book

After a hiatus during 1949, the next edition of the *Guide Book* appeared in 1950. The date on its title page reads "1951–1952," and this edition marked the first time that one edition was to represent pricing for a two-year period. The cover design had been altered so that "4th Edition" appeared in place of the year of issue. This alteration may have been due to the dual-year edition, or to enable copies to remain on the shelves for a longer period of time. Whatever the reason, printing only the edition number and not the applicable year on the cover would remain the *Guide Book* style through the 15th edition.

Yeoman again wrote a preface that was positive about the market. This time he said, "In almost every series, adjustments both upward and downward will be found . . . but changes for the most part are small, and the market is expected to remain reasonably stable for some time."

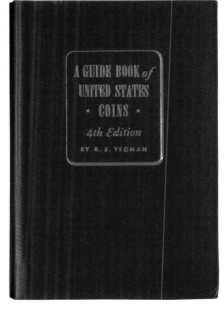

Values of the Fourth Edition

Year/Edition	Issue Price	VG	F	VF
1951/52 (4th ed.)	$1.50	$55	$110	$160

Dollar Price Performance

Year	Very Fine	Uncirculated	Proof
1895-P	$25	$60	$85
1903-O	50	175	Not applicable

No new varieties had been added to this edition, but—as Yeoman noted in the preface—there was a complete revision of the section on silver dollars from 1794 through 1803. Now it was expanded to include additional listings of varieties, particularly those from 1798 through 1803. To accommodate the extra two pages of this section while keeping the book's page count at a consistent 256 pages, the listings of some coins had to be compressed to take up less space. To accomplish this, the pricing information for the Bust half dollars from 1817 to 1833 and the Seated Liberty (today called Liberty Seated) half dollars was squeezed into two tight columns.

As the chart for the studied Morgan dollars illustrates, values were given for all coins in Very Fine condition for the first time in this edition of the Red Book. However, there was still no clear explanation of this (or any other) condition.

In April 1951 *The Numismatist* presented a lengthy and detailed review of this edition. Despite describing the Red Book as a "useful little manual," the (unsigned) review cast a skeptical eye on some "experimental" changes to the book's content, such as the expansion of the section on silver dollars. Noting that the new listings were "based on Bolender's recent book on that series," the reviewer sniffed that "this Bolender list of silver dollars is drawing it rather fine. I gravely doubt that it will be found easy to use . . . or that the divagations included could ever be called major varieties." Ultimately, he conceded, "the only effective test of this silver dollar revision will be time and the easy adoption or non-adoption of these designations by non-specialists." (In fact, the listings were not only kept; eventually they would be expanded upon, proving their usefulness.)

In other respects too the *Numismatist* response suggests that the Red Book was undergoing some growing pains. In a decidedly backhanded compliment, the reviewer acknowledged that "some of the more misleading errors found in earlier editions have been here corrected." Less-ambiguous praise greeted the new discussion of copies of colonial issues—"a subject neglected in the literature" that "is indeed a useful addition." The reviewer wrapped up his assessment with a judiciously weighed verdict: "judging by the improvements in this fourth edition, it is to believed that [remaining] errors will gradually be removed, and the result then will be a very helpful book correctly answering most questions non-specialists are likely to ask about the American series."

It is unknown how many copies of the fourth edition were printed. We do know that it is more readily available than the third edition. This may be because there were more printed, or there may have simply been more saved in Very Good or better condition. It was, after all, two years since the previous edition. Nice copies are available today, and although they are not common, they appear on the market with fair regularity.

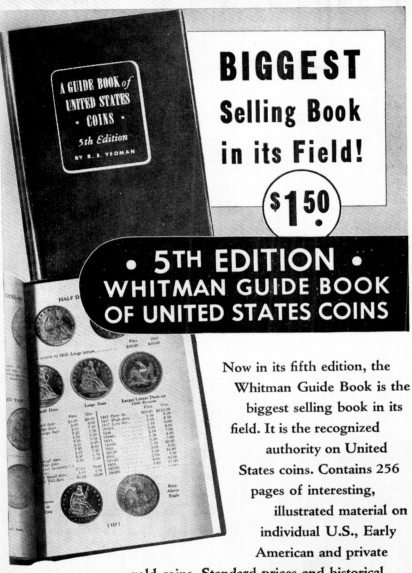

BIGGEST
Selling Book
in its Field!

$1.50

• 5TH EDITION •
WHITMAN GUIDE BOOK
OF UNITED STATES COINS

Now in its fifth edition, the
Whitman Guide Book is the
biggest selling book in its
field. It is the recognized
authority on United
States coins. Contains 256
pages of interesting,
illustrated material on
individual U.S., Early
American and private
gold coins. Standard prices and historical
references (1616 to date) are included. Cloth bound, with
gold stamped cover. Size 5⅛ x 7¾ inches.
Get your copy at your hobby dealer for only $1.50.

WHITMAN PUBLISHING CO.
RACINE, WISCONSIN

From the May 1952 *Numismatist.*

THE FIFTH EDITION (1952–1953)

The Year Was 1951, and . . .

Mint sets were sold once more, and would be produced every year until a two-year hiatus in 1982 and 1983. The George Washington Carver commemorative half dollar program began; it would end in 1954. The ANA established the Farran Zerbe Memorial Award, its highest honor. The award's namesake and former ANA president, Zerbe had died in 1949.

Inside the Red Book

In the preface to the fifth edition, Yeoman noted that there were revisions made throughout the entire book. He added, "Prices have advanced mainly in the early small cents, Buffalo nickels, Barber and Mercury dimes . . . and Three-Dollar gold pieces." Nearly all series (excluding modern coins) had increased in price.

One major change was the addition of Proof mintages. They were included alongside the total coinage, in parentheses. This was a major change in the information available to collectors. Yeoman showed that he was willing to be an innovator. It must have taken a great amount of time to accumulate this data.

A new entry added to the listing was the 1889, 9 Over 8, No Arrows Seated Liberty half dollar. (This coin was thought to be an *overdate*—struck with a die from a previous year that had been adjusted for current use—but was later determined to be a repunched date. It was removed from the Red Book in the seventh edition. This variety was also listed in Wayte Raymond's *Standard Catalogue* in 1951, and subsequently removed.) It was listed with a value of $15 in Uncirculated. Although there are no other notable additions to listed varieties, there are many changes to the valuations. Yeoman was determined to maintain a current listing, and he quickly added the new coin types, including (on page 183) the 1951 issue of the Booker T. Washington Memorial half dollar.

As the chart shows, the values for the selected dollars increased again.

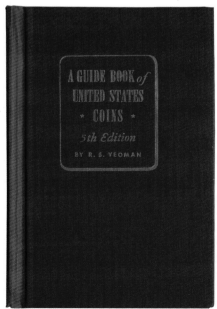

Values of the Fifth Edition

Year/Edition	Issue Price	VG	F	VF
1952/53 (5th ed.)	$1.50	$130	$260	$450

Dollar Price Performance

Year	Very Fine	Uncirculated	Proof
1895-P	$30	$75	$100
1903-O	50	200	Not applicable

This edition was reviewed by numismatic legend Walter Breen—a future Red Book contributor—in the May 1952 *Numismatist*. The tone of the review, like that of the preceding one, brings to mind a stern parent contemplating a less-than-stellar report card from a beloved child. The unspoken message was "I am pleased with what you have accomplished, but I *know* you can do even better than this!" Breen sniffily observed that "there are the same errors in text and illustrations as in the 4th edition" and went on to list them:

> The 1800 over 1798 and the 1800 over 1799 cents are represented as having the same obverse die (page 65). The date of the theft from the Mint Cabinet is given as 1850 (it actually happened August 16, 1858). The 1864 half dime is still listed in Fine and Unc. conditions, though it is a fact that only proofs were struck.

"In short," he concluded with an implicit sigh, "this edition still bears many earmarks of haste to report . . . price changes." After a detailed breakdown of the price changes represented in this edition, he ended on a note of patient optimism: "We believe it is not too much to expect that the remaining errors and rough spots will be gradually removed in subsequent editions, leaving a book equally well adapted for use of both the layman and the fairly advanced collector." Breen's diagnosis here does Yeoman the honor of recognizing that, despite the imperfections that are almost inevitable in a book of such scope (and an annual publication schedule), the Red Book had something to offer those at every point of the coin-collecting spectrum.

The fifth edition is one of the scarcest editions of the series. Indeed, the only book of the series that is less common to find is either printing of the first edition. According to numismatic book dealers such as Fred L. Lake, the low availability is due to a smaller-than-usual print run, occasioned by the paper shortage associated with the Korean War (see Jeff Starck's essay "In the 'Red'"). It should be noted, however, that in his essay "The Red Book Story" Yeoman himself asserted that the print run of every edition through the eighth actually *increased.* The longstanding difficulty of determining exact print runs for the Red Book makes it impossible to settle the question for certain, but whatever the reason, the fifth edition is notably scarce. Red Book collector and dealer Ed Lesniak noted in 1985, "Over the years we have found the hardest 'Red Book' to find in collectible condition is the fifth edition. . . . Our buy price for the fifth edition has surpassed our original retail price of just a few short years ago. At the moment we have more first editions in stock than we have fifths" (see Lesniak's "Collect 'Red Books' for Enjoyment First"). Numismatic book dealer Charles Davis told us, "I have twice sold an autographed contributor's copy [of the fifth edition] that bore evidence of use. . . . Perhaps these gentlemen were forced to use their signed copies as they were unable to purchase another for everyday use." Clearly, although the first edition still holds pride of place as the most valuable Red Book edition, the fifth edition continues to be a sought-after prize.

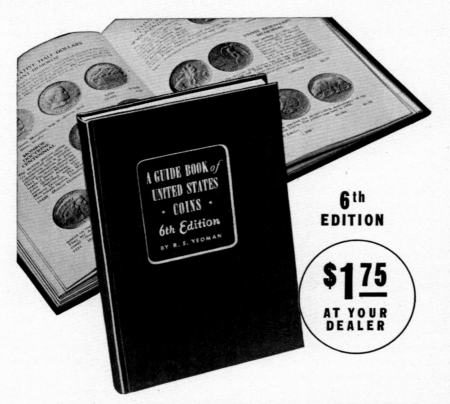

6th EDITION

$1 75

AT YOUR DEALER

THE RECOGNIZED AUTHORITY ON UNITED STATES COINS . . .

Whitman's Guide Book is the biggest selling book in its field . . . and for good reason! Coin collectors look to this book with confidence for authoritative information on United States coins. Over 250 pages of interesting, illustrated material on individual U. S., Early American and private gold coins. Standard prices and historical references (1616 to date) are included. Sturdily cloth bound, with gold stamped cover. Size 5⅛ x 7¾ inches. Get your new 6th Edition at your hobby dealer for only $1.75.

WHITMAN PUBLISHING COMPANY
RACINE, WISCONSIN

From the June 1953 *Numismatist*. The advertised price has risen to $1.75, but it would not increase again for more than a decade.

THE SIXTH EDITION (1953–1954)

The Year Was 1952, and . . .

The newspaper *Numismatic News* was founded by Chester Krause. R.S. Yeoman received the American Numismatic Association's Medal of Merit.

Inside the Red Book

The sixth edition, dated 1953–1954, was printed in 1952. It was a very different time period from today, one in which a fixed-price reference could be printed two years before the latest cover date. Yeoman's preface again paints a rosy picture of the coin market: "There have been no great price increases, but general advances have been necessary in Indian cents, Liberty nickels, Barber dimes, silver dollars, and almost all commemorative issues."

There were only minor changes to the listings. One that is readily obvious is the deletion of the 1894-S Barber half dollar High S and Low S varieties. These varieties were included in some early albums, but never became popular with collectors as an important part of the series that would be worthy of inclusion in most sets. This may be due to the fact there was no difference between the values of the varieties.

Another change occurred on page 65, with the deletion of the photo of the 1800 Over 1798 variety large cent. This was a logical move, because there was no way that the reader could have discerned the variety from the picture as shown in the earlier editions. The value of this coin was still listed, and the photos of the other varieties remained the same.

The price march for the 1895-P and 1903-O dollars continued, as shown in the chart. The prices either remained stable or increased slightly from the previous edition.

The review of this edition that appeared in the January 1953 issue of *The Numismatist* was an unprecedented length at over two pages. The unnamed reviewer followed in the footsteps of Walter Breen in his review of the previous edition: examining minutiae,

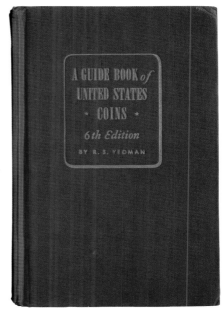

Values of the Sixth Edition

Year/Edition	Issue Price	VG	F	VF
1953/54 (6th ed.)	$1.75	$45	$65	$100

Dollar Price Performance

Year	Very Fine	Uncirculated	Proof
1895-P	$35	$90	$150
1903-O	50	250	Not applicable

taking the Red Book to task for various shortcomings, yet acknowledging its sound points—and emphasizing its potential to improve still further. It began on a faintly disappointed note:

> The present edition continues the trend of the last two, in that there have been some problematical changes and additions of types; and the improvements suggested by the reviewer of the last two editions have evidently been partly incorporated, though by no means consistently. Much of the new information presented appears to have sound factual basis but to have been slightly mishandled.

Albeit in a slightly patronizing way, the reviewer did indicate that the Red Book editorial staff were attentive to constructive criticism and continued to work to improve the book in response. As the review continued, it examined individual sections of the book and summarized the price changes therein, often pausing to dissect a particular price or condition listing that the reviewer found questionable. Of perhaps greater interest to the modern reader is the way the reviewer eventually came to determine where the Red Book was positioning itself with regard to an audience. "Type coverage is still rather superficial in most series," we read, but this assertion was followed by the more enlightened comment: "it begins to appear that this reference is now aimed at the general, unspecialized, collector of American coins rather than at the more advanced one." Likewise, in drawing the review to a close the writer made some insightful observations:

> Generally speaking, the Guidebook appears more and more to be crystallizing as a book aimed at the general collector of U.S. and cognate series. Its proposed readership thus differs more and more from that of the Standard Catalogue, which has begun to publish ever more and more specialized and recondite data on Americana, thus addressing a readership of what are usually termed "more advanced collectors." . . . For the Guidebook's apparent purpose there is certainly a place; but it is legitimate to ask that its accuracy be not therefore the less. . . . It is therefore hoped that next year's edition of this book will, as previous ones have, improve in this very important aspect of its presentation. It will then be a boon to the ever-growing newer membership of our Association, the fringe largely comprising just such unspecialized U.S. collectors.

The Red Book's practice of making coin-pricing information available not just to the numismatic elite but to the general hobbyist was clearly one that met with approval—and would make it increasingly popular.

Although the sixth edition is often considered the first regularly available edition, it is still typically valued at more than 60 percent of the value of a fourth edition. The price reflects the infrequent availability of books in Fine or better condition.

THE SEVENTH EDITION (1954–1955)

The Year Was 1953, and . . .

For the first time, sales of Proof sets broke the 100,000 mark (128,800). Issued at $2.10, the 1953 set currently sells for more than $300. The Carver/Washington commemorative half dollar saw its lowest-ever mintages at Philadelphia and Denver, with each mint producing only 8,003 coins.

Inside the Red Book

Yeoman's preface in the seventh edition was again positive. "The seventh edition has been revised throughout," he wrote. "There have been no great price increases, but general advances have been necessary in most categories, particularly scarce issues." The most notable change to the guide was in the listing for Lincoln cents. For the first time, there was a listing for a 1937 (Lincoln cent) "'Reeded Edge' (Reeding done outside of mint)." There was also a Buffalo nickel similarly listed as having a "'Reeded Edge' (Reeding done outside of mint)." (The process of reeding creates grooved lines on a coin's edge.) No price was listed for any grade. Rather than including the coin to assign a value to it, this was Yeoman's way of alerting the public to its existence.

The next change to the listings that should be noted was in the Morgan dollars. On page 134 there was a photo labeled, "Morgan dollar, 7 Tail Feathers." Actually, the photograph showed the reverse of a 1836 Gobrecht dollar (which could be found on page 131 of that edition of the *Guide Book*). This error was corrected for the eighth edition. Although interesting, it does not make for a collectible variety of the edition because all copies were issued this way.

The 1895-P silver dollar was listed with a mintage of 12,880, which included a Proof mintage of 880 pieces. For the first time, the editors apparently realized that the listed prices for the Uncirculated pieces were merely a dream and that there might not be any available, regardless of price. This year the prices for Uncirculated pieces were simply listed as dashes, reflecting the fact that there were no sales available for pricing of the issue. The value of this coin in Very Fine condition was also listed as a dash, because this coin was not known in this condition.

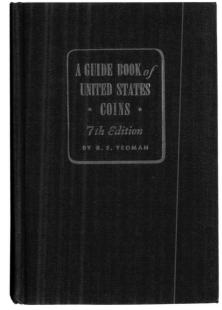

Values of the Seventh Edition

Year/Edition	Issue Price	VG	F	VF
1954/55 (7th ed.)	$1.75	$45	$65	$90

Dollar Price Performance

Year	Very Fine	Uncirculated	Proof
1895-P	—	—	$200
1903-O	$50	$250	Not applicable

THE EIGHTH EDITION (1955)

The Year Was 1954, and . . .

The original commemorative coin series, which had started in 1892 with the World's Columbian Exposition issues, saw its final year. It would be 28 years before the commemorative returned to production with the 250th anniversary of George Washington's birthday in 1982. The office of director of the Mint, vacant for a year, was filled when President Dwight Eisenhower nominated William H. Brett for the position. The coin collection of King Farouk of Egypt was auctioned off, except for the 1933 double eagle, which was withdrawn at the request of the U.S. government.

Inside the Red Book

The eighth edition, published in 1954 with a cover date of 1955, resumed the single-year dating convention of earlier Red Books. Yeoman's preface again provided a glimpse into the previous year in the world of coin collecting. "Changes of standard prices in this edition are more extensive than any previous one. . . . Only the larger denomination gold pieces show decreases, in the common dates. This is a reflection of the world gold market, which weakened greatly in 1954."

The number of contributors grew to 37. Among other numismatic notables, Walter Breen—whose review of the fifth edition (previously excerpted) had been decidedly mixed—was included in this list. A prominent place was given to the holder of a new position: Glenn B. Smedley, "Co-ordinator, Panel of Contributors." Smedley, a listed contributor to the previous edition, would hold the position of coordinator through the 15th edition. His function was key to one of the Red Book's primary goals: presenting the most accurate, unbiased, and up-to-date coin values each year. Ken Bressett described what this entailed in the June 1960 *Merchandiser.* As coordinator, Smedley performed the crucial task of assembling and collating all the pricing data provided by Red

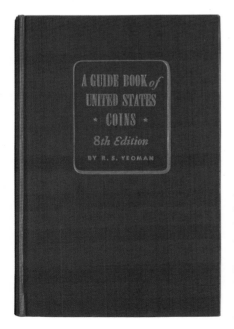

Values of the Seventh Edition

Year/Edition	Issue Price	VG	F	VF
1954/55 (7th ed.)	$1.75	$45	$65	$90

Dollar Price Performance

Year	Very Fine	Uncirculated	Proof
1895-P	—	—	$200
1903-O	$50	$250	Not applicable

Book contributors. In Bressett's words, Smedley's job was "to average out and tabulate a nightmare-full of prices and enter these figures on a master sheet to be used in the new edition"—a task that took "a good month."

Perhaps the most important (and recognized) change to the listings was in Lincoln cents. The editors decided that the 1922-D "Part D," which was valued in Good condition at half of the value of the 1922, No D, was not important or popular enough to be included. Accordingly, it was deleted from the listing. It would return in the 51st edition (1998), when the description was changed to "Weak D." Its reinsertion into the book would show that it had once again become a collectible and popular variety.

This edition corrected the photo on page 134, showing the proper 7 Tail Feathers reverse for the Morgan dollar of 1878. Another correction was finally made: a comma was added to "270,232,722 silver dollars were melted under the Pittman Act of April, 1918. 259 121,554 for export to India, and 11,111,168 for domestic subsidiary coins" so that it read "259,121,554." We can only wonder why Yeoman, usually such a careful editor, allowed this mistake to remain for so many editions.

As for the Morgan dollars we are studying, both the 1895-P and 1903-O continued to show impressive price gains.

In a departure from previous custom, the *Numismatist* review of this edition assessed the new Red Book side by side with its counterpart, the new (12th-edition) Blue Book. Assistant editor Elston G. Bradfield (who would go on to be *The Numismatist*'s editor for more than 12 years) opened his review of November 1954 with a strong indication that Yeoman had already made an indelible mark on numismatic literature:

> These two books are always eagerly awaited by all collectors of American coins; practically all dealers consult them and many base their auction estimates on them. . . . Handsomely printed and illustrated, they have the added advantage of being so reasonably priced that any collector can afford to have both in his numismatic library. In fact, it is difficult to see how he can get along without them if he is an active collector.

Bradfield observed that "although the text [of the Red Book] is practically the same as last year, some minor corrections and additions have been made." New collectors, he asserted, "will find the historical summary both interesting and instructional."

The eighth edition represents the end of an era in one respect: it was the last to be produced with the original dark-red cover material. Collectors should keep in mind that the first eight editions will differ in color from the more recent editions no matter what their condition.

From the September 1955 *Numismatist*. The Red Book illustration in the ad does not carry the edition number on the front, unlike the actual 9th edition. Perhaps in order to extend the life of its advertisements, Whitman Publishing would continue this omission in ads for the next six editions.

THE NINTH EDITION (1956)

The Year Was 1955, and . . .

The famous 1955 Doubled-Die Lincoln cent was released by the Philadelphia Mint. Legend has it that the error coins were discovered but released into circulation because the mint was closing due to the approach of a major hurricane. News of the rarity started a collecting mania. The San Francisco Mint ceased coining operations, and collectors rushed to hoard the last coins struck there. The U.S. Assay Office in Seattle closed. The Florida United Numismatists and the Professional Numismatists Guild were founded.

Inside the Red Book

The ninth edition continued the tradition of maintaining up-to-date pricing in a slowly changing coin market. This year, for the first time, Yeoman's preface was simply an edited version of the one from the previous edition. There was a major change to the descriptions in the Morgan dollar section. Yeoman added "1878 Philadelphia only" to the photo legend for the 8 Tail Feathers. In addition, a listing for Morgan dollars was added for the "1878 7 Tail Feathers over 8 Tail Feathers." The *Guide Book* again showed the importance of being flexible as the accepted popular varieties change and evolve. The contributor list in this edition featured a new designation: an asterisk by the names of those credited with "text and research." This annotation would not be continued in subsequent editions.

Yet the biggest, most interesting change to the *Guide Book* was the cover. Earlier editions had a cover made of maroon cloth that was susceptible to stains and wear. For the ninth edition, the cover was changed to a stippled plastic composition leatherette. This was an improvement: today, extant copies of the later editions are less likely to be faded from the sun and show fewer fingerprint stains than those made of cloth. However—and this is a big however—the cover of the ninth edition is very brittle. Since most collectors keep their copies on shelves, the normal tendency is to reach in and pull the books by the

This ninth-edition Red Book is in outstanding condition in many respects: the cover shows full gilt, and the binding is tight. However, improper handling has resulted in chipping at the top and bottom of the spine, so this book would have to be graded no better than Very Fine.

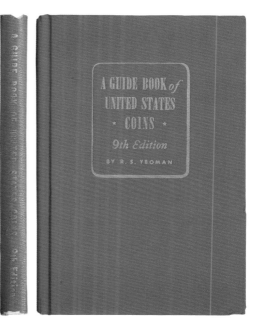

Values of the Ninth Edition

Year/Edition	Issue Price	VG	F	VF
1956 (9th ed.)	$1.75	$30	$40	$55

Dollar Price Performance

Year	Very Fine	Uncirculated	Proof
1895-P	—	(very rare)	$300
1903-O	$60	$300	Not applicable

top of their spines. For the well-being of the books, it is important to resist this temptation, especially with this edition. Pulling this book by its brittle cover results in a "chipping" of the top (and sometimes bottom) of the spine. (See chapter 3, "How to Be a Smart Collector," for a discussion of the proper handling of books.) Even very nice ninth editions often exhibit spine chipping. Copies that do not show any damage to the spine or cover are scarce and are worth a premium of about 50 percent over the listed prices.

Interestingly, Yeoman finally added additional grades and prices to some listings. In particular, he added these to the Barber quarters and Standing Liberty quarters. We can deduce that this change reflects the importance of additional pricing for dealers and collectors of the day.

The price march for the key-date Morgan dollars continued with the ninth edition. (*Key-date coins* are the rarest of a series.) There was, however, a break from tradition within these listings. Rather than being given a dollar value like that which accompanies most coins, the 1895-P was merely noted as being "Very Rare" by Yeoman. At the time, there had been no transactions to show the valuation in the marketplace.

This year Elston G. Bradfield was again the reviewer of this volume for *The Numismatist*, and again he discussed the Red Book and Blue Book in tandem. Almost the first observation in his review, from the November 1955 issue, was the change of the books' covers to "pyroxylin-coated covers designed to resist soiling." Sounding a theme that would be one of the primary distinctions of the Red Book, Bradfield noted that it was "recommended for the beginner as well as the advanced numismatist." After a brief description of the content of both volumes, he concluded his discussion of the Red Book by observing, "Admittedly it is difficult for any book of this type to keep up with a market that seems to change daily but this one will give the active collector a fairly accurate guide for his buying and selling."

RED BOOK RECOLLECTIONS
Joel Edler

My fondest recollection of the Red Book is how my friend and I mowed a lawn to make the $1.75 that our sixth edition cost. We shared the use of the book for the next year, at least. He kept the book for about 40 years, and I get to keep it for the next 40. I have had it for the last 14 years. In about 26 years, I plan to give it back to him.

I still remember the lawn we mowed, and occasionally drive by it when I get back to Freeport, Illinois.

THE 11TH EDITION (1958)

The Year Was 1957, and . . .

The popularity of Proof sets grew in leaps and bounds, as for the first year in history over one million sets were sold. B. Max Mehl, who had done so much to popularize coins and coin collecting with his ubiquitous *Star Rare Coin Encyclopedia*, died.

Inside the Red Book

For the 11th edition of the *Guide Book*, Yeoman's preface continued to assert that the state of the market was improving and that there was a "growing interest" in coin collecting. He noted that prices increased in all series except for silver dollars and higher-denomination gold coins, and that there had been a strong growth in the values for Proof coins.

With this edition, Lesher Referendum dollars made their first appearance in the Red Book. Yeoman also brought attention to early American pieces with known facsimiles, marking them with stars and including the name of the facsimile's maker where known. The next major addition was a clear microphotograph of the 1942, 2 Over 1 Winged Liberty Head (or Mercury) dime. This was probably the first time that this variety was illustrated in any reference manual. The 1918-S, 8 Over 7 quarter was also displayed in a clear microphotograph. Although photos of this coin had been included since the first edition, it had never before been displayed as clearly. In the opinion of this collector, these two photos justified the price of the entire book.

The Red Book received another warm writeup from Elston Bradfield in the August 1957 issue of *The Numismatist*. "Always awaited with intense interest," Bradfield said, "this book is indispensable to collectors of American coins." Among the enhancements to this edition, Bradfield singled out the new section on Lesher dollars and the new enlarged illustration of the 1918-D, 8 Over 7 five-cent piece. He also took the opportunity to

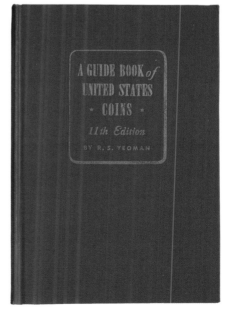

Values of the 11th Edition

Year/Edition	Issue Price	F	VF	New
1958 (11th ed.)	$1.75	$11	$20	$30

Dollar Price Performance

Year	Very Fine	Uncirculated	Proof
1895-P	—	—	$400
1903-O	$45	$400	Not applicable

recognize some of the behind-the-scenes talent responsible for that year's Red Book, noting: "The panel of contributors who assist in this [pricing] phase of the work is made up of numismatists from coast to coast and is representative of nationwide numismatic thought. Kenneth E. Bressett, LaVanch Burton, Ben Dreiske and Louis R. Karp are new members of the contributors panel." Interestingly, it would be two years before Ken Bressett, who would become so integral to the future of the Red Book, was actually listed in the book's credits.

The price changes for the described Morgan dollars were again dramatic. The value of the 1895-P Proof increased $100 (a 33 percent raise), while the value of the Uncirculated 1903-O increased $50 (a 14 percent raise). Strangely, the circulated 1903-O dollar again decreased in value. This time, it fell to $45—its lowest value since circulated prices were first listed in the fourth edition. Although, as the preface stated, values had lowered for silver dollars, it may seem arbitrary that the coin would increase in one condition and decrease in another—but such are the vagaries of the marketplace.

Note that the 11th edition is the first for which we list values in New condition. Although it is currently valued at not much more than many later editions, it is scarcer than its listed value suggests.

RED BOOK RECOLLECTIONS
Jesse Iskowitz

I first discovered the Red Book in 1955. I was at a friend's house, and his father was a collector and asked me if I knew any thing about collecting coins. I told him that I collected Lincoln cents. He asked me what years I had and what years I did not have. I was surprised to find out that there was more than one 1909-dated cent.

He told me what the rare coins were and wished me luck in my search for them in my pocket change. As I was leaving he gave me a copy of the 1955 Red Book, and boy was I surprised by the wealth of information that waited for me between the front and back covers. I was hooked on coin collecting and also trying to find the early editions of the Red Book at the library.

Over the years I have been able to collect a complete set of Red Books. I find that to this day I never get bored reading the early editions. And because of my love of early copies I have also collected copies of early catalogs—such as *The Reliable Coin Book* by C.F. Clarke & Co. (Le Roy, New York), *The Star Rare Coin Encyclopedia and Premium Catalog* by the Numismatic Company of Texas (copyrighted by B. Max Mehl in 1939), and the J.F. Bell sale of U.S. gold coins in April 1963—and any price list from the early years.

I was asked to do the pricing in the Red Book in the early '70s, and I am honored to be still doing it every year.

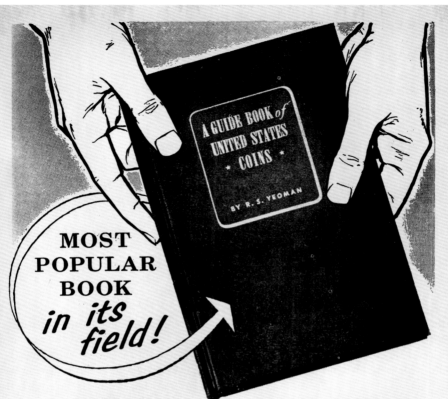

MOST
POPULAR
BOOK
in its field!

12th Edition...AT YOUR HOBBY DEALER

• Brief history of American coinage • Early American coins and tokens • Early mint issues • Regular mint issues • Private, state and territorial gold • Silver and gold commemorative issues • Proofs • Standard prices and historical references (1616 to date) • Pyroxylin-coated, soil-resisting hard cover.

ONLY $1 75

 PUBLISHING CO. • Racine, Wisconsin

From the November 1958 *Numismatist.*

THE 12TH EDITION (1959)

The Year Was 1958, and . . .

The Lincoln cent wheat-ear reverse entered its final year. Future generations of collectors would avidly search for them in circulation. A Lincoln cent with what would prove to be a very rare doubled-die obverse was released. Even 50 years later it would remain elusive.

Inside the Red Book

In the 12th edition, for the first time, the preface acknowledged the strange coin market of the day. It states that "late date proof sets . . . are somewhat lower as a result of recent over-promotion by speculators." This prescient comment foreshadows the unusual markets of later years.

The only significant addition to the listings was in the minor coinage. The different 1886 Indian Head cents were labeled Types 1 and 2 and described. Previously, Type 2 had been noted as "(2 var.)" with no explanation. These varieties had the same value, but the differences between the two coins were important and noteworthy. Now these differences were described: variety 1 featured "last feather points between I and C," and variety 2 had "last feather points between C and A." In a short time, these varieties would be included in most collecting albums and considered a standard part of the set.

Although this listing (the 1886 Indian Head cents Types 1 and 2) was the only unusual addition, this edition is still an amazing study of the coin market of the time. Readers should realize that when the editor refers to modern Proof coins, he is referring to those from 1936 to date. The decrease in speculative pricing that the preface remarked upon was evident in the 1936 and 1937 Proof sets, which had price decreases of $75 (to $400) and $20 (to $180) respectively. Proof sets for the other modern coins (from 1938 through 1955) had smaller decreases.

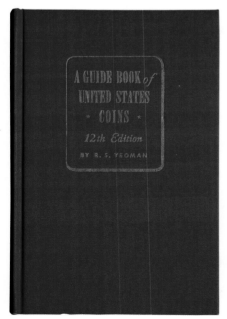

Values of the 12th Edition

Year/Edition	Issue Price	F	VF	New
1959 (12th ed.)	$1.75	$10	$15	$20

Dollar Price Performance

Year	Very Fine	Uncirculated	Proof
1895-P	—	—	$650
1903-O	$45	$400	Not applicable

The price change for the 1895-P Proof Morgan dollar was astonishing. The increase—63 percent—was huge and largely unheard of at the time. The extremely rare 1894-S Barber dime, for example, was listed at only $3,000 and had not had a price change for years. (However, this may have been due to a lack of sales of the 1894-S.)

Following the pattern of past years, Elston Bradfield gave the new Red Book a favorable review in *The Numismatist*, albeit a brief one. He wrote in the July 1958 issue, "Once again it is a pleasure to announce the arrival of the latest edition of the 'Red Book,' long familiar on the American scene and awaited each year by growing numbers of collectors of United States coins." Bradfield acknowledged that the book's function of providing current coin values "is difficult in an active market such as we have had in recent years," but added that "thanks to the help of the 41 contributors and advisers, this year's estimated prices are close to the current market." He also noted approvingly that "the low price of the book is continued in spite of rising printing costs," closing with the verdict that the new edition was "most attractive to every collector."

RED BOOK RECOLLECTIONS
John and Nancy Wilson

Richard "Dick" Yeoman was one of the greatest numismatists of our time. Very few have achieved what he did during his lifetime in the numismatic hobby. Mr. Yeoman was the recipient of just about every honor that could be bestowed on an individual from many numismatic organizations. Besides being a governor of the American Numismatic Association, he received their Medal of Merit in 1952 and the Farran Zerbe Award in 1956. He was installed in the ANA Hall of Fame in 1978. We can remember going to the Racine Numismatic Society meetings in the 1970s and 1980s. It was like a Who's Who at the RNS meetings. Some of the luminaries that attended regularly were Mr. Yeoman, Ken Bressett, Ed Metzger, and Neil Shafer. Of course, with Western Publishing located in Racine, many of these luminaries lived in the immediate area.

At one of these meetings the program was about how we got interested in the numismatic hobby. When it was Mr. Yeoman's turn, he talked about a time when he worked at a store as a young man and found when he was counting the money at the end of the day that he was short. Going through the change, he found a twenty-cent piece. He knew nothing about twenty-cent pieces and had mistakenly taken it in as a quarter. This made the till five cents short. He later found out that the twenty-cent piece had more value than the quarter, and that was one of his reasons for getting involved in the hobby.

Many years ago Mr. Yeoman and his wife visited Africa, and he was surprised to see his Red Book being used by traders in the market to value coins found in remote Africa.

We admired and thought very highly of Mr. Yeoman. He was always a gentleman. We had the opportunity over the years before his passing to talk and interact with this numismatic icon. As the author of the best-selling book in the hobby, the Red Book, and also due to his involvement with the coin board, his name will live on forever. He is one of the top 10 numismatists of all time.

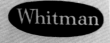
From the July 1959 *Numismatist*.

THE 13TH EDITION (1960)

The Year Was 1959, and . . .

In honor of Lincoln's 150th birthday, the Lincoln cent reverse was redesigned: the wheat ears were replaced with a view of the Lincoln Memorial in Washington, D.C. The design was met with mixed reviews. Kenneth E. Bressett took a full-time position at Whitman Publishing.

Inside the Red Book

For the first time, the preface was eliminated. It was replaced with a new section, "The Purpose of This Book," which provided an amazing snapshot of the year's coin market and economy. Yeoman explained the pricing process: "values listed in the *Guide Book* are averaged from data supplied by contributors several months before publication. The coin market is so active in some categories that values can easily change during this period." He then further explained the rapidly fluctuating prices. He expounded that price increases could be due to the inflationary economy, rapid growth in the number of collectors, and expectancy of sellers to realize profits. Prices could also decline, according to Yeoman, because of speculators looking to make a quick—rather than large—profit, as well as the sudden releases of hoards from either collectors or Federal Reserve vaults. Yeoman reassuringly concluded that "such conditions usually adjust themselves within a few months or years."

Meanwhile, the Red Book itself was thriving. The print run for this edition was an unprecedented 100,000 copies. The list of contributors continued to grow. Two new additions were particularly notable: Q. David Bowers and Kenneth Bressett were both listed in the credits for the first time. Bressett, the future *Guide Book* editor, had joined the Whitman staff full time in 1959.

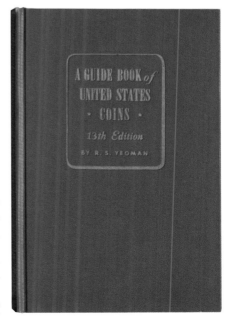

Values of the 13th Edition

Year/Edition	Issue Price	F	VF	New
1960 (13th ed.)	$1.75	$7	$9	$19

Dollar Price Performance

Year	Very Fine	Uncirculated	Proof
1895-P	$150	$350	$650
1903-O	90	500	Not applicable

The changes in the 13th edition showed a very active year for the editors. The first exciting addition was the inclusion of the 1955 Doubled-Die Lincoln Wheat cent, with an enlarged photo of the obverse. "Doubled-die" coins, a term coined by Ken Bressett and used in the 13th edition for the first time, were the result of a minting error (more specifically, a misalignment when the die used was created) that caused the coins' devices to look doubled. The 1955 Doubled Die had a listed value of $50 in Uncirculated condition and $30 in Extremely Fine condition. Also, added to the Lincoln cents section was the previous year's Memorial reverse. There were photos of the coin's obverse and reverse, but no legend. Additionally, an interesting new note accompanied the 1937-D 3-Legged Buffalo nickel variety: "Beware of counterfeits. (Removed leg.)" Evidently the popular variety had already attracted opportunists.

Yeoman also added a note of caution to the Morgan dollar section: "Beware of early strike Philadelphia mint uncirculated dollars being offered as proofs." In 1960, *prooflike* coins—non-Proof issues with exceptional reflectivity and detail—were not studied to the extent they are today. Clearly, the booming coin market of the day had provided con artists with a rich field for exploitation. Likewise, Yeoman appended an asterisk to the 1895 dollar, with the note "Beware removed mint letter."

In the Indian Head cents category, the 1873 Closed 3 and Open 3 varieties were added to the listings. Their addition meant they were finally recognized as accepted and important varieties that were needed for the series to be complete. Both varieties, unlike some others, continued to be recognized in the future.

We can see from the study of the 1895-P and 1903-O dollars that they continued to amaze collectors of the day. For the first time since the sixth edition, the prices for the circulated and Uncirculated 1895-P dollar reappeared. In the sixth edition, it had been listed at $35 and $90 for the Very Fine and Uncirculated grades, respectively. After vanishing for seven editions, the prices returned with a vengeance. The coin was listed at $150 in Very Fine condition and $350 in Uncirculated condition. These were 329 percent and 289 percent increases, a wonderful return that any investor would love. The 1903-O also jumped in value: it doubled in Very Fine condition and showed a 25 percent increase in Uncirculated. Although a fine increase, the 1903-O values pale in comparison to those of the 1895-P. Of course, we can only imagine how the editors arrived at the value for the Uncirculated 1895-P.

The August 1959 issue of *The Numismatist* contained a review of the new edition by longtime fan Elston Bradfield, who devoted almost an entire page to his review. He began with an affirmation of the Red Book's importance to the numismatic calendar: "Summer, for the collectors of U.S. coins, does not arrive until the annual 'Redbook' hits the street. Well, summer is here, because the 1960 'Redbook' has been published." Bradfield's review took note of the addition of the 1955 Doubled-Die cent and the replacement of the preface with the new section "The Purpose of This Book," and he quoted at length from Yeoman's explanations of the factors that cause coin prices to rise and fall. He also made note of Yeoman's statement that for the Red Book creators, the investment potential of collectible coins was secondary to the pleasure and educational benefits they offer. "With this," Bradfield concluded, "your reviewer heartily agrees."

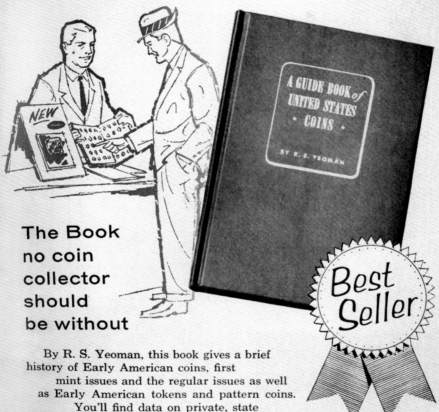

Just off the Press...

NEW 14th EDITION

The Book no coin collector should be without

By R. S. Yeoman, this book gives a brief history of Early American coins, first mint issues and the regular issues as well as Early American tokens and pattern coins. You'll find data on private, state and territorial gold issues, silver and gold commemorative coins plus information on proof coins. Includes standard prices and historical references from 1616 to present date. Pyroxylin-coated, soil-resistant hard cover.

NOW at your Hobby Dealer ... only **$1<u>75</u>**

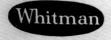 **PUBLISHING COMPANY, RACINE, WISCONSIN WORLD'S LEADING NUMISMATIC PUBLISHERS**

From the July 1960 *Numismatist.*

THE 14TH EDITION (1961)

The Year Was 1960, and . . .

The Lincoln cent was produced in both large- and small-date varieties. Russell Rulau coined the term *exonumia* for coin-related or coinlike objects (from the Latin *exo-*, "out of," and *numis*, for numismatics). The term was added to Webster's dictionary in 1965. The weekly newspaper *Coin World* was founded by J. Oliver Amos.

Inside the Red Book

As noted of the 13th edition, the preface had been deleted, and it remained absent from the 14th edition. In the new section, "The Purpose of This Book," Yeoman reiterated the information provided in the previous edition. He once again noted that investment profits were a secondary consideration (to collecting), realized over the long term and for coins in the best grades.

The panel of contributors had one major change. Kenneth Bressett was listed second, as editorial assistant. His dedication and importance to the *Guide Book* are clearly illustrated by his continued advancement in the credit listing.

The 14th edition boasted a significant new feature in the listed prices—the addition of an asterisk to mark speculative prices, particularly for coins that brought higher prices in rolls than in single specimens. The process by which the prices were updated was described by Ken Bressett in the June 1960 issue of the Whitman *Coin Supply Merchandiser:*

> This year the final work on the prices was done at a secret rendezvous completely free from interruptions and was finished in record time. The completed copy then goes directly to the typesetter and is always carefully guarded so that not a single price is ever known outside of this office until the books are finished and delivered. Even the panel of contributors who have submitted the prices can never know what the final results will be after their estimates are averaged together with all of the other prices. In this manner the prices in the GUIDE BOOK each year are a true reflection of the current market value of the coins.

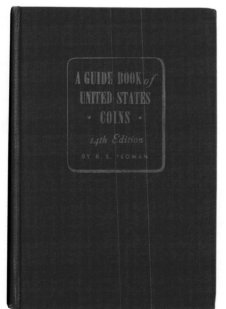

Values of the 14th edition

Year/Edition	Issue Price	F	VF	New
1961 (14th ed.)	$1.75	$4	$6	$16

Dollar Price Performance

Year	Very Fine	Uncirculated	Proof
1895-P	—	—	$700
1903-O	$90	$500	Not applicable

Although there were no major additions or deletions to any of the varieties popular with today's collectors, new coin listings had been added in the sections on colonial coins and territorial gold. In the colonial section, the listings for Connecticut, New Jersey, and Washingtonia had been "completely revised," according to Ken Bressett, writing in the *Merchandiser.* Enumerating further changes, he went on to say, "Our explanation of the 1943 copper cents will be of interest to everyone." New condition columns had also been added to various coin listings throughout the book. Among the changes to the illustrations was an addition to the Indian Head cent photographs, an illustration on page 81 of the date area for the 1873 Open 3 and Close 3 varieties. This was an important addition for students of the series.

The most striking new content was three new sections: "Coins and Tokens of Hawaii," "Alaska Rehabilitation Corporation Tokens of 1935," and "Philippines Under the Sovereignty of the U.S." The *Guide Book* continued to expand and add valuable new information that was otherwise not readily available.

Our study of the Morgan dollars shows the repeated alternation between pricing circulated and Uncirculated 1895-P coins and leaving these values blank when no information was available to the editors. The 14th edition, once again, left these prices blank. The 1895 Proof showed a small increase in price. Pricing of the 1903-O remained steady, with no increase.

In an unusual move, Whitman alerted its dealers to a number of errors in this year's Red Book. The December 1960 issue of the *Merchandiser* included a column humorously titled "Pardon Our Errrors" (*sic!*), which acknowledged some of the more "serious" goofs that had found their way into print despite the vigilance of the staff. These ranged from transposed photographs (of the 1826 large cents) to the presence of prices for a unique coin (the 1786 Connecticut cent with UCTORI legend). Interestingly, two of the reported errors were probably well-intended (if ignorant) *corrections* to apparent misspellings: on page 35, the 1776 Continental dollar of the rare CURRENCEY type was listed with the spelling CURRENCY; similarly, on page 37 the spelling of CONSTELLATIO was given as CONSTELLATION for the 1785 cent with pointed rays. The accurate reproduction of such quirkily spelled coin legends must be a continuing headache to the editorial team, to judge by such incidents as this one and the near-mishap that held up printing of the 26th edition (described later). Indeed, Yeoman would later look back on similar incidents in his essay "The Red Book Story":

> On several occasions urgent summonses would come from the pressroom to verify typographical errors. Some trips to the press were false alarms. After a few such incidents of press stoppings, however, those eagle-eyed craftsmen came to understand that aberrations such as the 1796 LIHERTY Cent and the 1800 LIKERTY Half Dime were actually historical and got there through someone else's carelessness, committed years before they were born.

As the *Merchandiser* list showed, though, not all of these second-guessed spellings emerged from the printer as they were intended to!

The column also proved that reader feedback was an important factor in the continuing evolution of the Red Book. It noted that "many questions" had greeted a change in the grade listings of Barber type coins: "Coins were priced in GOOD condition in the first column and in VERY GOOD condition in the second column. This was done intentionally because many dealers felt that the earlier dates in this series should be priced in a lower grade of condition." Even though this addition was not an error but a thoughtful attempt to provide readers with useful information, the editor conceded that the listing did "cause some confusion and may have to be changed next year."

Once again Elston Bradfield wrote a warm review for the new Red Book. In the August 1960 *Numismatist,* he noted that "among the new features are the replacement of many pictures with improved photographs, and extensive rearrangements of the colonial section." After going on to describe the other new features, he closed his brief review with a hearty endorsement:

> The "Red Book" needs no introduction to long time collectors of Americana. New collectors would do well to make its acquaintance. The price is low and the work is authentic. Recommended and—almost—required reading for all collectors of early American colonial and standard United States issues.

To echo the cautious wording employed by Bradfield, the new Red Book was receiving *almost* unqualified praise!

RED BOOK RECOLLECTIONS
Robert Rhue

I started collecting coins at the age of 10 in the mid-1950s. Anticipating the new edition of the Red Book each year became a highlight of my collecting.

Why? Because a good deal of the satisfaction that I got from collecting was seeing how much the value of my collection was increasing each year. Since the Red Book was basically the only pricing guide available at that time, each new edition, with its increased prices, brought an added measure of joy and satisfaction.

When I started collecting, one could find many valuable coins in circulation to fill the various holes in the much-used blue Whitman boards. And even when I had to buy coins from a dealer, they were relatively affordable (Dan Brown and Al Overton were my mentors and the only major dealers in Colorado).

For instance, most any Indian Head cent after 1880 could be had for a nickel. And most type coins from large cents through Liberty Seated half dollars could be had for $15 to $20 in choice to gem Uncirculated.

The years of steady increases in the prices listed in the Red Book made it seem as though the upward trend would never end. But it did, with the crash of the roll market in 1964, and the consequent leveling off of most other coins, for a period of perhaps six to eight years. That was a disappointing time for a collector like myself, because a good deal of my joy in collecting was derived from seeing the continual increasing value of my collection.

It's interesting to see the growth of the hobby and of technology from then until now. Back then, prices basically went up "once a year" with the release of the latest edition of the Red Book. Today, via the Internet and various electronic trading networks, they change weekly, daily, and sometimes hourly.

Even today I still enjoy perusing the Red Book for a ballpark indication of the value of most of the non-federal issues—that is, all those issues in the front and the back of the Red Book.

THE 15TH EDITION (1962)

The Year Was 1961, and . . .

Eva Adams was appointed 30th director of the Mint by President John F. Kennedy. Only the second woman to hold this office, she initially held coin collectors in disfavor. Over the course of her term, however, her attitude shifted, and *Numismatic News* would later credit her with doing "more to officially recognize this hobby than all her predecessors did combined." The Smithsonian established the first "modernized" exhibit of numismatic items. The American Numismatic Association, originally chartered by Congress in 1912, had its charter renewed in perpetuity. The International Bank Note Society was founded.

Inside the Red Book

Yeoman's preface continued to be sparse in the 15th edition. He alerted readers that, in the category of Indian Head cents, there was an 1869 recut date (9 Over 9) that should not be confused with the overdate 1869, 9 Over 8. Because of the insubstantial preface, readers had to view the data for further information and changes.

The Lincoln cents section was illustrated with the "hot item" of the day: the 1960 Large Date and Small Date varieties (distinguished by the size of the date on the coin). The differently sized dates were newly discovered, and many people searched hard to find a coin with a small date. These new listings came in direct response to collector demand: Whitman had actually conducted a survey to determine whether these varieties were popular enough to merit inclusion, and the response had been decidedly positive. The Large Date and Small Date cents were shown in enlarged photos, and prices were given for each, including Philadelphia Proofs. However, the editor believed that the given prices were questionable, and used an asterisk to note these values as speculative. This notation can be seen throughout the edition by the values of many modern (post-1950)

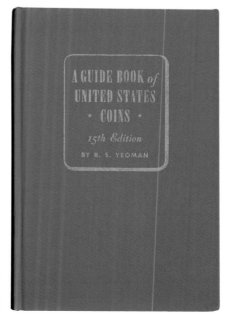

Values of the 15th Edition

Year/Edition	Issue Price	F	VF	New
1962 (15th ed.)	$1.75	$4	$5	$9

Dollar Price Performance

Year	Very Fine	Uncirculated	Proof
1895-P	—	—	$925
1903-O	$150	$600	Not applicable

issues, particularly for Proof prices. Time would show that these speculations were largely correct.

Also in response to their survey, the editors added another important variety: the 1945-S Microscopic S Mercury dime. The Micro S variety has a smaller S mintmark than the regular 1945-S, and Whitman had discovered that there was a "marked degree of interest" in this variety. This inclusion established the variety as an important addition to collections of Mercury dimes.

Survey results such as these helped the Red Book keep its finger on the pulse of the collecting public and determine which new varieties warranted inclusion. Red Book readers over the years may have wondered how the editors decided what newly discovered varieties would make the cut and which ones would be discarded. These decisions were based on careful research, as Ken Bressett explained in his column, whimsically titled "Interest Bearing Notes," in the *Whitman Coin Supply Merchandiser:* "Throughout the year a careful list is kept concerning information about overdates, minor varieties and other information that might be useful to readers of the GUIDE BOOK. Not all of these proposed listings are used each year, but they are each given consideration." The final determination was made after weighing a number of factors:

> Each year a conscientious attempt is made to see that all of the important numismatic discoveries are incorporated into each edition. . . . Listings in the GUIDE BOOK are not placed there arbitrarily. All of the normal mint coins are listed but sub-varieties are listed only when they are popular enough for collectors to want information and prices about them easily available. . . . By keeping up with the popular collecting trends, we feel that the WHITMAN PUBLISHING COMPANY will always be serving the needs of all classes of coin collectors.

Surveys provided the editors with important input about not only the popularity of specific coin varieties but also "the necessity of bringing controversial subjects to a vote before the collecting public." This attention to the collecting community's views has no doubt been one reason for the long and successful life of the Red Book.

Prices in the 15th edition followed an upward trend in general, and the changes to the gold series reflected the new popularity of that area. Also, the 1894-S Barber dime, which previously had not been priced, noted a specific sale—"Hydeman Sale 1961." The price given was a then-astonishing $13,500. Not all of the prices had risen, however: as Bressett observed in the *Merchandiser,* "a few prices went down because speculation had driven the price up beyond their natural level." The careful procedure through which Red Book prices were arrived at received emphasis in the June issue of the *Merchandiser,* in which Bressett stressed that "these prices are not merely arrived at by adding a flat percentage to last year's prices. Each coin is considered individually and values are arrived at by averaging together prices that have been reported by our panel of contributors."

As can be seen from the chart, the 1895-P and 1903-O Morgan dollars had been active. The 1895-P had another 32 percent increase in value. The 1903-O leapt 67 percent to $150 in Extremely Fine condition, while the Uncirculated version increased by another 20 percent to $600. Collectors of the day must have been shocked to see how high these values were going!

The popularity of the Red Book at this time can be gauged from the review of the 15th edition in the August 1961 issue of *The Numismatist*—the first review in seven years not to have been penned by Elston Bradfield, who was now the editor of the journal. Instead, his assistant, Glenn Smedley, stepped in. Smedley, as we have seen, was no stranger to the Red Book; as a credited contributor since the book's seventh edition, and coordinator of the panel of contributors since the eighth, he undoubtedly brought some bias to his reviewing. Nevertheless, his thoughts on the book that he helped produce offer interest and insight.

Smedley's review provides us the interesting information that "unusually heavy advance orders for the fifteenth edition of the popular 'Red Book' caused a two-week delay in initial shipments this year." At 15 years old, the Red Book was clearly riding high in popularity! Smedley went on to note specific changes from the year before: "There is increased space given to Confederate and Civil War items, and a few new photographs have been added. . . . At least one controversial piece, the doubloon dated 1742, has been eliminated entirely." With a whiff of nostalgia, he closed his review by taking a look back at the book's lifetime:

> Continuing the policy established with the first edition in 1946, the publisher exerts every reasonable effort to make the "Red Book" the best guide available to collectors of United States coins. Without making any spectacular changes from that first edition, when the unc. 1914-D cent was priced at $10.00 and the three-legged buffalo [nickel] wasn't even listed, the book's success continues to be unprecedented.

Now that more than 60 editions of the Red Book have appeared, it is almost amusing to see a 15-year landmark considered with such seriousness. But the sentiment was apt: the Red Book was indeed unprecedented, and the qualities that had allowed it to endure and prosper over its first 15 years would ensure its long life over decades to come.

An overprinted copy of the 15th edition has been recorded; see chapter 6 for details.

RED BOOK RECOLLECTIONS
Ron Guth

My earliest experiences as a coin collector revolved around the Red Book. I started collecting around 1963, just before America converted from silver to clad coins. My typical Saturday morning included going to the bank to purchase rolls of cents, dimes, quarters, and half dollars (depending on how much money I had in my pocket). Not knowing the values of anything, I relied on the Red Book to help me determine which coins were valuable and which were not. I soon learned to keep an eye out for a number of different date and mintmark combinations. For example, I soon learned that if I came across a 1909-S VDB cent or a 1916-D dime, I had hit a home run (sadly, I never did find a 1909-S VDB).

As my collecting advanced, the Red Book introduced me to obsolete types and series that could no longer be found in circulation—side roads that I traveled down with great enthusiasm: half cents, colonial coins, Seated Liberty silver dollars, Civil War tokens, and so much more. The Red Book, then and now, is a handy little book that gives a wonderful overview of the depth and breadth of American numismatics. It's the perfect guide for beginners, yet it still contains plenty of useful information for the advanced collector.

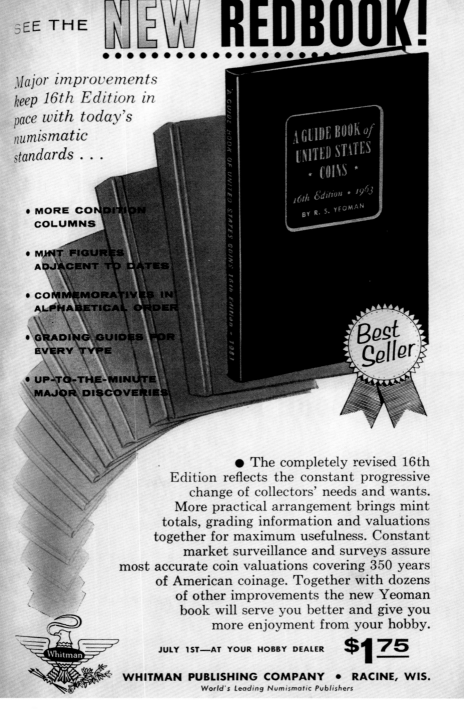

SEE THE **NEW REDBOOK!**

Major improvements keep 16th Edition in pace with today's numismatic standards . . .

- **MORE CONDITION COLUMNS**

- **MINT FIGURES ADJACENT TO DATES**

- **COMMEMORATIVES IN ALPHABETICAL ORDER**

- **GRADING GUIDES FOR EVERY TYPE**

- **UP-TO-THE-MINUTE MAJOR DISCOVERIES**

A GUIDE BOOK *of* UNITED STATES * COINS * *16th Edition * 1963* BY R. S. YEOMAN

Best Seller

● The completely revised 16th Edition reflects the constant progressive change of collectors' needs and wants. More practical arrangement brings mint totals, grading information and valuations together for maximum usefulness. Constant market surveillance and surveys assure most accurate coin valuations covering 350 years of American coinage. Together with dozens of other improvements the new Yeoman book will serve you better and give you more enjoyment from your hobby.

JULY 1ST—AT YOUR HOBBY DEALER   **$1.75**

WHITMAN PUBLISHING COMPANY ● RACINE, WIS.
World's Leading Numismatic Publishers

From the June 1962 *Numismatist*. The Red Book underwent a number of dramatic changes for the 16th edition, and this ad made sure that readers knew it. For the first time, the "Red Book" nickname is prominently displayed in *Guide Book* advertising.

THE 16TH EDITION (1963)

The Year Was 1962, and . . .

The San Francisco Mint's official designation was changed from mint to assay office. The numismatic world was shocked to learn about the existence of the King of Siam Proof set, which included the 1804 silver dollar—a coin that was studied in *The Fantastic 1804 Dollar*, by Eric P. Newman and Kenneth Bressett, in 1962). The set was originally presented to the king of Siam (King Ph'ra Nang Klao, also known as Rama III) by Edmund Roberts, U.S. envoy, on behalf of President Andrew Jackson, in 1836. Numismatic author Neil Shafer joined the Whitman staff. The first international coin-collecting convention was held in Detroit, Michigan, on August 14 through 18. About 40,000 visitors attended the convention, which was co-sponsored by the ANA and the Canadian Numismatic Association. The Philadelphia Mint discovered thousands of Morgan and Peace dollars in its vaults, and set about releasing them to the public.

Inside the Red Book

The 16th edition embodies many changes for the Red Book—what Yeoman would later call "major surgery"—and it is one of my personal favorites for a number of reasons. To start with, this year the cover and spine were changed to include the year as well as the edition number, so that this edition read, "16th Edition 1963." The addition of the year made it easier for collectors to distinguish among the editions on a bookshelf. A further alteration to the book's physical makeup was probably less noticeable to readers: the printing process changed from letterpress to offset lithography. The change, as Kenneth Bressett explained in the *Merchandiser*, meant faster printing. Another change that marked this edition was the promotion of Bressett to the position of coordinating editor.

Inside the 16th edition were many more changes. One of the most radical was the new placement of each issue's mintage (number of coins produced): previously these had

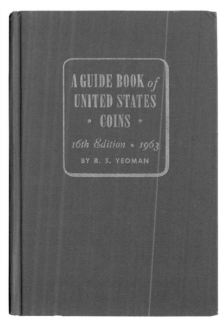

Values of the 16th Edition

Year/Edition	Issue Price	F	VF	New
1963 (16th ed.)	$1.75	$4	$5	$9

Note: See chapter 7 for discussion of error copies of the 16th edition.

Dollar Price Performance

Year	Very Fine	Uncirculated	Proof
1895-P	—	—	$1,500
1903-O	$400	$1,500	Not applicable

16TH EDITION GUIDE BOOK SHOWS MAJOR REVISIONS

R. S. Yeoman, author and editor of the GUIDE BOOK, inspects a press sheet during the current printing of the 16th edition.

One of the questions that many collectors will be asking concerns the latest numismatic discovery, the 1938 D over S Buffalo nickel. Because of the importance of this coin, it will be listed in the new book.

The reorganization of the GUIDE BOOK extends far beyond the printed copy that you will be selling. Unseen changes include a new method of selecting price contributions. Approximately 40 qualified dealers and collectors throughout the country are used for sources for price information. Starting this year approximately 20 per cent of these sources will be changed each year in a program to allow new people to participate in supplying information. This will give a much broader base to the prices and assure an accurate average of prices used throughout the country. All of the information submitted by the panel of price contributors has been averaged together in our office and the final tabulation gives the prices used in the book.

The method of printing the GUIDE BOOK has also been changed. This year we have switched from letterpress to offset lithography. Two giant high-speed presses are used to print the books. 64 pages are printed on a single sheet and the sheets are then transferred to the second press where the other side of the sheet is printed with another 64 pages. This gives a total of 128 pages on each enormous sheet of paper and thus only two sheets of paper are used for an entire 256-page book. This faster method of printing was necessary to produce enough books to be able to supply all jobbers with their initial requirements of the GUIDE BOOK. After this first surge of business is over, additional

quantities of the book will be printed to take care of the entire year's needs.

This year brilliantly printed window streamers are being packed in every case for initial shipments. These window streamers announce the fact that you have Red Books available and indicate some of the major revisions in this edition.

As dealers, you will realize the importance of passing along the good word about the revised GUIDE BOOK. Our recent survey indicated that many collectors purchase this book only every two or three years. We feel that this is the year that nearly every collector will want to have the new revised edition. Do not be caught short and miss out on sales because of lack of sufficient merchandise.

Members of the Coin Division inspect the Pack-O-Matic shipping facilities which speed the packing process.

The new 16th edition of A GUIDE BOOK OF U. S. COINS by R. S. Yeoman is now on the press and running on schedule so that it will be ready for shipment to all jobbers and will reach them by July 2. Collectors all over the country will be looking forward to this new edition with great anticipation because of the many special features that are being offered in this revised edition. The shipping of these books will be carried out on an exacting schedule so that dealers throughout the country will be able to receive their books on nearly the same day and be able to take care of the many collectors who want to be the "first" to get a look at this new book.

This year's Red Book has been enriched with numerous improvements. Some of these include more condition columns, mint totals' adjacent to the date, grading guides for each coin type, alphabetical arrangement of commemoratives, new pictures, latest coin discoveries and accurate coin valuations.

The *Whitman Coin Supply Merchandiser* from June–July 1962 provided an in-depth description of the "major revisions" that were made in the 16th-edition Red Book. In the photograph at the lower right, R.S. Yeoman and Kenneth Bressett oversee the new "Pack-O-Matic" system.

been grouped together in their own section in the rear of the book, but now each mintage figure was located adjacent to the date of the issue. The discussion of "Mints and Mint Marks" was inserted on page 59, with the new section "Proof Coins" and a modern listing—which included coins from 1936 and after—on the next page. The "Proof Coins" section included a discussion of what a Proof coin was, an explanation of how these coins were made, and a listing of dates and values.

Another important addition to the book's interior—in Yeoman's words, "the frosting on the cake"—was the inclusion of Brown and Dunn grading guides within the listings for each coin type. The general "Condition of Coins" section was still located at the front of the book, but the new descriptions were specific to each type and explained what to look for when distinguishing between the different grades for each coin. For example, the following standards were now given on page 111 for grading the Winged Head Liberty type:

Good—Letters and dates clear. Lines and diagonal bands in fasces (the bundle of rods on the coin's reverse) are obliterated.

V. Good—One-third of sticks are discernible in fasces.

Fine—All sticks in fasces are defined. Diagonal bands worn at center high points only.

Ex. Fine—Diagonal bands complete, with only slight wear. Hair braids and hair before ear show clearly.

Within the listed varieties, there was one important addition. In the Buffalo nickels section, the 1938-D, D Over S variety was shown for the first time. The *Merchandiser* issue of June–July 1962 showed that the Red Book team had anticipated that there would be a great deal of interest among collectors in whether this "latest numismatic discovery" would be incorporated into the Red Book. "Because of the importance of this coin, it will be listed in the new book," the article assures us. The microphotograph was top quality. Valuations, apparently unknown at the time, were simply listed as dashes. This variety was destined to become extremely popular in future years.

These changes—the "Proof Coins" section, the mintage listing, and the individual grade descriptions—were the most important to occur to the book in years. Further tweaks included the addition of more condition columns and new pictures. The result was a more modern *Guide Book*, which would continue to evolve through the years.

One innovation in the 16th edition, however, would prove controversial. The commemorative coin section, which had previously been organized chronologically, was now arranged in alphabetical order. The thinking behind this change was later explained by Yeoman: "The shift was made to conform to dealers' advertisements, which had assumed this arrangement for practical reasons," he wrote in the 1972 edition's special section on commemorative coins. "It seems that the old-timers knew the dates of each issue, but the great body of new collectors and dealers had not accepted the old system so well." Somewhat ingenuously, perhaps, he added, "The change was accepted without criticism." In future years the arrangement of this section would in fact draw criticism (see chapter 2), and would ultimately revert to chronological order.

Other changes took place behind the scenes and were not visible to readers. Ken Bressett told the dealers who received the *Merchandiser*:

> The reorganization of the GUIDE BOOK extends far beyond the printed copy that you will be selling. Unseen changes include a new method of selecting price contributions. . . . Starting this year approximately 20 per cent of [our] sources will be changed each year in a program to allow new people to participate in supplying information. This will give a much broader base to the prices.

As he had for the previous edition, Glenn Smedley reviewed the new Red Book in *The Numismatist*. His writeup, from the August 1962 issue, emphasized the importance the annual guide had taken on for numismatists. His review began: "'How is it priced in the new Red Book?' is an all important question which can be answered now." He goes on to observe that there are "many changes in prices and many improvements in arrangement and illustrations in this edition, bringing it up to date and making it easier to use." After a summary of price trends in the volume, Smedley wrapped up his review with a combination of praise and prophecy: "we predict that this improved edition will outsell any previous one because Whitman has spent money and effort to give the purchaser more value for the same price."

Let's look again at the two Morgan dollars, the 1895-P and 1903-O. In an amazing price jump, the value of the 1895-P Proof increased 62 percent, to $1,500. The 1903-O in Extremely Fine condition increased 167 percent in value to $400; in Uncirculated condition, the coin's value increased 150 percent to $1,500. These were amazing times for these two dates. Thankfully, there was no value given for the Uncirculated 1895-P, since this date does not exist in that condition.

The 16th edition is noteworthy for existing in an error edition. Early in the print run, page 237 was omitted, and a duplicate page 239 was put in its place. The mistake was caught and corrected, but some of the misprints still found their way into release. (See chapter 7 for the full story of the episode, in Yeoman's own words.) This book is one of the most desirable error editions. It is scarce, particularly in collectible condition, and therefore valuable.

From the July 1963 *Numismatist*. The Red Book is now decreed the "World's most popular coin book," due to its "unequaled high standard of quality in both content and appearance."

THE 17TH EDITION (1964)

The Year Was 1963, and . . .

President Kennedy was assassinated on November 22, 1963—an event forever etched into the minds of those who lived through the event. Congress authorized a new design for the half dollar in honor of the slain president. As a consequence, after only 16 years the Franklin half dollar saw its final year of production. The *Coin Dealer Newsletter*, or "Greysheet," was founded.

Inside the Red Book

As had become the pattern in recent editions, the 17th edition's price changes were considerable, and in line with the continually evolving hobby. The valuations for most of the popular series increased, particularly for the key dates within each issue. It is interesting to note that many of the key dates—for sets including Barber dimes, Barber quarters, Buffalo nickels, and Indian Head cents—could still be obtained from circulation. This probably fueled interest in different series and caused the growth in the number of active collectors.

In preparation for this edition, Whitman sent out another survey, the results of which were summarized in the June 1963 *Numismatist* (pictured). As Glenn Smedley commented in his review in the August issue, the survey responses "indicated general satisfaction with the *Guide Book*, so there was no incentive for major changes." Indeed, of the 11 coin varieties the survey proposed as additions to the Red Book, not a single one received a majority of favorable responses—even though almost all of them would in fact be incorporated into future editions! Only a few of the varieties are still not represented in the Red Book, such as the "1961-D over horizontal D cent" and the "1867 over small 67 Indian cent." In Yeoman's words, "apparently there is not enough interest" in the proposed new listings "to warrant their inclusion." As a consequence, there

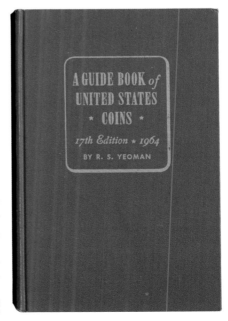

Values of the 17th Edition

Year/Edition	Issue Price	F	VF	New
1964 (17th ed.)	$1.75	$4	$5	$7

Dollar Price Performance

Year	Very Fine	Uncirculated	Proof
1895-P	—	—	$2,500
1903-O	$15	$30	Not applicable

Annual Red Book Survey Made

The Whitman Publishing Company has completed another sampling of collectors' opinions and wishes concerning the *Guide Book of United States Coins*. The results of the survey will serve as a guide for certain changes contemplated for the seventeenth edition of R. S. Yeoman's popular "Red Book."

Questionnaires were sent to thirty-five hundred subscribers, located in all parts of the country, of one of the popular numismatic publications. About one thousand replies were received, although a few did not answer all questions. Besides the answers to questions and comments requested, Whitman considers that the letters and notations received also reveal the attitudes and opinions of typical collectors. Specific questions asked and a summary of replies were as follows:

1. How often do you purchase a copy of the *Guide Book?* Replies indicated that 829 bought it every year, 111 bought it every other year, and 58 less frequently. Some bought more than one book a year.

2. Please give your opinions of the revisions and prices in the sixteenth edition. Almost everyone commented and most replies were favorable, especially to the moving of mintage figures into the listing and pricing by dates. Some constructive criticisms were offered.

3. Do you find the new grading guide helpful? Is it adequate? Of the 963 answers, only 24 replied "no" to the first part of the question. On the second part, most said it was adequate but some thought that it should be expanded to cover all grades of all series.

4. List changes that you feel would improve the usefulness of the *Guide Book*. As expected, replies gave personal opinions which were helpful but could not be tabulated easily and did not show general agreement on specific changes desired.

5. Vote on addition of the following items to the book:

	Yes	No
a. 1942-D over horizontal D nickel	228	595
b. 1955-D over S nickel	364	488
c. 1961-D over horizontal D cent	275	576
d. 1867 over small 67 Indian cent	295	524
e. 1905-O dimes with large and small mint marks	292	535
f. 1916 nickel with double obverse die	237	573
g. 1939 nickel with double obverse die	263	545
h. 1878 silver dollar with reverse of 1879 (slanting arrow feathers)	267	519
i. 1879-S silver dollar with reverse of 1878 (parallel arrow feathers)	266	519
j. 1880-CC silver dollar with reverse of 1878 (parallel arrow feathers)	269	510
k. 1900-O silver dollar with O over CC	371	427

As a result of this voting, Whitman does not plan to add any of these items to the seventeenth edition of the "Red Book."

6. List coins that you feel should be taken out of the book. There were 307 votes to remove the 1892-O micro O half dollar, against 247 votes to retain it. Others mentioned in fewer replies were the 1937-D three legged buffalo nickel, 1955 double die cent, 1942 over 41 dime, 1938-D over S nickel, and the 1945-S micro S dime.

To the seventh question, 588 (60%) indicated membership in some numismatic organization and 384 (40%) replied that they were not. Several of the smaller group indicated an intention to join a coin club or having already applied for membership.

Two specific comments seem to sum up the many received with the questionnaires returned: "The sixteenth edition was far better than the fifteenth; keep up the good work" and "The Guide Book does all that it was designed to do and more."

The Numismatist of June 1963 disclosed the responses to Whitman's survey on the Red Book.

were no additions to the variety listings for the 17th edition, although a new half-page section was devoted to the coinage of Puerto Rico.

The only change made in response to the survey, in fact, was a deletion: the removal of the 1892-O Micro O half dollar. In answer to an open-ended query about what varieties should be removed, 307 respondents voted to drop this coin (as against 247 who voted to retain it). Among the other varieties some responders suggested deleting were the 1937-D three-legged Buffalo nickel and the 1955 Doubled-Die Obverse cent, both of which escaped elimination and still appear in the Red Book to this day. The 1892-O Micro O half dollar would later be reinstated, and it too is listed in the current Red Book (see the discussion of the 49th-edition Red Book).

Smedley's review of the 17th edition makes delightful reading for the Red Book collector, not just because it is positive (which, indeed, is hardly unusual) but because Smedley was inspired to open it with a bit of laudatory whimsy. "Many things are taken for granted," he philosophized: "that the sun will rise each morning, that winter will be followed by spring and summer, and that the new edition of the 'Red Book' will immediately precede the Fourth of July." As he had two years before, Smedley took the reader down memory lane, musing about the changes collectors had seen since the first edition came out in 1946: "Just think, there wasn't any double die cent then; the three-legged buffalo [nickel variety] didn't appear in the first two issues; and at the 1946 price, you could buy a roll of 1914-D cents for the cost of just one coin today." One wonders how long it would be before he and his fellow collectors would become nostalgic for the 1963 price of a 1914-D cent!

Getting down to brass tacks, Smedley took note of the "general house cleaning of minor errata" evident in the new edition, as well as the numerous price changes. He ended by referencing the recent survey and its evidence that the Red Book had no need to make major changes, adding, "besides, enlarging or major revisions of the book would be costly, and the modest price at which it sells is certainly an important factor in its continuing popularity."

The 1963 price for the 1895-P Proof dollar could not be called modest, however. Its valuation increased 67 percent over the previous year's, to a total of $2,500. This is amazing, considering that the weekly income for most families at this time was around $125.

The 1903-O valuation was equally astounding—although not in a way that pleased sellers of the coin. This coin was suddenly $15 in Extremely Fine condition and $30 in Uncirculated condition. Respectively, this represented *decreases* of 96 percent and 98 percent! This shocking development occurred because of the great Treasury hoard releases of 1962 to 1964, when bags of Uncirculated dollars were released at face value. As a result, Yeoman deleted the notation at the end of the type listing—present since the second printing of the first edition—that read, "which probably accounts for the scarcity of the 1903 O."

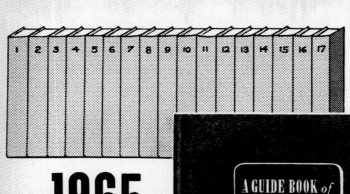
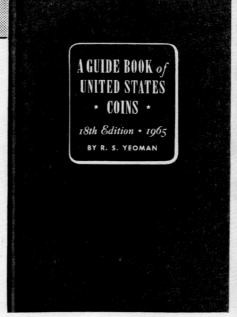
From the July 1964 *Numismatist*. The ad assures readers that the 18th edition contains "the Kennedy half dollar . . . and other late discoveries."

THE 18TH EDITION (1965)

The Year Was 1964, and . . .

America experienced its worst coin shortage since the Civil War. With the price of silver risen to precipitous heights, and the Treasury stock of silver coins running low, the government declared its intention to replace the silver coinage with copper-nickel clad coins. Moreover, Silver Certificates would no longer be redeemable for silver dollars. The public hurried to hoard the last silver coins, including the popular new John F. Kennedy half dollar. The proliferation of new coin-vending machines placed further demands on the shrinking supply of circulating coins. Mint Director Eva Adams held coin collectors responsible for the shortage, and the Treasury instituted measures to discourage collecting: eliminating mintmarks, discontinuing production of Proof sets, and placing a date freeze on new coins until the shortage was resolved. This year also saw the founding of *COINage* magazine and the ANA's Numismatic Hall of Fame, as well as the resignation of Mint chief engraver Gilroy Roberts, who was succeeded by Frank Gasparro.

Inside the Red Book

The country lost President John F. Kennedy in 1963, and 1964 saw the quick release of the Kennedy half dollar. The 18th edition added this new coin to the listings. Another major change was the addition of the rare 1786 Immunis Columbia New Jersey cent. As noted in the *Merchandiser* of July 1964, "This coin has long been known to exist, but was generally unlisted in all catalogs because of its rarity and its somewhat questionable authenticity. With the appearance of a new specimen, leading authorities are now able to determine that the variety is legitimate." The Feuchtwanger cent received its own listing, complete with illustration and values, due (as the *Merchandiser* reported) to the popularity of the piece and the "repeated inquiries" of Red Book readers. To make room

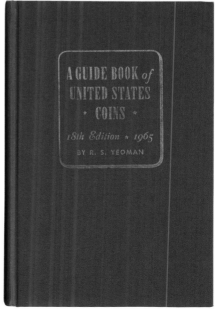

Values of the 18th Edition

Year/Edition	Issue Price	F	VF	New
1965 (18th ed.)	$1.75	$3	$4	$6

Dollar Price Performance

Year	Very Fine	Uncirculated	Proof
1895-P	—	—	$3,250
1903-O		$40	Not applicable

for the new listing, the section on Lesher Referendum dollars was reduced. The 1896 20-centavos coin of Puerto Rico had been removed because its existence was unproven.

Another important adjustment to the listings was in the description of the 1922 "plain" Lincoln cent. Previously, it had been listed as "1922 Plain (Filled die, D missing)." It was changed to read, "1922 Plain (Defective die, D missing)." Evidently the "filled die" variety was not popular or important enough to maintain its Red Book listing. (For a discussion of the three accepted 1922 No D varieties, the reader should consult Q. David Bowers's *Guide Book of Lincoln Cents* [Whitman, 2008].) Although the term "defective die" is misleading, the importance of the variety was understood, and as a consequence its value increased.

The 18th edition was also the first to list a value for the 1870-S Seated Liberty dollar. Prices for extremely rare pieces are added to the Red Book when their values can be determined from auction results. The appearance of this coin in the 1963 sale of the Samuel Wolfson Collection meant that the price could be added to the listing: a then-substantial $12,000. (In the 2009 Red Book this piece listed at $35,000 to $70,000.)

The continued study of the 1895-P and 1903-O dollars is fascinating. The 1895-P rose another $750, or 30 percent, to $3,250. This is remarkable in an era when common-date $10 gold coins sold for a mere $32.50. The 1903-O rose in price to $40, still a far cry from its value two years earlier, when it was priced at $1,500! For this coin in circulated condition, no price was given. It was evidently considered too common for a premium.

As usual, *The Numismatist* reviewed the new edition, and again the reviewer was Glenn Smedley. That the Red Book had become a fact of numismatic life is evident in his opening statement: "It won't be news or a surprise to anyone that the new 'red book' came out July 1," he told readers in the August 1964 issue, "but it should be recorded as a matter of fact." He then went on to offer a capsule portrait of the book's status at the ripe old age of 18:

> This book has served both collectors and dealers as the bible of the coin collecting hobby since the first edition came out in 1946. It has been praised, criticized, credited and blamed far more than any other numismatic book, but the proof of the pudding is in the eating, and the red book continues to be a best seller. . . . Nearly half of the original fourteen contributors are deceased, but the work which they helped Editor Yeoman instigate has grown through bust and boom times and continues to be the "must" for collectors of U.S. coins.

Smedley's close observation of the details of the new edition extended even to its binding! He pointed out "the addition of a head band, a cloth strip at the spine which protrudes slightly at the top and bottom. This makes for a stronger and more durable binding but is usually seen only on much more expensive books." The *Merchandiser* disclosed that the addition of the band was made possible through "new high-speed equipment capable of handling this operation at a relatively small expense." Collectors can easily find this feature by looking at the top or bottom of the book where the bound pages meet the book cover (see illustration).

Smedley did not exaggerate when he called the Red Book a best seller. This edition, in fact, set a record for Red Book sales that has yet to be broken, selling 1.2 million copies!

Red Book

(1967 ... 20th edition)

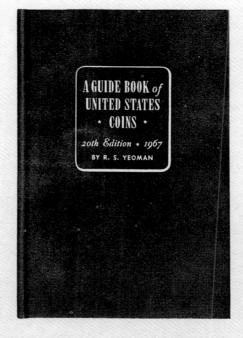

Over the years, no standard reference book has been of greater value to coin collectors than R.S. Yeoman's best-selling RED BOOK. This 20th edition affirms its position as the numismatist's indispensable authority on U. S. coins. The 1967 RED BOOK (it's also known as "A Guide Book of United States Coins") contains many changes and updatings from the 19th addition. Cataloging the vast field of American coinage from 1616 to the present, it features the latest coin values in 7 condition columns, gives mint figures adjacent to dates, lists commemoratives in alphabetical order and has grading guides for every type. 256 pages, gold-stamped soil-resistant hard-cover. **At your dealer's and other stores. $1.75. No. 9051.**

50ᵗʰ Anniversary

Whitman Publishing Company, Racine, Wisconsin

From the July 1966 *Numismatist*. A newly minimalist look distinguishes this ad for the 20th edition of the Red Book. Notice the logo marking the 50th anniversary of Whitman Publishing.

THE 20TH EDITION (1967)

The Year Was 1966, and . . .

President Lyndon Johnson appointed Eva Adams to a second term as Mint director. The ANA held a groundbreaking ceremony for its new headquarters in Colorado Springs, Colorado. *COINage* magazine began monthly, instead of quarterly, publication.

Inside the Red Book

For coin collectors, the year 1965—first reflected in the 20th edition—is one that will live in infamy. This year saw the release of the now-ubiquitous clad coinage for dimes and quarters, which meant that these were coins were being produced without silver. As a result, the listings for these coins were noted as "Clad Coinage." Interestingly, although half dollars still contained 40 percent silver, there was no notation to suggest this.

As opposed to the dramatic additions of accepted varieties that other recent editions had shown, most of the 20th edition's considerable changes were to the valuations of the various types. We can see this price growth by looking at the Morgan dollar series. Much like Sherman in his March to the Sea, the 1895-P Proof dollar continued its take-no-prisoners advance. Its impressive 6 percent value increase of $250 resulted in a hefty $4,750 price tag. Compared to the price increases of previous years, however, it was a timid advance.

The *Numismatist* review of this edition appeared in the September 1966 issue. The reviewer, identified as E. Moller, offers an unemotional description of the new edition of "the most popular reference on the retail value of United States coins." He notes a bit vaguely that "this year's edition features descriptions of popular varieties of older United States coins not discussed previously" and observes, likewise without offering specifics, that some mintage figures "have been corrected for this edition." The major change: "For the first time, clad coinage makes its appearance in the Red Book."

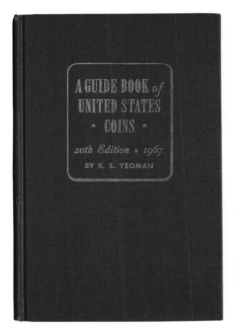

Values of the 20th Edition

Year/Edition	Issue Price	F	VF	New
1967 (20th ed.)	$1.75	$3	$5	$8

Dollar Price Performance

Year	Very Fine	Uncirculated	Proof
1895-P	—	—	$4,750
1903-O	$25.00	$37.50	Not applicable

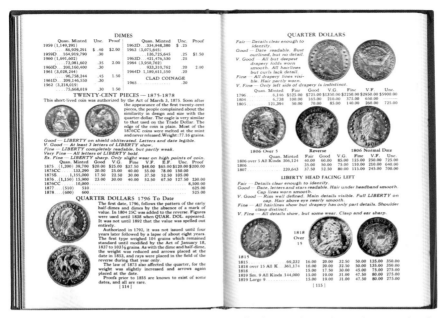

In 10 years the opening pages of the quarter dollar listings have changed tremendously. The pages are now packed with information, including grading descriptions, mintages, and values for six grades.

Moller's inoffensive writeup marks the beginning of the end of the era of personal, even emotional, reviews: in future years, the amount of space devoted to discussing new books would be devoted more to neutral description than to evaluation. There would be exceptions, as when Smedley returned to write a few more reviews, but for the most part Red Book historians and collectors will have to look elsewhere from this point on for a barometer of the cultural and popular status of the Red Book.

The 1903-O continued to mystify with its pricing. It increased, in Uncirculated condition, to $37.50, a nearly 6 percent increase—but considering the thousands that were released by the Treasury in 1962 through 1964, the price should have been somewhat static. (It did, in fact, remain static for coins in Very Fine condition.) Perhaps it was the former mystery of the rareness of this date that provided price support, resulting in a value considerably higher than that of a common date (which was listed at $2.50 in Uncirculated).

THE 21ST EDITION (1968)

The Year Was 1967, and . . .

On June 24, Congress passed a law that permitted the redemption of Silver Certificates for silver bullion for silver bullion for a period of one year. The legislation also restored the Denver and San Francisco mintmarks. This was due in part to Mint Director Adams, who had had a change of heart about "those little D's and S's."[23] The Mint announced that it would resume production of Proof sets in 1968.

Inside the Red Book

The 21st edition contained a new section for Special Mint Sets, on page 60 under the Proof coin listings. They were generally listed at their issue prices, with only a slight premium for the 1966 set. The Mint continued to produce these sets through 1967.

Generally, there were only minor changes to the 21st edition. One such change was in the organization of half cents: 1793 half cents were now designated "Head Facing Left" and separated from the 1794 to 1797 type half cents (now described as "Head Facing Right"). The only other alteration of note was in the Washington quarter listings. Previously, the 1934 quarter had been divided into the categories "Light Motto" and "All Kinds." For this edition, the categories were designated "Light Motto" and "Heavy Motto." The most noticeable change to the 21st edition, according to the August 1967 review in *The Numismatist*, was that "a greater number of price changes are reflected than in any previous edition." Most of the writeup was confined to a summary of price trends reflected in the new edition, but it did contain the telling assertion that the guide "is regarded as the bible of the numismatic field." One other change marked the 21st edition: a small rise in its price, from $1.75 to $2.00.

The value of the 1895-P Proof dollar remained steady for the first time since the *Guide Book* was first printed. The 1903-O had bounced around since the 17th edition (1964), when it had drastically dropped from $1,500 to $30, and in this edition it expe-

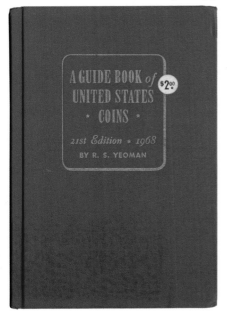

rienced a 27 percent decrease to $27.50 in Uncirculated condition, with similar decreases in the other listed grades. Collectors were clearly uninterested in this date.

Values of the 21st Edition

Year/Edition	Issue Price	F	VF	New
1968 (21st ed.)	$2	$3	$5	$10

Dollar Price Performance

Year	Very Fine	Uncirculated	Proof
1895-P	—	—	$4,750
1903-O	$18.50	$27.50	Not applicable

22nd Edition

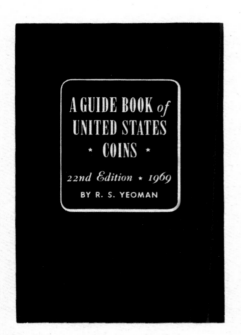

Red Book '69

Another year has rolled around and again Whitman offers a new edition of its prestigious **Guide Book of U.S. Coins,** so well known as the **Red Book.**

Over the years, no standard reference book has been of greater value to coin collectors than Mr. R. S. Yeoman's Red Book. The 22nd edition affirms its position as the numismatist's indispensable authority on U.S. coins.

Cataloging the vast field of American coinage from 1616 to the present, the Red Book features the latest coin values in seven condition columns, gives mint figures adjacent to dates, lists commemoratives in alphabetical order and has grading guides for every type. 256 pages, gold-stamped soil-resistant hard cover.

Now at your dealer's. $2.00 No. 9051.

 Whitman Hobby Products from WESTERN PUBLISHING COMPANY, INC. Racine, Wisconsin

From the September 1968 *Numismatist.*

THE 22ND EDITION (1969)

The Year Was 1968, and . . .

Proof sets were reintroduced. For the first time, they were minted in San Francisco and bore an S mintmark. The price was increased from its 1964 level of $2.10 to $5.00 per set.

Inside the Red Book

Times change, and so do coin types. Even the humble Lincoln cent evolved. In 1959, a design of the Lincoln Memorial replaced the wheat ear reverse, but *Guide Book* editors waited until the 22nd edition to acknowledge the change in a section heading. Here the category "Lincoln Type, Memorial Reverse 1959 to Date" finally gave formal recognition to the reverse type. Also new to this edition was an enlarged photo of the 1937-D 3-Legged variety in the Buffalo nickel section. This important addition probably helps account for the variety's popularity to this day. The nickel section had also been supplemented with an illustration of the 1968 Jefferson nickel showing the mintmark on the obverse.

Proof sets resumed production in 1968. This was also the first year that these sets, originally minted at the main mint in Philadelphia, were minted at the San Francisco branch mint—where they continue to be produced to this day. The 22nd edition Red Book, prepared in 1968, was able to include them in its listings. The 1968-S dimes, quarters, and half dollars were only released as part of the Proof sets, so these coins were listed with the notation, "Proof only." The 1968-S cents and nickels, on the other hand, were released both in the Proof sets and for circulation.

There were no other major changes to the different type coin listings, but prices generally continued to advance. The 1895-P Morgan dollar remained at $4,750. However,

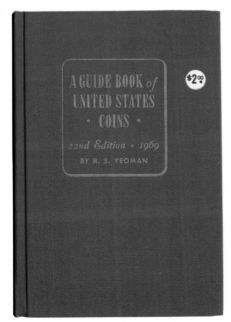

Values of the 22nd Edition

Year/Edition	Issue Price	F	VF	New
1969 (22nd ed.)	$2	$3	$5	$10

Dollar Price Performance

Year	Very Fine	Uncirculated	Proof
1895-P	—	—	$4,750
1903-O	$20	$30	Not applicable

the 1903-O rebounded slightly. In Very Fine and Uncirculated conditions, it averaged a $2 increase.

The 22nd edition received an eloquently enthusiastic review in the November 1968 issue of *The Numismatist*, with the return of Glenn Smedley to the reviewing post. Following his preference for taking the long view, Smedley opened his discussion with a glimpse back in time:

> "A low-priced standard reference book of United States coins and kindred issues has been a long-felt need among American collectors . . . It is believed that this volume will appeal to that group." Thus spoke R.S. "Dick" Yeoman in opening the preface to the first edition of the Red Book in 1947 [*sic*]. He planned well, for twenty-one years later the most popular of all numismatic books follows its original format and is the "low-priced standard reference book of U.S. coins."

Smedley noted that each new edition "is awaited mostly for the up-to-date retail prices which are based on reports from a panel of fifty of the country's leading dealers," and went on to summarize the price changes to be found in this edition. But at the end of the review his appreciation for the Red Book broke out again: "To say that the quality of the book itself, including binding, cover, paper stock, illustrations, etc., has not deteriorated is like saying that the quality of sterling has not been impaired," he declared. Summing up the range of the Red Book's appeal, he concluded that "shops will again sell thousands of this edition at $2.00 each to inveterate as well as to novice collectors, and to persons having or handling coins without any numismatic interest in them." According to Smedley's evaluation, practically every American had a reason to purchase a new Red Book!

RED BOOK RECOLLECTIONS
Lawrence S. Goldberg

My first contribution to the famous Red Book was in the 1970 edition. I remember how proud I felt when seeing my name in the most famous coin book ever. Richard Yeoman would always attend every ANA convention. I would say hello and shake his hand, and he always called me Lawrence.

My first ANA convention was at the Los Angeles Statler Hilton Hotel in the early 1960s. I first met Richard Yeoman at the San Diego ANA convention. I can't remember what year it was, but Richard asked me if I could get him a hotel reservation in Las Vegas. I said no problem, and for several years he thanked me for this.

Richard Yeoman was not only a gentleman but also a very important person for all coin dealers. His Red Book was the most important U.S. coin reference book. I remember waiting every year to receive my special copy of the Red Book. We would get it two weeks before anyone else, and the prices listed were very important to all of us.

I have been working with the Red Book people for over 38 years.

Fast change artist

The 1970 Red Book: your best guide to the rapidly changing coin market.

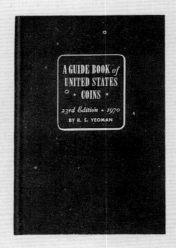

23rd Edition. No other reference book in the world of coins is more eagerly expected than the successive editions of R. S. Yeoman's, **A Guide Book of United States Coins.** The revised volume for 1970 is especially important because of extensive fluctuation in coin values. In this edition, each change is faithfully noted according to auction and sale prices and expert opinion at the time of printing. Coin values are given in up to seven condition columns for American coinage, 1616 to the present. To the careful collector, accurate information on even a single item can result in a saving many times over the purchase price of the new Red Book. **Now at your dealer's.**
$2.50 No. 9051.

**Whitman Hobby Products from
WESTERN PUBLISHING COMPANY, INC.**
Racine, Wisconsin 53404

From the September 1969 *Numismatist*. Advertising for the 23rd edition of the Red Book emphasized its ability to keep abreast of the coin market's rapid fluctuations.

THE 23RD EDITION (1970)

The Year Was 1969, and . . .

A major rarity, the 1969-S Lincoln cent with doubled-die obverse was minted. President Richard Nixon appointed a new Mint director: Mary Brooks, the third woman to hold this office.

Inside the Red Book

The 1970 *Guide Book* (which was actually printed, of course, in 1969) reflected a very quiet time for both coin collectors and the book itself. Aside from some minor changes in value for some Proof coins, there were not many changes made beyond the normal addition of the previous year's coinage. The year's only change of note was the addition of a legend to the Morgan dollar photo. The new legend explained that the photo was of the 1880-CC 80 over 79.

The Morgan dollars were relatively calm, too. The 1895-P Proof dollar value moved from being asleep to being in a coma as there was again no price movement. However, the 1903-O was still actively gyrating in price. Its prices increased dramatically, with a 50 percent increase to $30 in Very Fine condition and a 33 percent increase to $40 for Uncirculated pieces. The available supply of these dollars from the great Treasury hoard had dried up, and collectors were again seeking them.

As usual, price trends were the major focus of *The Numismatist's* review of the new edition. In the August 1969 issue, "PR" returned for a short review of the "new edition of the leading authority on American coins." After describing the increase in values for many coin types, the writer noted dryly that "prices not only climbed on the inside, a new price of $2.50 can be found on the cover" of the Red Book. Ken Bressett had broken news of the price increase in the July 1969 *Merchandiser*, saying that "manufacturing costs have increased to a point where the price of the Red Book must be raised this year. Labor settlements and raw materials have all contributed to this necessity and undoubtedly the increase must be passed on to the consumer." Nevertheless, *The Numismatist's* reviewer concluded that the book was "still the leader, still a tremendous buy."

Collectors should note that this year saw the release of an authorized edition of the *Guide Book* celebrating *Coin World* magazine's 10th anniversary. See chapter 6 for further discussion of this book.

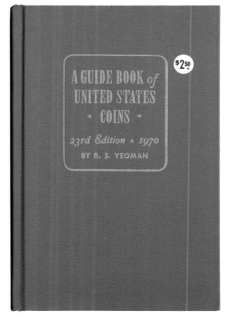

Values of the 23rd Edition

Year/Edition	Issue Price	F	VF	New
1970 (23rd ed.)	$2.50	$3	$6	$11

Dollar Price Performance

Year	Very Fine	Uncirculated	Proof
1895-P	—	—	$4,750
1903-O	$30	$40	Not applicable

RED BOOKS MAY COME AND GO... BUT THE 24th EDITION IS ONE YOU'LL SAVE!

A GUIDE BOOK *of* UNITED STATES · COINS · *24th Edition · 1971* BY R. S. YEOMAN

The 1971 Guide Book of United States coins, in addition to the usual value revisions, has something special for the first-timer, old-timer, or the in-betweener.

Readers have come to expect new grade columns and other refinements in each new addition. Average valuations from our top-notch panelists are expected and accepted. All this is there in the 24th, and more.

The real news is a special, added, nine-page progress report and analysis on 65 selected U.S. coins from the first to 23rd edition. Get your copy and see how sleepers and glamour coins get that way and make it or break it in the coin market.

The Red Book '71 is special . . . get yours today!

$2.50   No. 9051

Whitman Hobby Products from
WESTERN PUBLISHING COMPANY, INC.
Racine, Wisconsin 53404

From the July 1970 *Numismatist.* **This ad sets the 24th edition apart from its predecessors by high-lighting not its timeliness but a new feature notable for taking the long view: the "special, added, nine-page progress report and analysis" of the performance of 65 coins over the life of the Red Book.**

THE 24TH EDITION (1971)

The Year Was 1970, and . . .

The final silver half dollars with 40 percent silver content were minted, and released only in Mint sets. Today the coin is considered key to the set of Kennedy half dollars. Only 2,150,000 were minted, less than the number of Proof sets sold that year (2,632,810). An estimated 2,200 Proof sets were released with the dime lacking a mint-mark. Today this seemingly insignificant error is valued at well over $1,000. The Lincoln cent was minted with both large and small dates.

Inside the Red Book

In 1970, the year in which this edition appeared, author Al Overton finally released his long-awaited revised edition of *Early Half Dollar Die Varieties*, a reference guide to the Bust half varieties. This important book would influence future editions of the *Guide Book*. For the 24th edition, however, there is little to note. From layout to valuations, much of this edition remained unchanged from the previous year. There were few changes apart from the standard updates to values and the addition of new price columns in the quarter dollar section. The 1845-O dime in Uncirculated condition, always described as scarce, received a dash in its listing to indicate the possibility of its being unique—a contingency raised by the April 1969 sale of the R.L. Miles specimen.

One new feature, however, is still of particular interest to Red Book collectors and historians—a section called "Old Red Books Never Die," located on pages 236 to 244. (The private gold section was edited down to make room for this new content.) In order to demonstrate the usefulness of a library of old Red Books, the chapter contained tables that illustrated the performance over the past 23 years of more than 60 coins from five denominations—much, in fact, like the present volume's continuing illustration of the changing values of the Morgan dollars. (See chapter 2 for more on "Old Red Books Never Die.")

For this edition, the Morgan dollars remained quiet. Although there was increased interest in dollar varieties and some increased study of Morgan dollars because of the publication of *The Comprehensive Catalog and Encyclopedia of United States Morgan and Peace Dollars*, by Leroy Van Allen and A. George Mallis, there was little activity in the market. The 1903-O dollar showed nothing but a minor adjustment to the price in circulated condition.

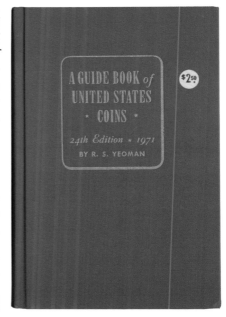

Values of the 24th Edition

Year/Edition	Issue Price	F	VF	New
1971 (24th ed.)	$2.50	$3	$4	$6

Dollar Price Performance

Year	Very Fine	Uncirculated	Proof
1895-P	—	—	$4,750
1903-O	$27.50	$40.00	Not applicable

The Numismatist's review of this edition—which appeared, rather tardily, in November 1970—made special mention of the "featured innovation" of the "Old Red Books Never Die" chapter. In a welcome return to reviewing duty, Glenn Smedley gave a detailed breakdown of the major trends noted in the new Red Book and spoke strongly for the usefulness of the new edition: "The $2.50 price of the book could easily be saved in the purchase or sale of a single coin by being up-to-date in valuations," he asserts. "By the way," he adds, after listing the standard places where one could purchase the book, "a few drug and notions stores carry the Red Book—such is its popularity."

Only one other observation needs to be made regarding this edition: it was the last to be prepared before the retirement of R.S. Yeoman. Although he would continue to be listed as the Red Book's author—and indeed would contribute to future editions—after this year editor Ken Bressett would take up the reins. The milestone passed without making a visible mark on the Red Book.

TABLE 1 — CENTS

	1909S VDB	1914D	1922 No D	1923S	1926S	* 1931D	* 1931S	1947S	1949S	1950S	1951S	1952	1952S	1955 Dbl. Die	1955S
1st/1947	15.00	10.00	—	9.00	6.50	3.00	1.35	.05							
2nd/1948	16.50	15.00	V.G. 3.50	11.00	6.50	3.50	1.50	.05	—						
3rd/1949	16.50	16.50	3.50	12.00	7.50	3.50	1.75	.05	.05	—					
4th/1951-52	12.50	20.00	3.50	15.00	6.50	3.50	1.60	.05	.05	.05					
5th/1952-53	13.50	27.50	3.50	17.50	7.50	4.00	1.50	.05	.05	.05	.05				
6th/1953-54	13.50	35.00	3.50	20.00	8.50	4.00	1.75	.05	.05	.05	.05	.05	.05		
7th/1954-55	17.50	47.50	3.50	25.00	9.00	4.50	2.00	.05	.05	.05	.05	.05	.05		
8th/1955	20.00	65.00	4.50	32.50	12.00	5.00	3.50	.10	.15	.05	.05	.05	.05		
9th/1956	30.00	80.00	Fine 7.50	40.00	13.50	6.50	4.50	.15	.25	.10	.10	.05	.10		
10th/1957	40.00	110.00	7.50	55.00	17.50	8.50	7.00	.20	.35	.20	.15	.05	.15		.05
11th/1958	60.00	150.00	Unc. 10.00	65.00	20.00	12.50	14.00	.20	.35	.25	.25	.05	.20		.05
12th/1959	77.50	200.00	100.00	110.00	35.00	17.50	18.50	.25	.50	.35	.35	.15	.30		.15
13th/1960	85.00	250.00	125.00	130.00	45.00	20.00	18.00	.30	.75	.50	.60	.25	.35	E.F. .50 Unc. —	.25
14th/1961	97.50	275.00	165.00	140.00	55.00	28.50	21.00	.60	1.25	.75	.80	.50	.70	E.F. .45 Unc. .80	.40
15th/1962	115.00	310.00	185.00	150.00	65.00	35.00	25.00	.50	1.15	.65	.75	.45	.65	E.F. 55.00 Unc. 95.00	.40
16th/1963	165.00	410.00	275.00	180.00	75.00	45.00	42.50	.65	1.50	.90	1.00	.55	.80	E.F. —	.50
17th/1964	310.00	500.00	325.00	200.00	80.00	60.00	72.50	.80	1.75	1.00	1.35	.60	1.00	E.F. — Unc. —	.90
18th/1965	335.00	700.00	600.00	250.00	140.00	85.00	85.00	1.25	2.25	1.10	1.50	.70	1.25	E.F. — Unc. 250.00	1.00
19th/1966	350.00	775.00	800.00	285.00	160.00	87.50	95.00	1.50	2.50	1.40	1.80	.85	1.25	E.F. 200.00 Unc. 350.00	1.25
20th/1967	300.00	700.00	850.00	265.00	160.00	80.00	85.00	1.25	2.25	1.20	1.50	.75	1.00	E.F. 235.00 Unc. 435.00	1.00
21st/1968	240.00	585.00	700.00	225.00	105.00	60.00	60.00	.75	1.50	.80	.95	.65	.65	E.F. 235.00 Unc. 400.00	.75
22nd/1969	220.00	560.00	700.00	225.00	105.00	60.00	60.00	.75	1.50	.80	.95	.65	.65	E.F. 235.00 Unc. 400.00	.75
23rd/1970	220.00	560.00	675.00	225.00	100.00	55.00	60.00	.70	1.50	.75	.90	.60	.60	E.F. 245.00 Unc. 430.00	.75

*See text

[239]

TABLE 6 — GROWTH

	CENT 1924D (2.52 Million)		NICKEL 1926S (.97 Million)		DIME 1926S (1.5 Million)		QUARTER 1927S (.396 Million)		HALF 1923S (2.2 Million)	
	Fine	Unc.	Fine	Unc.	Fine	Unc.	Fine	Unc.	Fine	Unc.
1st/1947	.50	8.00	6.00	35.00	2.00	7.50	5.00	27.50	2.50	18.00
2nd/1948	.60	9.00	6.00	60.00	2.00	10.00	5.00	60.00	2.50	25.00
3rd/1949	.60	9.00	3.00	65.00	1.50	12.50	5.00	60.00	2.50	30.00
4th/1951-52	.60	9.50	3.00	70.00	1.50	15.00	6.00	75.00	2.50	35.00
5th/1952-53	.60	10.00	3.00	75.00	2.50	17.50	7.50	85.00	2.50	45.00
6th/1953-54	.75	11.00	4.00	80.00	3.50	22.50	9.00	90.00	3.50	70.00
7th/1954-55	1.00	12.00	5.00	90.00	3.50	30.00	12.50	100.00	3.50	85.00
8th/1955	1.50	15.00	7.50	95.00	3.50	35.00	15.00	110.00	4.00	100.00
9th/1956	2.50	20.00	9.00	100.00	5.00	40.00	15.00	150.00	5.00	115.00
10th/1957	3.00	27.50	8.50	125.00	6.50	45.00	12.50	175.00	6.00	125.00
11th/1958	4.00	35.00	10.00	140.00	7.50	50.00	15.00	200.00	4.00	150.00
12th/1959	4.00	45.00	10.50	150.00	9.00	57.50	17.50	210.00	4.50	152.50
13th/1960	4.50	50.00	12.50	165.00	8.00	60.00	11.00	235.00	4.50	165.00
14th/1961	5.50	60.00	14.00	175.00	9.00	70.00	13.50	275.00	4.50	175.00
15th/1962	6.00	70.00	15.00	210.00	6.00	72.50	13.50	390.00	4.50	175.00
16th/1963	7.75	82.50	18.00	225.00	7.00	87.50	17.50	450.00	4.50	175.00
17th/1964	7.50	110.00	19.50	275.00	8.00	95.00	20.00	550.00	4.50	175.00
18th/1965	27.50	200.00	20.00	325.00	9.50	150.00	17.50	575.00	5.00	195.00
19th/1966	27.50	250.00	21.00	400.00	10.00	250.00	17.50	700.00	5.25	220.00
20th/1967	22.50	225.00	21.00	430.00	10.00	250.00	17.50	750.00	6.00	250.00
21st/1968	16.50	175.00	17.00	435.00	10.00	275.00	15.00	725.00	4.50	300.00
22nd/1969	16.50	175.00	17.00	440.00	10.00	300.00	15.00	725.00	4.50	350.00
23rd/1970	13.50	180.00	16.50	440.00	11.50	320.00	15.00	750.00	6.00	365.00
Growth Multiple	x27	x22.5	x2.75	x12.6	x5.75	x42.7	x3	x27.2	x2.4	x20.4

[244]

Two tables from Yeoman's "Old Red Books Never Die" essay, showing the progress of coin values as charted in past editions of the *Guide Book*.

R. S. Yeoman   Aubree E. Bebee   Malcom O. E. Chell-Frost   Kenneth W. Lee

Arthur Kagin

Abner Kreisberg

On its Silver Anniversary, Red Book salutes the panel!

The 1972 Silver Anniversary Edition of the **Guide Book of United States Coins** is now available. Like those preceding it, the 25th edition derives a large measure of its authority from Whitman's Panel of numismatic experts. This Panel represents some of the most respected names in coins, and their familiarity with the subject and the market make them supremely qualified. The gentlemen on this page have all served as panelists for twenty years or more. Our congratulations and thanks. They have aided immeasurably in making the Red Book what it is—the one indispensable volume to the coin hobbyist—R. S. Yeoman, Editor.

See your dealer today. 256 pp. $2.50

Whitman Hobby Products from
WESTERN PUBLISHING COMPANY, INC.
Racine, Wisconsin 53404

Paul Kagin

Harold Whiteneck

F. K. Saab

Bill Mertes

Abe Kosoff

Norman Shultz

From the July 1971 *Numismatist*. As the Red Book turned 25, it paid tribute to contributors who had put in 20 or more years of service. Four of the men showcased here were listed contributors to the first edition: Aubrey Bebee, Malcolm O.E. Chell-Frost, Abe Kosoff, and Abner Kreisberg.

THE 25TH EDITION (1972)

The Year Was 1971, and . . .

Another error variety was created when the Mint released some Proof Jefferson nickels without a mintmark. An estimated 1,655 were issued, each valued today at more than $1,000. The Eisenhower dollar coins were released with great fanfare. They proved not to be particularly popular, except in casinos.

Inside the Red Book

What a difference a year makes! In contrast to the dearth of changes in the *Guide Book* of 1971, the next year's silver anniversary edition came with astonishing renovations. As the July 1971 *Merchandiser* observed, "On the occasion of the silver anniversary, Kenneth Bressett, who has been coordinating editor of the book since 1959, was determined to engineer additional changes major enough to warrant the claim of a completely revised edition." As a consequence, "nearly every page in the book was revised in one way or another."

This was the first edition in which the cover and spine lettering were not gold. In honor of the book's 25th anniversary, the color was changed to—you guessed it—silver, along with a special design and a notation that read, "Silver Anniversary Edition." The cover also broke new ground in featuring an illustration, also in silver: a circle of coin designs, including the Lincoln cent, Buffalo nickel, and Roosevelt dime.

The interior saw equally dramatic changes. In the front of the book facing the title page appeared a picture of R.S. Yeoman along with a facsimile of his autograph and a short biography describing his numismatic achievements. (Additional quantities of these books were printed late in the year, but without the end-sheet dedication to Yeoman.) For the first time, editorial assistants were credited: Neil Shafer and Holland Wallace. Moreover, most of the book's sections were completely revamped. The colonial section was "com-

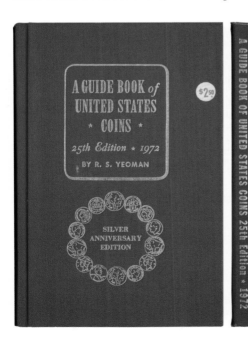

Values of the 25th Edition

Year/Edition	Issue Price	F	VF	New
1972 (25th ed.)	$2.50	$6	$9	$12

Dollar Price Performance

Year	Very Fine	Uncirculated	Proof
1895-P	—	—	$4,900
1903-O	$27.50	$40.00	Not applicable

pletely revised" (again according to the *Merchandiser*) and deleted the listings for the New Hampshire copper with WM in the center, the New England stiver, the Connecticut "Wheel Goes Round" piece, and the Good Samaritan shilling ("long known to be spurious but included as a supplementary note"). Additions to this section included the Machin's Mill coinage, the Albany Church penny, and the New York Theatre token.

The large cent section also saw some major changes—"a complete face lifting," in the words of the *Merchandiser*, which credited the Early American Coppers Club with reorganizing the section and selecting varieties for inclusion or deletion. For the first time, it included both recognition and microphotographs of the 1794 Starred Reverse cent. (The 1794 Starred Reverse is an unusual one-cent piece that has 94 five-pointed stars along the perimeter of its reverse side.) Photos of both the Indian Head and Lincoln cents were added, to display the positions of their mintmarks. The Lincoln cent section also included the addition of photos of the newly discovered 1970-S Large Date and 1970-S Small Date.

Added to the listings for Jefferson nickels were two overpunched mintmarks: the 1954-S, S Over D and 1955-D, D Over S varieties. Both were illustrated with excellent photos. The *Merchandiser* predicted that "news of their existence will come as a surprise to many collectors and will prompt a search for additional specimens." My personal favorite coin, the 1893, 3 Over 2 Barber dime, was finally recognized (although no photo was provided). The 1942, 2 Over 1 Denver overdate was also listed for the first time, bringing acceptance to this variety.

Another important change was the revision of the Morgan dollar series to include the newly discovered 1880 overdates. The previous edition's overdate photo was replaced with three photos that clearly illustrated the design's three different reverse styles. To top off all these alterations, the entire Bust half dollar section was changed, taking its cue from Al Overton's important study of this variety. For the first time, there were close-up pictures of the different dates and popular varieties. Collecting of Bust half varieties advanced as a result of these photographs. A special section called "The United States Commemorative Half Dollar: A 25-Year Record" replaced last year's feature "Old Red Books Never Die." The new section compiled the values for these coins given in all editions of the Red Book to date and analyzed them to determine the causes of the price trends that had taken place. The section on the coinage of Puerto Rico was dropped "because of lack of popularity," according to Bressett in the July 1971 *Merchandiser*. The Hawaiian coin section had been revamped, and the fractional gold section had been expanded and was now three times its former size. The Eisenhower dollar also made its debut in the Red Book, with a listing that included commentary on both the copper-nickel and silver clad versions.

The Red Book also reached an enormous milestone with this edition: during production of the 25th edition, the ten millionth Red Book was printed. The landmark volume was greeted with a special ceremony and presented to author R.S. Yeoman by the president of Western Publishing, Gerald Slade, rather than being released for sale. Those present at the ceremony later autographed the book. A note identifying it was also added, which read:

TEN MILLIONTH COPY OF THE RED BOOK
1972 Silver Anniversary Edition

This book was determined to be the ten-millionth copy ever printed of *A Guide Book of United States Coins*. It came off the press on June 1, 1971, in the presence of all those who witnessed the event and signed the book as evidence of its authenticity.

R.S. Yeoman, author of the book

Ken Bressett, editor of the book

Neil Shafer, editorial assistant

Holland Wallace, editorial assistant

Ed Metzger, production manager

Bill Whaley, V.P. Whitman Publishing

Jerry Slade, President Western Publishing Company

No doubt many a collector today would give untold sums for this one-of-a-kind copy were it ever to come up for sale!

Sadly, the state of the coin market did not match the excitement surrounding this edition and its changes. To cite our favorite example, it seemed as though nothing could rouse the Morgan dollars market. The value of the 1895-P Proof dollar rose a bit to $4,900, but the 1903-O went back to sleep.

The silver anniversary edition received a detailed and typically enthusiastic review from Glenn Smedley in the September 1971 *Numismatist*. His review appeared under the heading "Ten Million Copies in 25 Years" and opened with the observation that "the Red Book is now among the top ten sellers in the non-fiction field, which is no surprise to coin collectors." What *was* surprising, he went on to observe, was that "each edition has been a definite improvement over its predecessor"—meaningful praise indeed from one who had reviewed the Red Book for many years and with such close scrutiny. Smedley's verdict on the 25th anniversary edition was that it "top[s] all others." He made special note of the addition of new photographs, particularly those that show enlargements, and singled out for praise "the addition of data on the physical properties of each coin type: size, weight, metallic composition, etc." The removal of listings for some colonial coins "of doubtful origin" also met with his approval. And, finally, one thing that had *not* changed came in for special attention: the price. Smedley noted that the cover price would be "approved by everyone" for remaining unchanged since the previous year. He closed his review with the respectful decree "The staff of *The Numismatist* and this reviewer add our congratulations to the many others tendered to Red Book editor 'Dick' Yeoman."

Although the 25th edition is valued as a common printing, there is evidence that copies in New condition may be fairly scarce. Careful study of Internet sales shows that it is infrequently encountered in New condition. Future study and sales results are likely to show that it is underpriced in today's market.

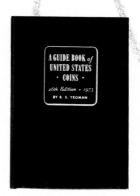

From the August 1972 *Numismatist.*

THE 26TH EDITION (1973)

The Year Was 1972, and . . .

Another national treasure hunt began when the Mint released the 1972 doubled-die obverse Lincoln cent. The "Granite Lady," legendary former home of the San Francisco Mint, gained a new identity as an office building for the federal government; it also housed a small numismatic museum. This year also saw the founding of the American Numismatic Association Certification Service (ANACS).

Inside the Red Book

After the scope of changes and updates in the 25th edition, it was surprising to see the necessity of making any adjustments, aside from pricing, for the following year. Nevertheless, the *Numismatist* review of September 1972 (by J.D. Ferguson) stated that "there have been revisions of every section in the 26th edition of the red book." One notable addition was the inclusion of a close-up photo of the 1830, 30 Over 29 Capped Bust dime "to help identify this difficult variety," per the July 1972 *Merchandiser.* Photos of the 1880-CC Morgan dollar overdates were also added. This edition also saw a new focus for the rotating nine-page section that spotlighted a different issue every year: this year's analysis was devoted to Morgan silver dollar collecting and price trends since 1946. The colonial section was rearranged to present the coins in each series in order of denomination, from lowest to highest, rather than in chronological order. A new listing had been added: the 1865, 5 Over 4 two-cent piece. Some varieties of early silver dollars had been removed "because of a general lack of interest and the fact that there was no difference in the values between many of the varieties of any given date." The *Merchandiser* went on to assure the reader, "All varieties of significant interest or value will continue to be listed," and "the space gained by removing some of these older varieties has been put to good use in the Morgan Dollar section, where the most popular new varieties have been added." In the area of pricing, readers learned that "establishing new prices in the Gold section has been particularly difficult this year" because of the rising price of gold bullion.

Values of the 26th Edition

Year/Edition	Issue Price	F	VF	New
1973 (26th ed.)	$2.50	$4	$5	$7

Dollar Price Performance

Year	Very Fine	Uncirculated	Proof
1895-P	—	—	$5,000
1903-O	$27.50	$40.00	Not applicable

The book's physical presence had also seen some changes. Not only did the cover printing revert to its usual gold (after the silver printing used for the previous year's anniversary edition), but the paper on which it was printed was different. As Ken Bressett explained in the *Merchandiser*, the new paper was "a more expensive and durable variety designed to eliminate glare, accept ink markings more readily (for those who are inclined to make notes in their books), and above all, form a better bond with the backing so that pages will not tear loose."

We will continue to observe the 1895-P and 1903-O Morgan dollars. There was a slight improvement in the price of the 1895-P Proof dollar, an increase of $100 (2 percent) to $5,000. The price of the 1903-O remained constant.

Behind the scenes, an overconscientious (and underinformed) staffer nearly caused a delay in the book's release. This account of the incident appeared in the *Merchandiser*:

> Soon after Western Publishing Company's gigantic Cottrell press began printing the books, one of the pressmen noticed a misspelled word and immediately called for the press to be shut down and a correction made. The "misspelled" word was on page 23 in the listing of the 1788 Vermont cent with backward C in AUCTORI. Fortunately, one of the Whitman editors was checking the printing progress soon after that and explained to the pressman that this was indeed how the coin was inscribed and how it should be listed in the book. Happily, the presses started to roll again immediately without further delay.

Finally, one other change warrants mention here. On the list of contributors who had died the previous year, there was the notable addition of Al C. Overton. His contributions to the study of Bust half dollars cannot be overemphasized.

RED BOOK RECOLLECTIONS
Mary Sauvain

I first met Ken Bressett in 1980 when we were both employed by Donald Kagin in Des Moines, Iowa. Due to my interest in Gobrecht dollars, I asked to update that section in the Red Book. I enlisted Robert Julian due to his great U.S. Mint research capabilities, and my first contribution to *A Guide Book of United States Coins* became a joint effort to revamp the Gobrecht dollar section of the 1984 Red Book. By that time Ken was the director of ANACS (American Numismatic Association Certification Service) in Colorado Springs, and communication on this work was conducted long distance with both Robert and Ken. This section remained the same until slight modifications in the 2004 edition, mainly adding die alignments as defined in Q. David Bowers's works.

Over the years my main work with Ken each year on the Red Book has been joining him and other individuals to help compile and tabulate all figures submitted and gathered by the numerous contributors into the final columnar figures used for the annually released *Guide Book of United States Coins*.

It is always an experience to see how auction prices realized as well as day-to-day transactions figure into Red Book tabulations. Of course, another experience is to meet the last-minute deadlines that are always part of the process!

'74 Red Book

27th Edition

A GUIDE BOOK OF UNITED STATES COINS — R. S. YEOMAN

Most dramatic coin value increases in its 27-year history...

Are coins becoming a glamour investment? Soaring prices of gold and silver coins, all-time highs of type coins and a general interest in "coins as an investment" brought the most dramatic price increases the Red Book has ever seen. While the 27th edition's all-important feature is the faithful recording of these values in up to seven condition columns, the complete book has been revised and updated with all significant numismatic developments. Several new over-dates and varieties have been added, and the number of price columns increased in many areas. This year's special 9-page feature section is appropriately a record of type coin values to show the long-term price trend of these blue chip coins. This is one edition you can't afford to miss.. get your copy today.

Still only $2.50 No. 9051.

Whitman Coin Products from
WESTERN PUBLISHING COMPANY, INC.
Racine, Wisconsin 53404

From the August 1973 *Numismatist.* Advertising for the 27th edition used both text and graphics to emphasize the dramatic increases in listed values.

THE 27TH EDITION (1974)

The Year Was 1973, and . . .

The General Accounting Office (GAO) commenced selling silver dollars that were found in inventory. Many of these were bags of Carson City silver dollars. Five sales would be conducted from 1973 to 1974, but sales were lackluster. Legislation was passed to commemorate the U.S. Bicentennial by changing the reverse designs on quarter, half dollar, and dollar coins struck from July 4, 1975, through January 1, 1977. A nationwide competition was held, and nearly 1,000 entrants submitted designs for the coins.

Inside the Red Book

The first significant change to the 27th edition was on the title page: Kenneth Bressett was now listed as editor. The passing of the torch was now official.

The 1974 edition continued the tradition of updating the listings to include new and important coin varieties. The hottest new item was the doubled-die error on the 1972 Lincoln cent, which had received so much publicity from the national wire services that even non-collectors were eagerly sifting their pocket change in hopes of finding one. By the time of the book's release in mid-1973, the value for this variety had settled at a still-considerable $75. The new listing included a close-up photo of the doubled legend "In God We Trust" and a notation that the given values were for pieces with full doubling of the legend. This note was probably a response to the popularity of "poor man's doubled-die" coins, which bore an error that appeared to be a doubled die but actually exhibited signs of *die deterioration doubling*—when the image appears doubled because the die was worn and became distorted. These coins are not very rare and not worth as much as true doubled-die coins, so this is an important distinction.

Values for many coins were up significantly, as the July 1973 *Merchandiser* reported: commemoratives "were breaking new records every week during the period of Red

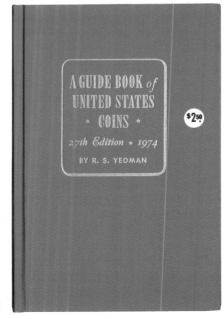

Values of the 27th Edition

Year/Edition	Issue Price	F	VF	New
1974 (27th ed.)	$2.50	$2	$4	$6

Dollar Price Performance

Year	Very Fine	Uncirculated	Proof
1895-P	—	—	$6,000
1903-O	$29	$42	Not applicable

Book price compilation and it was next to impossible to find stable values. . . . All are up dramatically over last year's book." Recent sales of colonial coins, including some from the Massachusetts Historical Society, had reawakened interest in these issues and provided new sale information from which to update values, and as a result some rarer colonial pieces had seen significant price increases in the Red Book.

How did our two Morgan dollars fare this year? With the previous year's push of the 1895-P Proof dollar to $5,000, the demand continued as collectors strove to obtain the coin before the price went completely out of their reach. This push resulted in a massive 20 percent increase, to $6,000. (There had not been an increase like this since the 19th edition [1966], when the piece's price bounded up $1,250—38 percent—to $4,500.) A 20 percent increase is great in any year. But this was 1974, when a full-time bank manager only earned about $150 a week! Regardless of inflation, this price increase was extraordinary. In contrast, the 1903-O saw increases that were nowhere near as impressive. Its values went up 5.4 percent (or $1.50) and 5 percent (or $2), to $29 and $42, in Very Fine condition and Uncirculated condition, respectively.

The Morgan dollars section also saw improvements with the insertion of two new varieties: the important 1887, 7 Over 6 and 1887-O, 7 Over 6. Neither was given a specific value. The Eisenhower dollar listings included new information on varieties of the type. Along with the additions came a subtraction. The 1865 overdate two-cent piece—added just the year before—was dropped "on the grounds that it is too questionable for attribution," according to the *Merchandiser*. (In the current Red Book, mention of this variety appears in a footnote.)

Like a number of the coins it described, the Red Book was riding high. "Business is bullish not only in coins, but in Red Books too," proclaimed the *Merchandiser*: "the 1973 book has been sold out for the past two months. . . . We sold out everything we printed and regretted that we didn't have more. We will be printing quite a few more this year, and our advance orders show that we're right in our thinking, because they're up by over 20 percent."

However, drama behind the scenes had almost derailed these heady preparations:

> The Red Book operation nearly suffered a major setback April 16 [1973], when fire broke out in the composing room where the type was being set.
>
> It was a near-disaster, although just a minor fire in the ventilating system. The sprinklers went off and flooded the composing room, and there was about $10,000 worth of damage.
>
> We almost panicked, because our original copy, with all the price changes, was in the room—and if that had been destroyed it would have really set us back. Fortunately, everything was well protected.
>
> As it was, the fire and water damage set back operations perhaps two days and the July 1 issue date was met, as promised.

This year's nine-page historical analysis section focused on the performance of type coins since 1946—"a topic whose timeliness is underscored by the gains these coins have posted this year alone."

The unsigned review that appeared in the September 1973 *Numismatist* offered a methodical breakdown of many of the changes to the new edition, noting that it "has incorporated some new photos" and that "an extra fine column has been added to half dimes and quarters where necessary to bridge the widening gap between VF and Unc."

An overprinted edition of the 1974 *Guide Book* was issued; see chapter 6 for details.

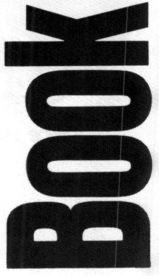

From the August 1974 *Numismatist.*

THE 28TH EDITION (1975)

The Year Was 1974, and . . .

The sale of silver dollars by the GAO was concluded. Millionaire LaVere Redfield died, leaving among his assets an estimated 351,000 to over 400,000 silver dollars. The coins were purchased by A-Mark Coins and encased in special holders for sale. President Nixon appointed Mary Brooks to a second term as director of the Mint.

Inside the Red Book

This edition presented an improved picture of the 1918-D, 8 Over 7 Buffalo nickel. As opposed to the hazy pictures previously used, the new photo was sharp and showed a clear overdate. The nine-page special section this year was devoted to modern Proof sets; in addition to the historical perspective it provided, it gave collectors the procedure for obtaining sets directly from the Mint.

The market experienced some increases in pricing, but the majority of changes were in the key dates, and were minor. Our regulars, the 1895-P and 1903-O Morgan dollars, replicated the market conditions. The fairly common 1903-O did not increase in price, while the key-date 1895-P increased a very respectable 11 percent.

The Numismatist did not offer a review of this edition until its December 1974 issue. The unknown reviewer praised the Red Book as "the most up-to-date published reference guide on all United States coins for collectors" and added, "many new headings and photographs are used." He (or she) also pointed out the new feature of giving weights in net troy ounces for gold and silver, for the use of readers who wanted to calculate bullion value of coins.

Perhaps the most interesting part of the review from the historical perspective is the statement that "demand for the new edition of Whitman's Red Book has increased this year and . . . the entire first printing of nearly one half million copies has already been

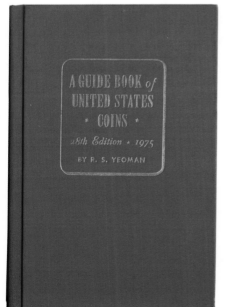

distributed to dealers through the country." Although the price had risen to $3.00, the reviewer maintained that it is "perhaps a bigger bargain than ever before, considering the ever-rising costs of labor and materials." He concluded stoutly, "the 1975 Red Book is one that no collector can do without."

Values of the 28th Edition

Year/Edition	Issue Price	VF	New
1975 (28th ed.)	$3	$4	$5

Dollar Price Performance

Year	Very Fine	Uncirculated	Proof
1895-P	—	—	$6,750
1903-O	$30.00	$47.50	Not applicable

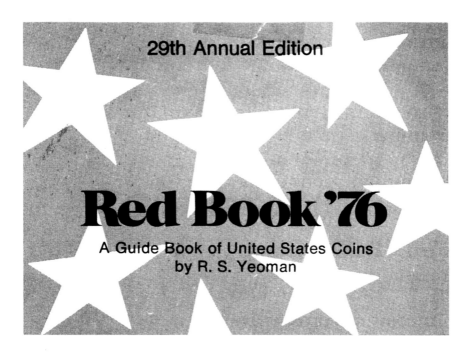

From the August 1975 *Numismatist.* Advertising for the 1976 Red Book adopted the theme of the American Bicentennial. Presciently, the ad notes that "this Bicentennial Edition might very well become a collectors [*sic*] item by itself."

THE 29TH EDITION (1976)

The Year Was 1975, and . . .

An extreme rarity was created when some Roosevelt dimes without mintmarks were released in Proof sets. The number released before the Mint discovered its error is unknown, but minute. Today's value for this coin is about $45,000 in Proof-65 condition. The Mint started production of the Bicentennial coins. There would be no 1975-dated quarters, half dollars, or dollar coins.

Inside the Red Book

To celebrate the U.S. Bicentennial, the Red Book was released with a decorative cover for the first time since the silver anniversary edition. Below the standard text can be seen a bicentennial banner surmounted by stars and an eagle. Despite the fancy cover, some collectors were disappointed in the book because it was not printed on the high-quality glossy paper that had previously been used.

Listings for the new Bicentennial coinage were added to the quarter, half dollar, and dollar sections. Each section included a narrative that described the design of the new coin and listed its designer and metal content. The coins celebrating the U.S. Bicentennial were minted in 1975 and 1976, but dated 1776–1976. The interest generated by these commemorative quarter, half dollar, and dollar coins and special silver Proof sets, however, did not have much of an impact on interest in the other sets of U.S. coins. After all, the coins were not yet circulating to a large extent (although they would be released in vast numbers throughout the next year); had they been, they may have brought more attention to the other circulating coins.

This year's *Guide Book* also introduced a picture of the 1942-D, 2 Over 1 Winged Liberty Head (or Mercury) dime. The large microphotograph was of superior quality and extremely clear.

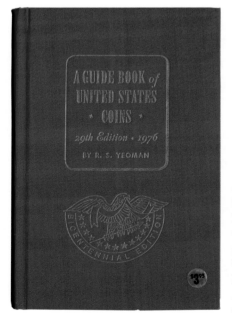

Values of the 29th Edition

Year/Edition	Issue Price	VF	New
1976 (29th ed.)	$3.95	$4	$5

Dollar Price Performance

Year	Very Fine	Uncirculated	Proof
1895-P	—	—	$8,000
1903-O	$35	$55	Not applicable

The studied Morgan dollars awoke with a bang. The 1895-P leapt to $8,000, for an increase of $1,250, or 18.5 percent. The 1903-O also did well, with a Very Fine value of $35 (up 17 percent) and an Uncirculated value of $55 (up nearly 16 percent). The coin market was waking up—it probably saw many new collectors from the introduction and dispersal of the Bicentennial coinage.

The Numismatist's very brief writeup on this edition in the August 1975 issue observed that it contained "more price changes than have ever before appeared in its entire history of publication," and that the new prices "represent a greater percentage of increase than has ever been seen." With regard to other content, the reviewer noted that "new coin illustrations have been added and many photos have been replaced for clearer and sharper detail." As Glenn Smedley had observed in an earlier review, the Red Book continued to improve with every edition, and even this briefest of "reviews" reflected the fact.

RED BOOK RECOLLECTIONS
Doug Winter

I can't remember exactly when I received my first *Guide Book*, but I'm certain that it was obtained as a result of nagging my Mom, who controlled the family purse strings at that time. I do know that I was about seven or eight when I got my first copy (which I still have) and that I read it every night until I had mintage figures memorized for most coins. My set of Red Books includes at least the last 35 editions, and they are a prized part of my numismatic library.

What I loved about the *Guide Book* then is what I still love about it today: its elegant simplicity. It is truly *the* complete one-volume coin library, and I think it has become an underrated reference in this era of numismatic specialization. It remains in a prominent place on my desk, and it's a rare day that I don't refer to it at least once.

I became a contributor to the *Guide Book* in 1983. I had just started working for Steve Ivy, and being the new kid at his firm, I was told to do Steve's pricing when a packet arrived for him one day. I can remember telling Steve that I'd be happy to do it but I wasn't going to be his ghost-pricer and that if I did do the work I wanted credit for it. Steve did his own pricing, but this began a tradition for me of pricing United States gold coins for the *Guide Book* that has now gone on for a quarter of a century.

The pricing, of course, has witnessed an evolution of technology. For years, I remember filling in new prices with a pen and sending in dozens of sheets to the editors with my price changes and suggestions. Today this is done via computer. But I still really enjoy the chance to analyze what I think coins are worth, and I take my duties as a consultant to the *Guide Book* very seriously.

I would have to regard the *Guide Book* as one of the great contributions to 20th-century American numismatics, right up there with coin folders and coin albums. Think of the millions of copies of the *Guide Book* that have been sold and think of how many prominent dealers and collectors began their lifelong obsession with American coins as a result of this incredible book. I should know, because I'm one of them.

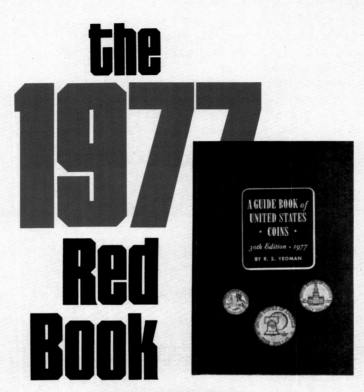

the 1977 Red Book

30th Edition

A Guide Book of United States Coins by R. S. Yeoman

No generation gap here! The 30th Edition of the number one coin book of all times is still "right with it". From the newest coins, illustrated on its quality bright red cover, to the latest, increased coin values, the Red Book is as up-to-date as ever. Numerous editorial revisions have been added, as well as new varieties, excellent illustrations, and new pricing columns. The Colonial section is presented in a much handier format. This year's six page special feature section covers all aspects and historical background of the interesting 1848 Quarter Eagle with CAL. made from California gold.

  After 30 years Whitman's 1977 Red Book is as new as today...at your favorite store. **No. 9051—$3.95**

Whitman Coin Products from
WESTERN PUBLISHING COMPANY, INC.
Racine, Wisconsin 53404

From the July 1976 *Numismatist*. As the Red Book reached its 30th edition, Whitman Publishing took pains to emphasize its continued relevance—although then-current expressions like "with it" would have a short shelf life.

THE 30TH EDITION (1977)

The Year Was 1976, and . . .

Numismatic Scrapbook, founded in 1935 by Lee Hewitt, ceased publication. The ANA convention in New York set an attendance record of 21,900, which would stand until the 1990s. The grading service ANACS relocated from Washington, D.C., to Colorado Springs, Colorado, where the ANA had its headquarters.

Inside the Red Book

For the 30th edition, the cover was redesigned to include pictures of the Bicentennial coinage from the previous two years. The quarter, half dollar, and dollar coin reverses were displayed in actual-size photos. The material of the cover was changed as well: it had a less glossy, more cardboardy finish than earlier covers. Today, as a result, even copies fresh out of the box usually display white rub marks on their covers. Copies without these marks are very rare, extremely desirable, and worth a high premium over listed prices. Unfortunately, the lower-quality paper used for the 29th edition was used for this edition as well, and new copies frequently also have yellowing pages.

There were not many changes to the listed varieties. There was, however, the addition of the 1949-D, D Over S Jefferson nickel. The desire to keep the listings of varieties contemporary remained active, and of utmost importance.

From the previous year's edition, pricing had remained basically stable, even for scarce key-date coins. However, some of the valuations for the Morgan dollars were again active. The 1895-P increased by $250—which was actually only a 3 percent increase for the expensive coin. The 1903-O increased $10 (to $65) in Uncirculated condition, while the price for the circulated version did not fluctuate.

Interestingly, this edition listed the value for a "1908S, V.D.B." Lincoln penny. This coin doesn't exist—the listing was supposed to read, "1909S, V.D.B." Although Internet sales have erroneously offered this entry as evidence of a scarce error edition, no premium should be paid for it: all copies have the same typographical error.

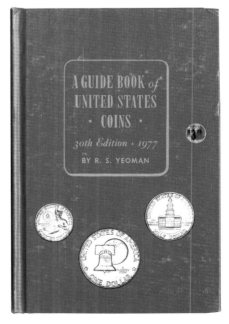

Values of the 30th Edition

Year/Edition	Issue Price	VF	New
1977 (30th ed.)	$3.95	$4	$25

Note: As stated in the text, the use of a lower-quality composition for the cover of the 30th edition resulted in white streaks across the front and back of the book's cover. New-condition copies without these streaks are truly scarce and infrequently offered for sale.

Dollar Price Performance

Year	Very Fine	Uncirculated	Proof
1895-P	—	—	$8,250
1903-O	$35	$65	Not applicable

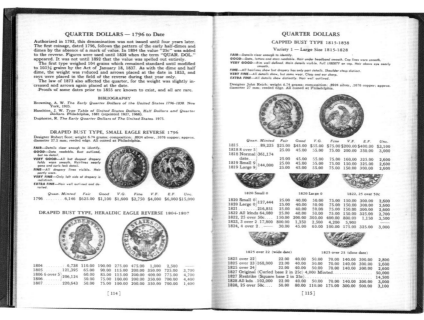

Compared to that of a decade before, the 1977 Red Book's quarter dollar section boasts an additional grade column (Extremely Fine) and a more efficient use of space: now many variety photographs are cropped to make room for more content.

RED BOOK RECOLLECTIONS
Wayne Homren

Why collect outdated editions of the *Guide Book*? Aside from the fun you'll have marveling at the antiquated pricing levels and grading systems, the books provide valuable pricing history that can guide collecting decisions today.

I recall the day I was walking through a coin show and spotted a special coin in a dealer's case—a Scott restrike of the Confederate half dollar. To me, it was the most interesting piece in the whole show, and I decided to buy it. But the $2,000 price tag gave me pause: was I willing to spend that much on a single coin for my collection? I knew the dealer and asked if I could put a deposit on the coin while I slept on my decision, and he agreed. Back at home that night, I raced to my library and pulled out all of the old Red Books I could find. I grabbed a piece of paper and charted the price history of the coin. Not once did the value ever go down—year after year the value increased, at a fairly steady and impressive interest rate. Seeing the figures in black and white made it clear to me that I could easily justify my purchase as an investment. Mind you, I didn't have a wife to convince in those days, so it would have been an easy choice regardless. But the Red Book convinced me.

The next day I returned to the show and purchased the coin. Several years later I sold it along with the rest of my Civil War numismatic collection, where the coin realized $8,625. Those old Red Books helped me more than quadruple my numismatic investment.

THE 31ST EDITION (1978)

The Year Was 1977, and . . .

The designs of the quarter, half dollar, and dollar coins returned to the pre-Bicentennial designs. President Jimmy Carter appointed Stella Hackel Sims as Mint director and Azie Taylor Morton as treasurer of the United States—the first African American to hold this office. The Central States Numismatic Society (CSNS) dubbed its May 14 convention "Dick Yeoman Night" and honored the Red Book author with the unprecedented Extraordinary Numismatic Ambassador Award. August saw the death of distinguished former *Numismatist* editor Elston G. Bradfield.

Inside the Red Book

For the 31st edition, the cover reverted to its usual style. The illustrations were eliminated and the previously used better-quality material was reinstated for the cover. To the relief of many collectors, the publishers also reverted to the better paper for the book's interior.

Pricing remained fairly static, except for important key dates in popular collections. Dates such as the 1916-D Winged Liberty Head (or Mercury) dime and the two over-dates in the Winged Liberty Head dime collection increased in value, as did the 1916 Standing Liberty quarter. Most of the other coins remained quiet. The study of the two Morgan dollar dates shows little activity. Only the circulated 1903-O changed at all—a 14 percent, or $5, increase.

One major addition to the listings was the 1944-D, D Over S Lincoln cent. No value was listed, but its inclusion gave the variety instant importance and credibility. A new section, "Hard Times Tokens," was also added, with illustrations and values for many issues. These tokens originated in the period from 1832 to 1844, when President Andrew Jackson's withdrawal of all government funds from the Bank of the United States resulted in the bank's collapse. All bank notes were discredited, which led to the hoarding of all hard currency, including copper coinage. The privately produced copper pieces that replaced the federally minted coinage became known as Hard Times tokens. These tokens are popularly collected by type and include satirical pieces that denounce the day's Jacksonian politics. The new Red Book section included eight pages of historical discussion and variety listings—just the tip of the iceberg, but a great starting point for collectors.

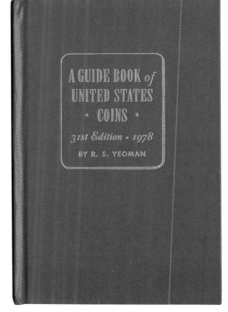

Values of the 31st Edition

Year/Edition	Issue Price	VF	New
1978 (31st ed.)	$3.95	$4	$5

Dollar Price Performance

Year	Very Fine	Uncirculated	Proof
1895-P	—	—	$8,250
1903-O	$40	$65	Not applicable

THE 32ND EDITION (1979)

The Year Was 1978, and . . .

The Eisenhower dollar entered its last year of release; it had never been popular with the general public and was rarely used. The ANA recognized R.S. Yeoman by naming him to the Numismatic Hall of Fame, along with Victor D. Brenner, designer of the Lincoln cent. Public Law 95-447 authorized production of a dollar coin portraying Susan B. Anthony, the first nonmythical woman to appear on a regular U.S. circulating coin.

Inside the Red Book

In 1979, the year after the 32nd edition was prepared, prices would begin to surge for silver and gold. Because the *Guide Book* was completed in 1978, however, the 1979 runup in the prices of silver and gold was not reflected in the listings.

Nevertheless, there were a number of improvements to the book. For the first time, the coin grades incorporated a numerical system of grading. A detailed, illustrated explanation of this system—"The Importance of Coin Grading Today"—appeared on pages 242 to 244. The grading system used a 70-point system as defined by the *Official ANA Grading Standards for United States Coins*. (Interestingly, *Guide Book* editor Ken Bressett edited this book as well.) As before, each coin was valued in different conditions, such as Mint State (MS), Extremely Fine (EF), and Very Good (VG). Now, however, these conditions were specified precisely. A normal Very Good coin, for example, might receive a numerical value of VG-8. A coin of the same grade but in slightly better condition, on the other hand, could be indicated by the value VG-10.

In the nickel section, the 1943, 3 Over 2 Jefferson variety was finally listed. This was a personal triumph: I had been waiting for this addition for years. In the early 1970s, I had shown this variety to a number of coin dealers. They all stated that no such overdate was listed in the Red Book, and therefore it must not exist. I had no real rebuttal

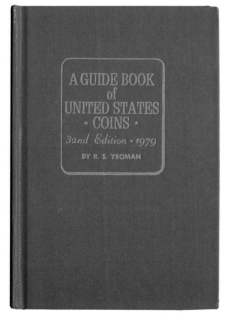

Values of the 32nd Edition

Year/Edition	Issue Price	VF	New
1979 (32nd ed.)	$3.95	$4	$6

Dollar Price Performance

Year	VF-20	MS-60	Proof-60
1895-P	—	—	$9,000
1903-O	$45	$70	Not applicable

to offer until the 1979 edition of the Red Book. No value was listed for the variety, but there was an excellent picture of the coin on the next page. The 1939 doubled-die Jefferson nickel was also newly listed, complete with values.

The entire large cent section was reformatted, with new close-up photos of many varieties, including small dates, large dates, and overdates. The Washington quarter section was also revamped. Two doubled dies, the 1934 and 1943-S, were added to the listings, as were two over-mintmark dates (the 1950-D, D Over S and the 1950-S, S Over D). Out of these four, only the 1934 doubled die carried a value (in Extremely Fine condition and MS-60). There were also many other varieties added this year.

Finally, the Morgan dollars were again showing a bit of liveliness. The 1895-P Morgan dollar's value increased $750, while the 1903-O dollar's value increased $5 in each grade. Although this was a period of inflation, the 1895-P Proof dollar's growth of $750 was worth noting.

RED BOOK RECOLLECTIONS

Phil Bressett

I was first asked to join the Red Book pricing session in 1978 for the 1979 edition. That year I believe that the group included Dad (Ken Bressett), Neil Shafer, Don Kagin, and Dick Thompson. Gold and silver had started to go up, so there were a lot of changes. It seemed like every coin in the book had gone up in value, and I remember thinking, this is a lot of work!

By the next year, the 1980 edition, silver had hit nearly $50 per ounce and gold had hit $850 per ounce. This made last year's changes look easy. Just about every coin in every grade had gone up in value in this edition. The changes were endless. I also remember that the 1980 edition sold out quickly and today is worth a little more that the other Red Books from those years. By the next year gold and silver had settled back down, so just about everything had to be adjusted again, mostly down this time.

After those first few hectic years, things seemed to settle down, and for the most part prices have been slowly and steadily rising every year. It's hard to believe that 30 years have passed and that the 2010 edition has been released. It looks like gold and silver are once again on the move and exciting times are here again! I feel very lucky to have been a part of Red Book history and hope to continue for a long time to come.

Phil Bressett has worked on the Red Book with his father, Kenneth, for more than a quarter of a century.

THE 33RD EDITION (1980)

The Year Was 1979, and . . .

The Susan B. Anthony dollar coin made its debut, but it never gained popularity with the public and would vanish after a puny three-year production run—only to resume minting 18 years later. The GAO resumed the sale of silver dollars from its inventory, but due to the rising price of silver, bid minimums were constantly changed, resulting in confusion. The sale of the first coin to realize a half million dollars was made: the Brasher Doubloon with EB on wing sold at auction for $725,000.

Inside the Red Book

Although the prices of silver and gold were on the rise, this was not yet reflected in the *Guide Book*. There were small corrections to the prices of common-date silver coins—for example, the value of the Roosevelt dime increased in circulated condition from 60 to 65¢—but no major increases were shown.

Buffalo nickels received a boost with the addition of the 1916 doubled die, which included prices in three grades. There was also a clear microphotograph of this variety. No other major varieties were added to the edition, but prices continued to slowly rise, especially for key-date coins. There was also the addition of a new section: a discussion of mint errors written by Bill Fivaz and "Lonesome" John Devine, two experts in the field. This nine-page essay, "An Introduction to Mint Errors," brought new respect to error collecting, and the field would never be the same.

The Morgan dollar prices shot up as though attached to a rocket. The 1895-P Proof dollar nearly doubled: it rose from $9,000 to $17,500! The 1903-O increased $5 in Very Fine condition and $40 in Uncirculated condition. The market was fully awake.

At one time, the 1980 edition was scarce, and its current values still reflect this. As numismatic book dealer Charles Davis notes, the escalation of bullion prices in late 1979 and early 1980 "sucked every 1980 Red Book off the market. It was simply unavailable after Christmas 1979, and it became an expensive edition." Most of the books had been purchased

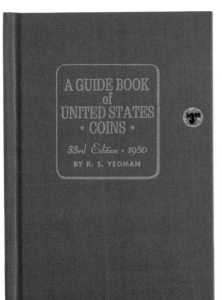

Values of the 33rd Edition

Year/Edition	Issue Price	VF	New
1980 (33rd ed.)	$3.95	$4	$10

Dollar Price Performance

Year	VF-20	MS-60	Proof-60
1895-P	—	—	$17,500
1903-O	$50	$110	Not applicable

by non-numismatists who wished to check their silver coins for valuable dates before selling the coins for their melt value. Eventually many of these copies found their way back to the marketplace via yard sales, flea markets, and the like. As it became apparent that it was no scarcer than other Red Book editions, its premium disappeared except in crisp, unused condition, as none were unsold at the end of the release year.

RED BOOK RECOLLECTIONS

Ginger Rapsus

My first Red Book was the 1967 edition. I had just discovered coins and collecting, and I was happy to find a guide to every United States coin I could find, and some I had never heard of. I still have that 1967 Red Book, along with a number of other editions.

I saved every copy of the Red Book, and if a local dealer wanted to get rid of his stock, I was happy to take them off his hands, for something like 50¢ each. I learned that a few other collectors liked the Red Book, too, which led me to research and write an article for *The Numismatist* on how collectible and desirable older copies could be.

This was 1989. Since then, the Red Book has come into its own as a collectors' item. Hardcover and softcover varieties have been issued each year since 1993. Some buy the hardcover edition every year, to keep their collection more uniform. Others buy the softcover or spiralbound book, for the price and the convenience. The completist will buy both versions every year!

When researching my story, I found that a few books with errors exist, giving Red Book collectors a challenge. Since then, many different editions have been issued, including some with special covers commemorating the ANA and FUN conventions and the SS *Central America*, as well as a scarce leatherbound edition given to members of the Numismatic Literary Guild at their banquet. As an NLG member, I am sorry I missed out on that one.

The ANA World's Fair of Money was held in Denver in August 1996. While at the show, I spotted a specially covered Red Book to commemorate the 50th anniversary of the Red Book, in the old-fashioned maroon cover. A little souvenir booklet was also available, a small cardboard holder shaped like a Red Book, with spaces to hold dimes dated 1946 and 1996. I picked one up to keep with my Red Book set, and found out after the show that some of the holders had silver 1946 dimes already placed inside.

The banquet held at the World's Fair of Money is always a fun time, and part of the fun is seeing what kind of goodies you'll find at your table. A Red Book with a special ANA cover appeared at the 1992 banquet. The 2000 banquet in Philadelphia had a special giveaway, too—copies of the 2001 Red Book with the first page embossed with the Liberty Bell and the date.

Red Book fans will also want to own a copy of the reprinted 1947 edition. The back of the book features a guide to the many changes in the Red Book, prices, and the coin market in general, making this a must for any numismatist interested in the historical aspect. It's also interesting to see the low prices of coins in the 1947 edition. They all seem like such bargains now!

The Red Book will always be a favorite. Collecting these books can be interesting, challenging, and fun—just like collecting coins.

THE 34TH EDITION (1981)

The Year Was 1980, and . . .

The final silver dollars in the government's inventory were sold. The price of silver hit an all-time high of $49.45 per ounce, and gold reached a high of $850 an ounce during the same period. When the markets collapsed, the Hunt brothers, who had tried to corner the silver market, lost billions and were forced to liquidate many of their assets. The Mint began striking the congressionally mandated American Arts series of gold bullion medals; this series would end in 1984. The Numismatic Bibliomania Society, a nonprofit organization to promote the use and collecting of numismatic literature, was founded by George F. Kolbe and Jack Collins.

Inside the Red Book

The 1980 explosion in gold and silver prices was reflected in the 34th edition. For the first time, all common-date coins (including Barber dimes, quarters, and half dollars) were priced with italic numbers. A section at the back of the book (pages 250 through 252) noted that these values, which had been calculated with silver priced at $35 an ounce, were contingent upon the current value of silver. Listings for coins containing gold (which had been calculated with a value of gold at $650 an ounce) were similarly qualified, but these prices were not italicized. A chart on page 252 illustrated these meltdown values. Suddenly, common-date dimes were valued at $3, which was 30 times their face value! On the other hand, quarters were worth $6.25, or only 25 times face value. There was no explanation for this discrepancy in value.

Another innovation appeared in this edition. The last two pages of the *Guide Book* displayed a listing of U.S. type coins and their values in various grades. There were price increases in a number of key-date coins.

In the interim, the Morgan dollars were still a good hedge against the inflation of the times: the 1895-P dollar rose another $2,500 (or 14.3 percent) to a simply incredible $20,000. Compared to the 1895-P, the 1903-O barely made a noticeable change—and yet it showed increases of more than 300 percent in both grades. In Very Fine condition, the coin rose to $175 (from $50); in MS-60 (Uncirculated condition), it rose to $350 (from $110). The times were indeed changing.

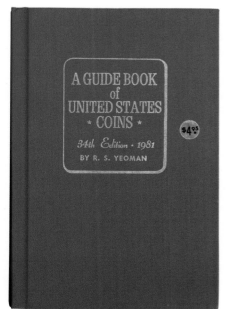

Values of the 34th Edition

Year/Edition	Issue Price	VF	New
1981 (34th ed.)	$4.95	$2	$5

Dollar Price Performance

Year	VF-20	MS-60	Proof-60
1895-P	—	—	$20,000
1903-O	$175	$350	Not applicable

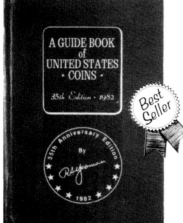

From the July 1981 *Numismatist.* The 35th edition of the Red Book was distinguished by a special anniversary cover emblem, which is prominently displayed in the ad.

THE 35TH EDITION (1982)

The Year Was 1981, and . . .

The ill-fated Susan B. Anthony dollar coins were released only in Mint sets. They would not be minted again for 18 years. The gold and silver markets returned to somewhat normal conditions. President Ronald Reagan appointed Donna Pope as Mint director and Elizabeth Jones as chief sculptor and engraver—the first woman, as well as the first internationally acclaimed sculptor, to serve in this position. Decades of Treasury hostility toward commemorative coins were ended when President Reagan signed legislation approving an issue to commemorate the 250th anniversary of George Washington's birth. It would be the first commemorative coin issued by the Mint in almost 30 years, and opened the floodgates for a surge of such releases.

Inside the Red Book

There were several revisions to this edition in honor of the Red Book's 35th anniversary. A large commemorative emblem bearing a replica of R.S. Yeoman's signature was added to the cover. As in the silver anniversary edition, a photograph and short biography of Yeoman were added opposite the title page. In the contributor credits, Neil Shafer had moved from editorial assistant to coordinating editor.

In late 1980, after the 34th edition had already gone to press, the price of both gold and silver fell. When the 35th edition was compiled, silver was priced at $12 an ounce and gold at $550, and the *Guide Book* made a note of these going rates. Silver dimes, for example, were reduced from $3 a coin to a mere $1.25. Coins affected by the collapsing silver prices showed prices in italics to indicate that they were speculative. Speaking of prices, the cover price of this edition was now $4.95.

The saga of the Morgan dollars did not cease. Although the price of the 1895-P Proof was static, it was still worth $20,000! At the same time, the 1903-O surged in value. In

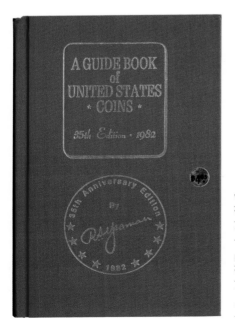

Values of the 35th Edition

Year/Edition	Issue Price	VF	New
1982 (35th ed.)	$4.95	$2	$5

Dollar Price Performance

Year	VF-20	MS-60	Proof-60
1895-P	—	—	$20,000
1903-O	$310	$600	Not applicable

Very Fine condition, the coin increased $135, or 77 percent, while Uncirculated versions were suddenly worth $600, an increase of $250 or 71 percent. Not since before the great Treasury hoard release of 1963 had prices for the 1903-O reached these values.

The Lincoln cent section had the first addition to the listings, with a listing and photo of the 1969-S doubled die. Then the Jefferson nickels added the 1942-D, D Over horizontal D variety, although no photo was provided. The study and acceptance of varieties was still very important to the editors, and care was taken with every coin added.

For the annual special section, attorney David Ganz provided an essay called "Investing in Coins: Planning Your Rare Coin Retirement." In the essay Ganz explained that, at the coin market's current state, investing $7,500 in certain rare coins every year for a 25-year period would accrue into $1.3 million dollars. Unfortunately, the market did not continue its upward trend forever. However, Ganz's contribution marked the start of a tradition of yearly essays by different writers.

Although the Red Book had not received a review in *The Numismatist* for years, the 35th anniversary edition was singled out as an exception. The August 1981 issue described the special anniversary features and the changes to the new edition; by now, no fewer than 60 "expert panelists" were noted to have contributed to the price listings. The unnamed writer assured readers that "the usual helpful features of every Red Book are present in the 1982 edition," including "thousands of facts about coins that help collectors realize the fullest enjoyment from their hobby."

RED BOOK RECOLLECTIONS

Denis Loring

I've been contributing to the Red Book for many years, always in large cents, and in other small areas as I develop knowledge about them. I can also tell you one story involving collecting Red Books and Blue Books:

New York City, where I used to live, has an annual street fair, "New York Is Book Country," consisting only of books—retailers, publishers, and used book dealers. I would go every year. On September 19, 1993, I was browsing at that year's fair. I saw a used-book dealer who had, sitting on the street, a plastic milk carton labeled "Coin Books, $1." The entire carton consisted only of Red and Blue Books. The ones on top were from the '70s and '80s. I dug down and they got older, going back into the 1960s, then 1958 and 1957. As I got toward the bottom, I saw one that looked older than the rest—it was a third edition, 1949, one of the rarities. It even had some old notes and advertisements folded inside the front cover. Finally, at the very bottom of the carton, was the prize: 1947 first edition, first printing, used but undamaged. I bought the 1947, 1949, 1957, and 1958 editions for a total of $4. A good day at the fair!

THE 36TH EDITION (1983)

The Year Was 1982, and . . .

The U.S. Assay Office in New York City closed. Midway through the year, the Mint began to strike cents in copper-plated zinc instead of bronze. As a result of this change and the use of both large- and small-dated dies, there are eight different 1982 cents (including Proofs) available for collectors. No Uncirculated Mint sets were officially sold by the Mint. To take the place of the official Mint sets, Uncirculated Souvenir sets were packaged and sold in Philadelphia and Denver. The George Washington 250th Anniversary half dollar, designed by Elizabeth Jones, was released; although the equestrian portrait of the president was admired, the hefty selling price—$10.50 for Proofs, $8 for circulation strikes—was not. Between this year and the end of 2006, more than 80 commemorative types would appear, leading to widespread head-shaking over the state of the commemorative-coin program.

Inside the Red Book

The *Guide Book* continued to offer valuable information for collectors, including its new presentation of essays about the coin market. The 36th edition provided an essay by George Klabin entitled, "A Survey of Coin Storage and Preservation Methods." As always, the unique education provided by the *Guide Book* was not readily available elsewhere.

The prices of silver and gold continued to spiral downward. Melted down, common-date coins were now worth $9 per ounce for silver coins and $400 per ounce for gold coins. A silver dime would fetch $1; a quarter could get its owner $2.50.

There were not many changes to the listings in this edition. The most notable addition was the 1909-S, S Over Horizontal S Lincoln cent. Also, an improved photo of the 1969-S doubled die was added. A change behind the scenes was visible in the list of contributors, where a new coordinating editor, Dolores Toll, was listed. From this edition forward, the position of coordinating editor would be filled by a staff member whose function was secretarial rather than numismatic.

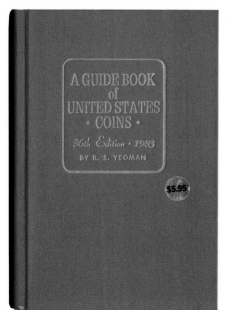

Values of the 36th Edition

Year/Edition	Issue Price	VF	New
1983 (36th ed.)	$5.95	$2	$5

Dollar Price Performance

Year	VF-20	MS-60	Proof-60
1895-P	—	—	$24,000
1903-O	$250	$325	Not applicable

The values of most key dates—except for the Morgan dollars—continued to increase at a steady pace. The 1895-P Proof dollar added $4,000 to its value, for an increase of another 20 percent. But the 1903-O declined to $250 in Very Fine condition and $325 in MS-60 (Uncirculated condition)—continuing its roller-coaster pricing.

RED BOOK RECOLLECTIONS
Dennis Tucker

Do you remember the first rare coin you ever laid eyes on? I remember mine—an old "nickel" that was special for two reasons: because it was so strange and exotic looking, and also (this was more of a *feeling* than a conscious thought) because it was a gift from my eldest brother. Mike was (and is) 13 years older than me, so when I was a tyke going into kindergarten, he was leaving home to join the U.S. Marine Corps—definitely someone to look up to!

One day, home on leave, Mike gave me a coin from the steamer trunk that held his collection. We sat down and he showed me a copy of the Red Book. Together we looked up this unusual coin, and compared its physical traits to the grading standards listed. I was excited to learn that it was in Very Good condition—that sounded promising! He patiently explained that *Very Good* was better than *Good* (which made intuitive sense), but not as good as *Fine*. Okay; obviously I had a lot to learn, but with the Red Book I had the right resources, and thanks to that "rare coin"—actually, a super-common 1937 Buffalo nickel, worth all of $0.30 at the time—I was hooked on this great hobby. I read the book from cover to cover, absorbing its arcane and wondrous knowledge.

Since then I've enjoyed numismatics, from United States types to world coins (and most recently focusing on European medals and tokens). Now, years later, I'm living a collector's dream: hired as Whitman's publisher in 2004, I actually get to work as a hands-on member of the Red Book team. I never guessed that my career in corporate communications and publications would lead me to Whitman Publishing, the maker of the famous scarlet tome. I count among my coworkers Kenneth Bressett and Q. David Bowers—how much more fortunate can a numismatist get? Ken's *Guide Book of English Coins* was the first world-coin book I ever bought, back when I started to branch into British and European material. And of course there was many a Bowers title on my numismatic bookshelf. I'm honored to work with the hundreds of pricing contributors and researchers—now including Jeff Garrett as valuations editor—who make the Red Book so unique.

Working here, I feel a sense of history and a connection to other coin collectors. I can't help thinking of the thousands—*millions*—who have been introduced to the hobby by Whitman coin folders, and sustained and nurtured through their learning process by Whitman books.

I still have that 1937 Buffalo nickel, and also the first Red Book I purchased on my own. I wouldn't trade either one for an 1804 dollar. I hope your journey through the hobby—and your experience with Whitman Publishing and in particular the Red Book—is equally enjoyable.

THE 37TH EDITION (1984)

The Year Was 1983, and . . .

The first Prestige Proof set was sold by the Mint. It included an Olympic commemorative dollar coin. With a release price of $59, total sales were 140,361. An unknown quantity of Proof sets were released with a dime from which the mintmark was missing—today an eagerly sought error. Once again, no Mint sets were sold, and future prices would reflect the lack of saving of the date. Q. David Bowers began his term as president of the ANA. Kenneth Bressett was apointed director of ANACS. The Mint released a number of 1983 Lincoln cents with a doubled-die error. This would become a major variety, although it was not as popular as earlier doubled dies since the doubling is on the reverse.

Inside the Red Book

The *Guide Book* continued its new tradition of including relevant and insightful essays. R.S. Yeoman himself provided the 37th edition's essay, entitled, "The Red Book Story— Chapter One: A Retrospective." In it he shared his adventures and trials during the development and production of the *Guide Book*, and offered some insights and little-known historical facts about the book over the years. Interestingly, he also discussed the increasing prevalence of collectors of the Red Book. The essay concluded with Yeoman's "Roll of Honor," a list of every person who had contributed to the *Guide Book*, from the first edition to the current one. He had intended to add to his story: the Roll of Honor was followed by the statement "A second and concluding chapter of *The Red Book Story* is planned for a later edition." Unfortunately, the second chapter of "The Red Book Story" was never written. This was also the last essay included in the *Guide Book* until the 48th edition.

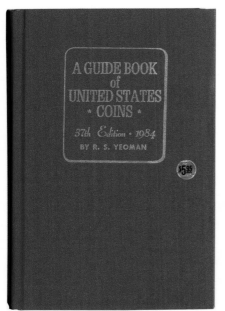

Values of the 37th Edition

Year/Edition	Issue Price	VF	New
1984 (37th ed.)	$5.95	$2	$5

Dollar Price Performance

Year	VF-20	MS-60	Proof-60
1895-P	—	—	$25,000
1903-O	$175	$275	Not applicable

Valuations of common-date silver and gold were listed at $15 an ounce and $500 an ounce, respectively. Common-date dimes were worth 12.5 times face value, and quarters and half dollars were listed at 12 times face. Added to the *Guide Book* was the listing and illustration of the 1982 Large Date and Small Date Lincoln cents. No other major varieties were added to the edition, but all prices were updated and, for the most part, increased.

Not for the first time, the Morgan dollar series both elated and confused coin enthusiasts. The 1895-P Proof dollar rose another $1,000 to a grand total of $25,000 (for a mere 4.1 percent rise). The 1903-O continued to baffle collectors. Seemingly at random, it declined $75 in Very Fine condition and $50 in Uncirculated condition. Such was the market.

The new Red Book was not without errors, as eagle-eyed readers were quick to discover. *Coin World* pointed out a mistake in this edition: on page 257 where the silver bullion content of U.S. coins was given, the figures were shifted over by one column, so each coin type was paired with the wrong silver content. A more obvious error was the illustration for the 1783 Georgius Triumpho token, on page 51: the obverse view of the token was shown reversed, so that Washington faced the viewer's left, and the inscription ran backward.

The September 1983 issue of *The Numismatist* contained a detailed writeup on the new edition and is of particular interest because it contained comments from editor Ken Bressett on the current state of the coin market. "If a single observation is to be made about the new price levels of the Red Book," he was quoted as saying, "it is that values have at least stabilized." For this edition the prices were credited to a "select numismatic panel" of no fewer than 70 members. The review also observed that the gold coin section received "special attention" in this edition, and Bressett pointed out that "many [gold] pieces not seen in recent years can now be valued because of auction prices established at the historic 'U.S. Gold Coin Collection' sale." Better known by the name of the collection's late owner, Louis E. Eliasberg Sr., this milestone 1982 sale featured an example of every regular-issue U.S. gold coin.

Also in this issue of *The Numismatist* was an intriguing article by Q. David Bowers, "The Guide Book Revisited." This delightful nostalgia piece took the newly released 37th edition as a launching point for reminiscences, anecdotes, and revelations about Red Book history from the perspective of a longtime contributor. (See Bowers's foreword to this book for some of these historical nuggets.) In addition, Bowers discussed the sometimes overlooked virtues of this long-lived reference. "Much can be gained by those who take the time to actually study the book," he pointed out, for "no other numismatic reference crams so much information into such a compact volume." He added,

> I have used the *Guide Book* as the main textbook for my Summer Seminar class, "All About Coins," because it is a good jumping-off point for those having specialized interests in different areas. . . . One of the most concise and informative histories of American coinage can be found in the *Guide Book*, pages 5 through 12. Every year or so I [re]read it, just to refresh my memory concerning the development of the country's monetary system.

"The next time you have an hour or two to spare," he concluded, "why not reacquaint yourself with this helpful reference? As a strong foundation of the numismatic hobby, it deserves close reading."

THE 38TH EDITION (1985)

The Year Was 1984, and . . .

The Philadelphia Mint produced yet another Lincoln cent with doubled-die obverse. Although not as popular as the previous ones, due to the fact that the doubling was at Lincoln's ear, today it is popular and collectible. The Mint released its first gold coin in over 50 years, the $10 Los Angeles Olympic commemorative coin, which was also the first coin to bear the W mintmark of the West Point Mint. The Mint's official name changed from the Bureau of the Mint to the United States Mint.

Inside the Red Book

From 1980 to 1984, the *Guide Book* had included a different topical essay in each edition. Without explanation, this practice was concluded, and the 38th edition contained no essay.

Values for bullion coins were again based on going rates of $15 and $500 per ounce for silver and gold, respectively. Prices for common-date silver dimes, quarters, and half dollars remained the same as in the 37th edition.

There were two major additions to the constantly changing list of varieties: the 1983 Doubled-Die Lincoln cent, which had made headlines in the press when it was discovered the previous year as a new and valuable variety, and the 1942-D, D Over S Walking Liberty half dollar. Changes were also made to the Morgan dollar section. Values for the Proof dollars—except the 1895-P—were reduced to a footnote to make room for additional values and more grades. These coins were worth $800 in Proof-60 condition, $2,000 in Proof-63, and $5,500 in Proof-65.

Yet again, the value of the famous 1895-P Proof dollar rose—an increase of $5,000. A 20 percent growth is always welcome, but at this level it is truly amazing. The coin was now worth $30,000. The 1903-O remained dead in the water, and slowly sinking. The only change in value was in Uncirculated condition, which had a decrease of $25, or 9.1 percent.

An authorized edition of the 38th-edition *Guide Book* was also released; see chapter 6 for details.

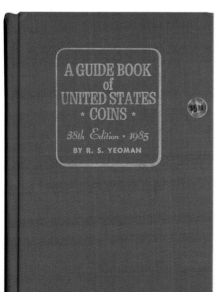

Values of the 38th Edition

Year/Edition	Issue Price	VF	New
1985 (38th ed.)	$5.95	$2	$5

Dollar Price Performance

Year	VF-20	MS-60	Proof-60
1895-P	—	—	$30,000
1903-O	$175	$250	Not applicable

THE 39TH EDITION (1986)

The Year Was 1985, and . . .

The Statue of Liberty Coin Program was authorized to commemorate the statue's centennial on half dollars, silver dollar coins, and $5 gold coins, all of which would be issued the following year. The $5 coin, or half eagle, had not been minted in over half a century. After searching for decades, Mel Fisher finally discovered the remains of the Spanish treasure ship *Nuestra Señora de Atocha*, sunk in 1622. Fisher had become famous for his unswerving belief that he would find the treasure, expressed in his refrain, "Today's the day."

Inside the Red Book

For the 39th edition, the price of bullion continued downward: silver was priced at $8 an ounce; gold at $350 an ounce. Dimes were worth 10 times face value, while quarters and half dollars were priced at 9 times face value.

The *Guide Book* listings did not see any dramatic changes this year. The coin market as a whole was generally quiet. Even most key dates showed little or no change. However, there were some key dates—such as of the Indian Head cents, Lincoln cents, and Buffalo nickels—that showed slight declines in value. The 1916 Doubled-Die Buffalo nickel, on the other hand, was red hot this year. Its values had increased by a factor ranging from 250 percent (from $400 to $1,000 in Fine) to a staggering 375 percent (from $200 to $750 in Very Good). In Extremely Fine, it had skyrocketed from $850 to $2,200!

In our Morgan dollar series, however, values were generally unchanged. The 1895-P remained at $30,000 while the Uncirculated 1903-O had a small increase of $10. The values of the other Proof dollars were given as footnotes, as in the previous edition.

The new edition received a writeup in the September 1985 *Numismatist.* The unsigned piece detailed the contents of the new Red Book and summarized the price changes—including the one to the book itself, which was now offered at $5.95.

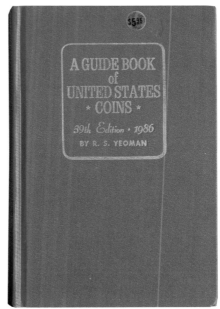

Values of the 39th Edition

Year/Edition	Issue Price	VF	New
1986 (39th ed.)	$5.95	$2.50	$5

Dollar Price Performance

Year	VF-20	MS-60	Proof-60
1895-P	—	—	$30,000
1903-O	$175	$260	Not applicable

THE 40TH EDITION (1987)

The Year Was 1986, and . . .

The Mint began the American Eagle silver bullion program. The 1-ounce silver coins, with a face value of one dollar, featured the Walking Liberty design from the half dollar of 1916 to 1947. Gold bullion American Eagle pieces were created in four denominations, containing gold in the amounts of 1 oz., 1/2 oz., 1/4 oz., and 1/10 oz., and bearing a slimmed-down version of Augustus Saint-Gaudens's Liberty. The Professional Coin Grading Service (PCGS) was founded, and quickly popularized the encapsulation ("slabbing") of rare coins in a sealed plastic holder. Ken Bressett, at the invitation of Mel Fisher, dove at the *Atocha* wreck site to view and study the recovered coins and artifacts.

Inside the Red Book

The 1987 edition celebrated 40 years of the *Guide Book* with a new cover design. A round emblem had been added, which read, "40th Anniversary Edition 1946–1986," and featured a miniaturized reproduction of the book's standard cover design. (The dates in the anniversary logo refer to the actual years of publication, rather than the cover dates of each edition.) This edition also came with a special offer: by mailing in a special gold sticker from the cover, along with a form on the book's last page, buyers could purchase a limited-edition silver medal honoring the *Guide Book*'s anniversary.

The next 10 editions of the Red Book would feature a similar offer, with the final one appearing in the 51st (1998) edition. Simultaneously, the Blue Book included similar mail-order offers for commemorative silver rounds. (For additional information about the limited-edition silver medals, see chapter 8.) From the limited number of these medals that are seen today in auctions and at dealers' tables, we can infer that not many readers took advantage of the offer. This may have been because it required owners to remove the last page of their *Guide Book*. Both new and used copies of the 11 editions

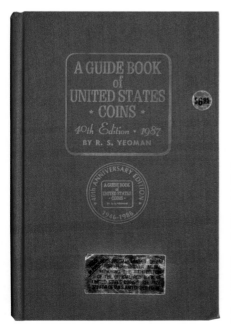

Values of the 40th Edition

Year/Edition	Issue Price	VF	New
1987 (40th ed.)	$6.95	$3	$6
Special ANA cover		500	1,000

Note: See chapter 5 for discussion of the ANA special edition.

Dollar Price Performance

Year	VF-20	MS-60	Proof-60
1895-P	—	—	$35,000
1903-O	$175	$260	Not applicable

The opening pages of the Red Book's quarter dollar listings have made a particularly significant new addition over the space of a decade: the 1987 edition, unlike that of 1977, contains a table of type coin values at the start of the section. Notice also the less crowded arrangement of the layout, which lets both text and images breathe.

with the original sticker still attached are more valuable than ones without the sticker. Those without the sticker are considered used books and should not be purchased as New books.

For the first time in its 40-year history, the Red Book's total page count was changed. The addition of 16 pages resulted in a total length of 272 pages, up from the traditional 256 pages. Among the new contents were a section on Mint sets, which was placed after the Proof set listings on page 62, and a description on page 235 of the then-upcoming American Eagle bullion coins. Aside from these new sections, the added pages went toward a general reorganization, necessitated by all the coins that had been added to the listings since 1946. The extra pages permitted sections to be aired out, so they were less crowded and easier on the eye.

There was little change in the values from the previous year. Morgan dollars were quiet as well, with one notable exception. The 1895-P Proof dollar had a $5,000 (or 17 percent) increase. The 1903-O remained static in both conditions.

A special-edition *Guide Book* was also released this year in honor of the ANA. See chapter 5 to read about this edition.

THE 41ST EDITION (1988)

The Year Was 1987, and . . .

Coins salvaged from the Spanish galleon *Atocha* were sold at auction. The Numismatic Guaranty Corporation of America (NGC) was founded.

Inside the Red Book

The 41st edition of the Red Book offered another limited-edition silver medal. This year's design was based on the Spanish milled dollar, also known as the "piece of eight" for its value of 8 reales. This coin had been given a place of honor in the Red Book since the third edition. The 41st edition's cover featured a picture of the coin, as well as the gold proof-of-purchase sticker that *Guide Book* owners would peel off and send in, along with the last page of the book, to purchase the medal.

The 41st edition included no new varieties, although the one-page section on American Eagle bullion coins (page 235) had been revised and updated to include coin images and value listings. One small change that may have gone unnoticed by many readers was a correction to the listing for the Gettysburg commemorative half dollar: the sculptor, Frank Vittor, was now unambiguously identified as hailing from Pittsburgh, rather than Pennsylvania, as had been stated in all previous editions. Although such a change may seem insignificant (except to Pittsburghers), it is a reminder of the painstaking process of improvement that went into every successive edition of the Red Book.

The values of the Morgan dollars remained constant except for, again, the 1895-P Proof dollar. This year's listed price of $37,500 was an increase of $2,500 (or 7 percent) over its value the previous year.

The 41st edition received not one but two lengthy and enthusiastic writeups. The first appeared in the October 21, 1987, issue of *Coin World* and was written by noted numismatist Col. Bill Murray. Its title summed up its author's position neatly: "'Red Book'

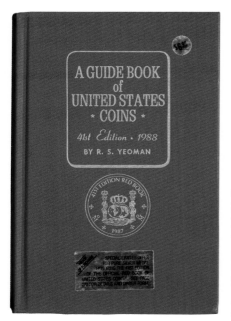

Values of the 41st Edition

Year/Edition	Issue Price	VF	New
1988 (41st ed.)	$6.95	$3	$5

Dollar Price Performance

Year	VF-20	MS-60	Proof-60
1895-P	—	—	$37,500
1903-O	$175	$260	Not applicable

Still an Informative Guide." The next month, an essay by Q. David Bowers appeared in *The Numismatist*. It, too, was embodied by its favorable title: "The Red Book: Great Value for the Money." (See chapter 2 for more on both these articles.)

Bowers's essay was not an unmitigated love letter, however. The author leveled a few constructive criticisms at the Red Book, suggesting that it "would do its readers a favor and increase sales among numismatists if it included a few more grades in the listings, such as AU-50, MS-63 and MS-65." (In future years such grades would in fact be added to many listings.) He added, "it wouldn't hurt if the book was more consistent," and pointed out the disparity in grade categories over different coin types.

On the whole, though, Bowers seemed to feel that these drawbacks were minor considerations for a volume that offered such "meaty reading" and "interesting tidbits of information." Bowers's final verdict was that the Red Book had "justly earned" its position among the 10 best-selling reference books of all time.

RED BOOK RECOLLECTIONS
Jeff Garrett

My work as valuations editor for the Red Book began just a few years ago. Whitman Publishing is very good to work with, and dedicated to making the Red Book the best rare coin reference possible. When the current owners purchased the Red Book, the data was stored on index cards. Whitman has since done much to bring the Red Book to modern standards. The pricing, which I am mostly responsible for, along with Ken Bressett, is carefully reviewed with our contributors to provide the most accurate numbers possible. Whitman is also constantly looking for ways to improve the Red Book, and there will probably be many more innovations to come. I am proud to be a part of this great team.

Much has changed over the last three decades in rare-coin pricing and numismatic literature in general. In the early 1970s, when I began, the Red Book was the key reference on United States rare coins. It is easy to see how the book got the nickname "the rare-coin bible." I can still remember the anticipation of each release of the Red Book. In early summer people would not price their coins until the Red Book arrived. Most of my early study of rare coins was the memorization of mintages, prices, and other bits of trivia gleaned from the Red Book. I still have those early dog-eared copies in my library.

Today's collectors have no idea of the wealth of knowledge they have compared to 20 or 30 years ago. One year's production at Whitman probably outweighs all the books available at the time.

Ken Bressett has done a great job over the years maintaining the integrity of the Red Book. He guards very carefully what is included in the book and has always avoided being manipulated by promoters. Compiling the prices for the Red Book is a huge endeavor, and Ken deserves much credit for his efforts.

Jeff Garrett (right) at work with Kenneth Bressett on the Red Book.

THE 42ND EDITION (1989)

The Year Was 1988, and . . .

The landmark reference *Walter Breen's Complete Encyclopedia of U.S. and Colonial Coins* was published. The West Point Mint, founded in 1937 as the West Point Bullion Depository, became an official branch of the U.S. Mint. The once and future San Francisco Mint, an assay office since 1962, regained its Mint status. An era ended with the death of Richard Yeo, better known as R.S. Yeoman, who left the numismatic world a poorer place with his passing.

Inside the Red Book

Like the two previous editions, the 1989 *Guide Book* included a mail-away offer for a silver medal. The coin replicated in the silver round, the Continental dollar from 1776, was illustrated on the book's front cover. Both the cover illustration and the silver round modified the original coin design to include the legend "42nd edition Red Book" and the date—the year of publication (1988), rather than the edition date. Once again, the Blue Book also offered a silver medal. Its design was of the Fugio cent.

This year, the *Guide Book* and the coin market both slumbered. There were few major additions to the book. Among the new listings were the U.S. Constitution bicentennial commemorative dollar and five-dollar coins, and a new variety of the 1873 Shield nickel: Large 3 Over Small 3. Also new to this edition was a close-up photo of the 1984 Lincoln cent with doubled-die obverse; the new picture clearly illustrated Lincoln's doubled ear. Other alterations were noted in *The Numismatist*'s review of October 1988, which observed that "editorial changes are especially evident in the colonial section, where recent research about certain pieces is included."

The listings showed numerous price decreases, including some for some key dates. In the Buffalo nickel section, for example, the value of the 1913-S Type 2 dropped five

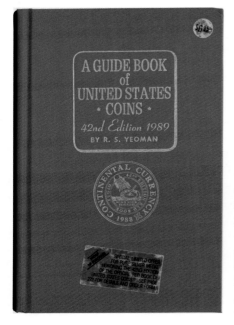

Values of the 42nd Edition

Year/Edition	Issue Price	VF	New
1989 (42nd ed.)	$6.95	$3	$8

Dollar Price Performance

Year	VF-20	MS-60	Proof-60
1895-P	—	—	$37,500
1903-O	$165	$260	Not applicable

dollars. At the same time, however, some of the other Buffalo nickel dates had minor price increases. In the Winged Liberty Head dime section, the 1916-D dime (in Good condition) fell $50 and the 1942, 2 Over 1 (also in Good condition) fell $15. In a January 1989 article about this edition, also in *The Numismatist*, Q. David Bowers commented that values for Barber coins were "homogenized," so that "they all come out fairly equal." He observed that the low premium for the rarer Barber issues reflected the disappearance of collectors specializing in them. Overall, the market was quiet but stable.

The Morgan dollars reflected the mood of the market. There was no price change for the 1895-P Proof dollar, while the 1903-O in Very Fine condition experienced a $10 decrease. These were very quiet days for the coin market in general.

By this time, the Red Book had attained the status of a landmark and a collectible in its own right. Collector interest in the reference extended, of course, at least as far back as 1970, when the 24th edition had acknowledged it in the chapter "Old Red Books Never Die," but it was definitely picking up momentum. In the year that this edition appeared, 1988, the September issue of *The Numismatist* ran a cover story about—you guessed it—the Red Book.

R.S. Yeoman died on November 9, 1988, and because the Red Book was released on July 1, there are some copies of this edition with his signature, although they are very scarce. For those who collect Red Books signed by Yeoman, this edition marks the end of the collection.

RED BOOK RECOLLECTIONS
Jeff Ambio

My experiences with the Red Book began at the age of 12 when my father bought me a copy of the 1988 edition at the local book shop on Staten Island to serve as the standard reference for my small coin collection. Through its pages I first learned about such classic United States coins as the Walking Liberty half dollar, Morgan dollar, and Peace dollar. I continued to acquire personal copies almost yearly until I became a professional numismatic cataloger in 1999. Now, I use the book almost daily while cataloging auction lots for companies such as Bowers and Merena and researching Steve Contursi's inventory at Rare Coin Wholesalers. It was a tremendous honor when I was recently accepted to serve as a contributor to the book that helped to launch my interest in numismatics as a child.

From the December 1989 *Numismatist*. The Red Book commemorative silver medal is prominently featured in the ad for the 43rd edition.

THE 43RD EDITION (1990)

The Year Was 1989, and . . .

The fifth known Albany Church token, discovered in the estate of a Vermont man, was auctioned. The King of Siam set sold for a reported $2 to $3 million. The bicentennial of the U.S. Congress was commemorated on a half dollar, dollar, and $5 coin.

Inside the Red Book

The death late in 1988 of R.S. Yeoman, whose contributions to the *Guide Book* were immeasurable, was reflected in the 43rd edition, which was published in 1989. The page facing the title page was dedicated to his memory, bearing a photograph of the late author and an unsigned but heartfelt tribute. The *Guide Book* was now in the hands of Kenneth Bressett. Followers of the *Guide Book*, aware that Bressett had been an integral part of the book for 30 years, were assured that the reference would continue to be a quality production. To this day, however, in recognition of his importance, R.S. Yeoman remains the listed author on the Red Book's cover and title page.

The offer of medals by mail order continued. This time, a version of the 1915 Panama-Pacific commemorative $50 round, with a reworked obverse, was offered. The stylized silver round is beautiful in its execution. The only price change of note is the increase of the 1916 doubled-die Buffalo nickel. Although its prices increased across all listed grades, it had an unusual increase of $50 (to $600) in Good condition.

The Morgan dollar section was again reworked. The editors removed the price column for MS-65 and inserted a Proof column. However, prices were listed only for PF-63. Prior to this year, the 1895-P Proof dollar in PF-60 condition was listed. Therefore, our table of comparative pricing will change accordingly. The previous year's value for the 1895-P in PF-63 had been $20,000, so there was no change this year. The 1903-O continued its sleep, perhaps falling into a light coma.

An authorized edition of the 43rd edition also exists; see chapter 6 for details.

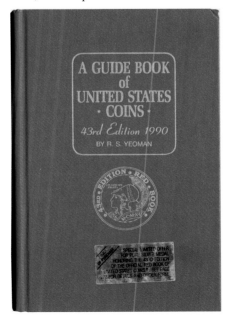

Values of the 43rd Edition

Year/Edition	Issue Price	VF	New
1990 (43rd ed.)	$7.95	$2	$7

Dollar Price Performance

Year	VF-20	MS-60	Proof-63
1895-P	—	—	$20,000
1903-O	$165	$260	Not applicable

From the July 1990 *Numismatist*. The Red Book's expanded length is spotlighted here, with the promise that "the Red Book is growing bigger and better."

THE 44TH EDITION (1991)

The Year Was 1990, and . . .

President George H.W. Bush signed Public Law 101-585, authorizing the issuance of annual silver Proof sets. An estimated 3,555 were produced. Once again the Mint goofed up some of the Proof sets; this time the Lincoln cent was missing the mintmark. Chief Engraver Elizabeth Jones stepped down after a distinguished Mint career, leaving what would become a permanent vacancy: the position would be abolished six years later during the Clinton administration.

Inside the Red Book

The coin featured by the 44th edition, both on its cover and on its commemorative silver medal, was the $20 gold coin, or double eagle, as issued from 1849 through 1907. The stylized design was changed to read "Whitman" on the crown instead of "Liberty."

The *Guide Book* was again expanded: it now included 288 pages. Among the new content was the section "Rare Coins as an Investment," which provided the reader with some excellent insights. In addition, the colonial sections were redesigned and supplemented with much new information.

The coin prices again remained relatively stable, with only minor changes. The noteworthy changes included some minor decreases in the values for Liberty nickels. The 1885 in Good condition, for example, decreased from $250 to $225. The only noted increase was for the 1916 Doubled-Die Buffalo nickel, which rose in Good condition from $600 to $800. Yet, as illustrated by the new picture of a 1961 Proof doubled-die Franklin half dollar, the world of variety collecting was certainly changing.

At the same time, the Morgan dollars fell out of favor, after so many years of hyperactivity. The 1895 Proof declined $1,000 (a 5 percent decrease), and the 1903-O fell in both grades (by $15 in Very Fine and $60 in MS-60). The times were changing for coin collectors who were accustomed to years of continued growth.

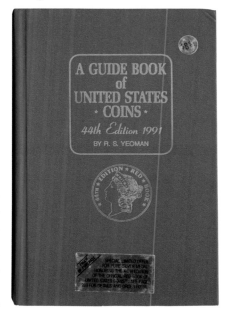

Values of the 44th Edition

Year/Edition	Issue Price	VF	New
1991 (44th ed.)	$8.95	$2	$5

Dollar Price Performance

Year	VF-20	MS-60	Proof-63
1895-P	—	—	$19,000
1903-O	$150	$200	Not applicable

THE 45TH EDITION (1992)

The Year Was 1991, and . . .

The Numismatic Bibliomania Society raised and donated $3,000 to the ANA to establish the Numismatic Literature exhibit category and endow the Aaron Feldman Award, to be given each year for the top numismatic literature exhibit. Commemorative coins honored Mount Rushmore, the United Service Organizations, and the 38th anniversary of the end of the Korean War.

Inside the Red Book

For the sixth year in a row, the Red Book's cover featured a stylized coin design, which was repeated on the promotional silver round offered through this edition. To celebrate 100 years since it was first introduced, the Charles E. Barber Liberty Head design, featured on dimes, quarters, and half dollars from 1892 to 1916, was offered. This year, the motto "Liberty" was left on the diadem (unlike in other years, when it was replaced with "Whitman").

There were no interesting additions in this Red Book, but all data was updated on current issues. A special edition honoring the ANA was also released (see chapter 5).

The Morgan dollar series continued to be of great interest to collectors. Surveys by coin publications note that the Morgan dollar was probably the most collected series of this year (surpassing the Lincoln cent). This year, the 1895 Proof dollar maintained its value of $19,000 in Proof-63. The 1903-O, however, fell out of favor, falling 10 percent in both Very Fine and Uncirculated conditions.

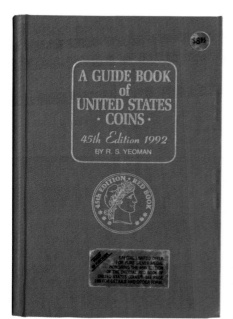

Values of the 45th Edition

Year/Edition	Issue Price	VF	New
1992 (45th ed.)	$8.95	$2	$6
Special ANA cover		150	275

Note: See chapter 5 for discussion of the ANA special edition.

Dollar Price Performance

Year	VF-20	MS-60	Proof-63
1895-P	—	—	$19,000
1903-O	$135	$180	Not applicable

The 46th Edition (1993)

The Year Was 1992, and . . .

Silver Proof sets were made once more. Sales were decent, but the asking price—nearly double the cost of the regular Proof set—was not attractive to collectors. President Bush appointed David J. Ryder director of the Mint. This year saw the release of commemorative issues in honor of the 25th Olympic Games, the 200th anniversary of the White House, and the quincentenary of Christopher Columbus's landing in America.

Inside the Red Book

The cover of the 46th edition displayed the first commemorative half dollar, the Columbian Exposition half dollar, in honor of its 100th anniversary. (The anniversary year was 1992, the year of the Red Book's publication rather than its cover date.) To the bust of Columbus was added the legend "46th Edition Red Book." As with the other books that offered corresponding silver rounds, the cover design paralleled the design on the medal.

The changes to the 46th edition were subtle, but they caused an increase in the number of pages. For the first time, the *Guide Book* exceeded 300 pages. There was an increase of 16 pages, bringing the book to a grand total of 304 pages. The extra pages were primarily used to accommodate the added listings of modern commemorative coins and Proof and Mint sets. There was also some added information on different varieties. The first major addition the reader encountered was close-up photographs of the 1917 and 1936 Lincoln cent doubled-die obverses. The Jefferson nickel received the new listing for the 1943-P Doubled Eye. Due to a typographical error, this variety is listed for less than a regular 1943-P in Very Fine and Uncirculated conditions. Other popular series also received updates. A favorite variety, the 1905-O Micro O dime, was finally listed as more than a footnote. For the first time, it received its own listing and value.

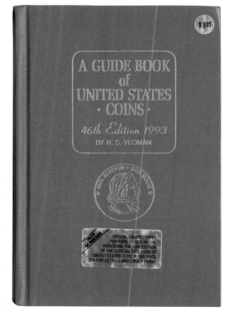

Values of the 46th Edition

Year/Edition	Issue Price	VF	New
1993 (46th ed.), Hardcover	$9.95	$2.25	$7
1993 (46th ed.), Softcover	6.95	1.00	5

Dollar Price Performance

Year	VF-20	MS-60	Proof-63
1895-P	—	—	$17,000
1903-O	$125	$160	Not applicable

The Roosevelt dime began to receive some attention, with the addition of the 1960 Proof Doubled-Die Obverse and the 1964-D Doubled-Die Reverse varieties. Both were illustrated. Then, in the Washington quarters section, the 1937 and 1942-D Doubled-Die varieties were both added, along with a clear illustration of each. Although not pictured, the 1943 Doubled-Die Walking Liberty half dollar and the 1974-D Doubled-Die Kennedy half dollar were both recognized. Doubled dies were the popular item for the issue, with the further addition of two Morgan dollar varieties, the 1888-O "Hot Lips" and the 1901 Doubled-Die Reverse. Both entries included pictures. The 1979-P Anthony dollars with wide or narrow rims were distinguished for the first time. The controversial 1869 two-cent piece with repunched date was deleted. There were other additions, but these were the most popularly recognized.

Both of the Morgan dollars we have been studying did not perform well in this edition. They took a backseat to the growing popularity of variety collecting. The 1895 dollar showed an 11 percent decline in value—from $19,000 to $17,000—and the 1903-O again slid in both grades.

Softcover Edition

By 1992 the increased costs of producing the Red Book required an increase in the cover price. The price on the front-cover sticker of the 1993 hardcover was $9.95, up $1.00 from the 1992 sticker price of $8.95. At the same time, however, Whitman offered readers a new, lower-priced alternative: a softcover *Guide Book*, which bore a cover price of $6.95.

The idea of a softcover coin book was nothing new to the hobby, since all versions of the *Star Rare Coin Encyclopedia*, published by B. Max Mehl (see chapter 1) were published in softcover format. Additionally, the *Handbook of United States Coins* had been changed from a hardcover to a softcover in 1982, with the release of the 1983 (40th) edition. In that

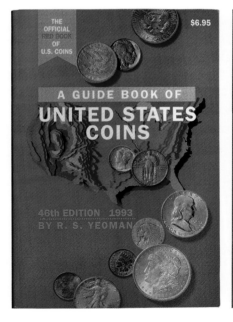

instance, the cost of the book actually increased, but the softcover was well worth the higher cost since the new release (as announced on the cover) was increased in size by 50 percent, from 128 pages to 192!

The Red Book's new incarnation was well received. Not only did the softcover edition offer convenience and portability, but now collectors could preserve their hardcover editions in pristine condition while enjoying day-to-day use of the softcover volume. In contrast to the new softcover Blue Book, the softcover Red Book was identical in content to its hardcover counterpart. However, it was released at a 30 percent discount from the cost of the regular edition. The cover design also created a striking contrast to the hardcover edition. Where the hardcover edition bore an illustration of the special-edition silver round (showing a version of the image of Columbus from the Columbian half dollar), the softcover featured a stylized topographical map of the United States, against which were displayed various popular type coins of all metallic compositions. The dominant color, naturally, remained red, but for the first time other colors were present as well.

A careful examination of the cover of this edition reveals an interesting historical note. At the top of the cover was an insert that read, "The Official Red Book of U.S. Coins." This was apparently the first official recognition on the book itself of its previously unofficial nickname. Although the *Guide Book* had been known to collectors for decades as the Red Book, this was the first time that the term had appeared on a copy.

Today, the 1993 softcover edition may still be located in New condition without difficulty from various online dealers and sellers. Do not settle for a used copy or one in less than New condition, since the cost savings will be negligible.

The obverse die for the 1992 Red Book medal still exists in the possession of Whitman Publishing, along with a number of other dies used in the making of the series of silver rounds. See chapter 8 for more on these medals.

From the August 1993 *Numismatist*. For the first time, Red Book advertisements feature two versions of the venerable reference: one hardcover, one softcover.

THE 47TH EDITION (1994)

The Year Was 1993, and . . .

Kenneth Bressett began his term as president of the ANA. The treasure seekers of Deep Sea Research located the remains of the steamship SS *Brother Jonathan*, which had sunk in 1865 and was later found to contain over 1,000 gold coins. The Bill of Rights commemorative coin series was issued: the obverses of the half dollar, dollar, and $5 coins all bore the portrait of James Madison. Also issued this year was a commemorative series marking the 50th anniversary of World War II; the coins in this series were all dated 1991–1995.

Inside the Red Book

The 47th edition honored the large cent of 1793, a topical choice given that 1993, the year in which this Red Book was published, was the 200th anniversary of this coin type. Once again, the primary cover device was the bust of Liberty, with a legend added to acknowledge the 47th edition of the *Guide Book*.

After the amazing revamping of the listings for the 1993 edition, most of the updating of this issue was restricted to updating the listed prices. However, the 1950-S, S Over D Roosevelt dime variety was added, although no illustration was included. In the Buffalo nickel section, the 1935 Doubled-Die Reverse was added to the listings. The editors also added the 1936 3-1/2 Legs variety, legitimizing it as a collectible variety. Other newly listed coins, as Q. David Bowers noted in his review of November 1993, included the 1868 large cent (identical to the 1857 large cent) and the 1795 Flowing Hair silver dollar with silver plug at center, "one of the more significant discoveries of recent years in American numismatics." Bowers also pointed out that the 47th edition "notes for the first time that 35,401 business-strike, high-relief 1922 Peace dollars were struck for circulation, but were melted at the Mint."

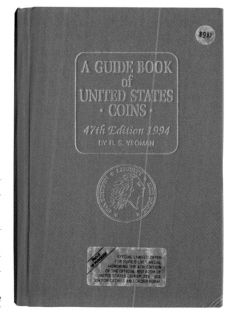

Values of the 47th Edition

Year/Edition	Issue Price	VF	New
1994 (47th ed.), Hardcover	$9.95	$1	$4
1994 (47th ed.), Softcover	7.95	1	4

Dollar Price Performance

Year	VF-20	MS-60	Proof-63
1895-P	—	—	$17,000
1903-O	$125	$160	Not applicable

Bowers's review, "Checking Out the 'Red Book,'" discusses not only these changes to the new edition but also the Red Book's unparalleled place in numismatic circles: "no other publication holds a candle to the 'Red Book' when it comes to combining illustrations, historical descriptions, prices in several grades and the general relationship of series. . . . I turn first to the 'Red Book' and second to other publications. To borrow a medical term, it is the book of 'first response.'" Although he points out that "space constraints prevent price listings for as many grades as I would like," he concludes his remarks on a note of warm enthusiasm: "Each year, when the latest edition of the 'Red Book' arrives, I curl up with it for an hour or two and appreciate all over again what a grand volume it is."

Collecting the new varieties seemed to be the order of the day. Once again, the Morgan dollars took a backseat. However, the market for them steadied: valuations of both the 1895-P Proof and 1903-O remained the same, which is always preferable to a decline.

Softcover Edition

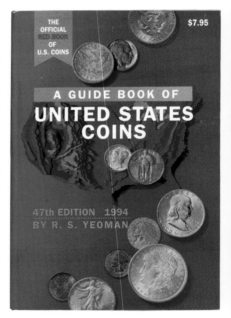

After the success of the 1993 softcover release, Whitman continued the new tradition of releasing two different cover formats of the Red Book. Except for year and edition number, the cover of the 1994 softcover edition was identical to that of the previous year. For its second year of issue, the price was increased to $7.95. Once again, the contents were the same as the hardcover edition.

Whereas the 1993 softcover edition is readily available, this softcover and those of subsequent years are more difficult to locate. A recent search for availability revealed that several dealers do have them in stock, but online auctions are few and far between. It may become apparent in future years that certain editions are actually relatively scarce and hard to locate in New condition. My personal search took several months, and I was outbid on the first few lots that I tried to win.

From the July 1994 *Numismatist.*

THE 48TH EDITION (1995)

The Year Was 1994, and . . .

In a return to past excesses of the program, six different individuals or events were honored on commemorative coins; counting Proofs as separate from circulation strikes, this created a total of 16 pieces for collectors, including two gold coins. President Bill Clinton named Philip N. Diehl as 35th director of the Mint. Longtime Red Book contributor Q. David Bowers was named to the ANA's Numismatic Hall of Fame.

Inside the Red Book

For the 48th edition, the Red Book's cover showed the obverse of the 1794 Liberty Cap half cent, which was replicated in that year's silver round. In this design, Liberty's head faced right, and the liberty pole was included in the design. The *Guide Book* increased in size, adding eight additional pages. Most of the additional space was used for a reordering of the listings, starting with the Kennedy half dollars. These updates in the book's layout continued to improve its ease of use.

The first notable variety that was added was the 1956-D cent with repunched mintmark (RPM). This was the first time that an RPM was listed in the *Guide Book;* these varieties had gone largely unstudied until the 1990 publication of John Wexler's *The RPM Book*. The only other notable addition was the 1945-P Jefferson nickel with doubled-die reverse, which had no illustration.

For the first time since the 37th edition, an essay was added to the back of the book. "The *Guide Book* as a Collectible" was a monumental section. It discussed the history of the *Guide Book*, printing errors, and special editions. It also offered a valuation guide to the Red Book's previous editions, listing three different condition grades. With this essay, collecting of the *Guide Book* was officially recognized.

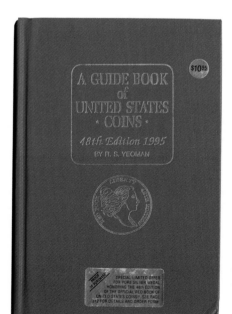

Values of the 48th Edition

Year/Edition	Issue Price	VF	New
1995 (48th ed.), Hardcover	$10.95	$1.50	$4
1995 (48th ed.), Softcover	7.95	1.00	3

Dollar Price Performance

Year	VF-20	MS-60	Proof-63
1895-P	—	—	$17,000
1903-O	$125	$160	Not applicable

The Morgan dollar market remained static for the year, with little or no interest shown for these varieties. This was truly a fantastic time for collectors to develop an interest in our two studied coins. Anyone who did was sure to profit in the long run.

An authorized edition of the 1995 *Guide Book* was also released; see chapter 6 for details.

Softcover Edition

Whitman continued to release softcover versions of the Red Book, and the 1995 edition featured the same cover design as its predecessors. As noted earlier, some editions are going to take some searching for and may be difficult to locate in New condition. A copy found for $3 in New condition might turn out to be one of the deals of the century. Only further study and experience will tell.

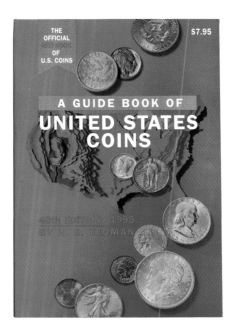

VALUATION GUIDE FOR PAST ISSUES OF THE GUIDE BOOK				
Year/Edition	Issue Price	Fine	V. Fine	New
1947-1st, 1st printing	$1.50	$250.00	$350.00	$500.00
1947-1st, 2nd printing	1.50	225.00	275.00	450.00
1948-2nd	1.50	85.00	125.00	250.00
1949-3rd	1.50	90.00	150.00	300.00
1951/52-4th	1.50	75.00	100.00	150.00
1952/53-5th	1.50	125.00	220.00	325.00
1953/54-6th	1.50	40.00	75.00	150.00
1954/55-7th	1.50	40.00	75.00	125.00
1955-8th	1.50	35.00	50.00	75.00
1956-9th	1.50	25.00	40.00	60.00
1957-10th	1.50	20.00	32.00	40.00
1958-11th	1.50	10.00	15.00	25.00
1959-12th	1.50	8.00	10.00	15.00
1960-13th	1.50	8.00	10.00	18.00
1961-14th	1.50	7.00	9.00	18.00
1962-15th	1.50	5.00	7.00	10.00
1963-16th	1.50	4.00	6.00	10.00
1964-17th	1.75	4.00	6.00	10.00
1965-18th	1.75	1.50	3.00	5.00
1966-19th	1.75	1.50	3.00	5.00
1967-20th	2.00	2.00	4.00	6.00
1968-21st	2.00	2.00	4.00	6.00
1969-22nd	2.00	2.00	4.00	6.00
1970-23rd	2.50	2.00	4.00	6.00
1971-24th	2.50	2.00	4.00	6.00
1972-25th	2.50	8.00	10.00	15.00
1973-26th	2.50	2.00	4.00	6.00
1974-27th	3.00	—	2.00	4.00
1975-28th	3.95	—	2.00	4.00
1976-29th	3.95	—	2.00	4.00
1977-30th	3.95	2.00	4.00	7.00
1978-31st	3.95	—	3.00	5.00
1979-32nd	3.95	2.00	4.00	6.00
1980-33rd	4.95	8.00	10.00	16.00
1981-34th	4.95	—	2.00	3.50
1982-35th	4.95	—	2.00	3.50
1983-36th	5.95	—	2.00	3.50
1984-37th	5.95	—	2.00	3.50
1985-38th	5.95	—	2.00	3.50
1986-39th	6.95	—	2.50	4.50
1987-40th, Special A.N.A. Cover	6.95	—	—	100.00
1987-40th	6.95	—	3.00	5.00
1988-41st	6.95	—	3.00	5.00
1989-42nd	6.95	—	3.00	5.00
1990-43rd	7.95	—	2.00	5.00
1991-44th	8.95	—	2.00	5.00
1992-45th	8.95	—	2.00	5.00
1992-45th, Special A.N.A. Cover	8.95	—	—	75.00
1993-46th, hard bound	9.95	—	2.25	5.50
1993-46th, soft bound	6.95	—	1.00	3.00
1994-47th, hard bound	9.95	—	2.25	5.50
1994-47th, soft bound	7.95	—	1.00	3.00

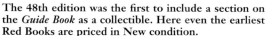

The 48th edition was the first to include a section on the *Guide Book* as a collectible. Here even the earliest Red Books are priced in New condition.

THE 49TH EDITION (1996)

The Year Was 1995, and . . .

The commemorative program exploded with the release of 40 pieces (counting Proofs) honoring three events. They included 32 pieces for the 100th anniversary of the modern Olympics and 10 gold coins. The Mint also released a special anniversary gold Proof set to commemorate the 10th year of the gold bullion program. Collectors were excited by the discovery of doubled-die obverses on 1995 Lincoln cents, although the error pieces soon proved to be more common—and thus less valuable—than initially supposed. New security features were introduced on the $100 bill to thwart counterfeiters. The redesigned bill, which included color-shifting ink and a larger, off-center portrait of Benjamin Franklin, would go into circulation the next year, paving the way for security-minded revamps of other denominations of U.S. paper money.

Inside the Red Book

Whitman Publishing's silver-medal offer continued with the 49th edition. This year's medal, and thus the emblem on the Red Book cover, was based on the obverse design of the 1795 to 1804 eagle, or $10 gold coin, which featured Robert Scot's Capped Bust motif. As with earlier selections for medal designs, the coin design's anniversary coincided with the year in which the book and silver round were released, rather than the stated edition year.

The section entitled "The *Guide Book* as a Collectible" continued, and included updated prices. The listings, following the 1995 addition of the 1956-D repunched mintmark, added the 1943-D "boldly doubled" mintmark to the Lincoln cent listings. More than 10 editions later, these listings still remain.

In the Barber half dollar listings, the 1892-O Micro O had been returned. This variety had been absent from the Red Book since the 17th (1964) edition, although it had later

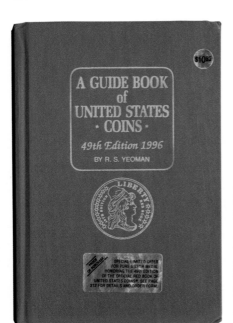

Values of the 49th Edition

Year/Edition	Issue Price	VF	New
1996 (49th ed.), Hardcover	$10.95	$1.50	$4
1996 (49th ed.), Softcover	7.95	1.00	3

Dollar Price Performance

Year	VF-20	MS-60	Proof-63
1895-P	—	—	$18,000
1903-O	$125	$160	Not applicable

been acknowledged in a footnote. Its replacement in the 49th edition meant that it regained its proper status as an important variety. There were no other new varieties listed.

The value of the 1895-P Proof Morgan dollar increased by $1,000. However, the 1903-O had no change in value.

The 49th edition received a short review in the September 1995 issue of *The Numismatist*, which referred to the annual reference as "the much-revered and relied-upon 'Red Book.'" The review noted that "the 1996 edition includes pricing information compiled from data provided by more than 90 of the nation's leading coin dealers." Kenneth Bressett was quoted as saying that price changes in the new edition were a reflection of the unsettled, "soft" condition of the coin market at that time. Interestingly, the unsigned review describes the regular hardcover edition of the new Red Book as "deluxe," presumably to distinguish it from the lower-priced softcover version.

Softcover Edition

For the softcover edition, both the cover and the price remained the same as in the previous year. It should be noted that most collectors purchased their softcover books to use for reference, and as a result, New copies of the softcover books are rarely available from collectors. The usual source is from dealers' remainder stock; however, sometimes the *Guide Book* collector may get lucky.

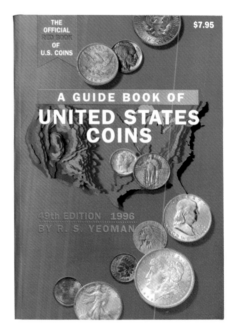

Recent observations of online auctions revealed that the sale of 1996 softcover editions is not a regular occurrence. Studies over a three-month period showed only one available, and it was in used condition. Considering its current availability, this may be another sleeper with the possibility of future increases in value.

THE 50TH EDITION (1997)

The Year Was 1996, and . . .

Deep Sea Research recovered the first gold coins from the treasure ship SS *Brother Jonathan*. The ANA named Red Book editor Kenneth Bressett to the Numismatic Hall of Fame. A new price record was set when a single coin sold for more than $1 million: the Eliasberg 1913 Liberty Head nickel, one of only five of these legendary rarities in existence. The final price, including buyer's fee, was an astounding $1,485,000. Commemorative coins were released to celebrate national community service and the 150th anniversary of the Smithsonian Institution. As a result of the proliferation of commemorative coins, legislation was introduced to limit future issues both in number and in mintage quantity.

Inside the Red Book

Many collectors were excited to see what Whitman would do with the 50th anniversary edition of the *Guide Book*, and they were not disappointed. Not only did the publisher release a special edition with an anniversary cover (see chapter 5), but the standard edition was also revamped to celebrate the event. Its entire front cover was redesigned to show a stylized outline of the continental United States and the American flag, along with a special emblem for the 50th anniversary. (Although the silver-medal promotion was still in operation this year, the Red Book cover parted from earlier practice and did not portray the design used for that year's silver round: the Roosevelt dime. See chapter 8 for details on the silver round.)

Inside, color illustrations had been added to many of the different series of coins. As Kenneth Bressett explained in a press release, "adding color this year was a feasibility experiment. The results, however, are so exciting that a decision has been made to continue in the future and expand color coverage throughout the book. Locating the thou-

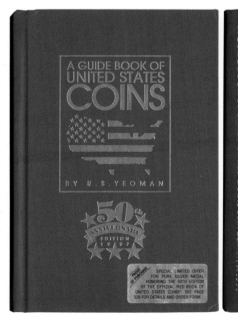

Values of the 50th Edition

Year/Edition	Issue Price	VF	New
1997 (50th ed.), Hardcover	$11.95	$1.50	$5
1997 (50th ed.), Spiralbound	8.95	1.00	5
Special anniversary cover	24.95	52.50	125

Note: See chapter 5 for discussion of the special edition with anniversary cover.

Dollar Price Performance

Year	VF-20	MS-60	Proof-63
1895-P	—	—	$18,000
1903-O	$125	$160	Not applicable

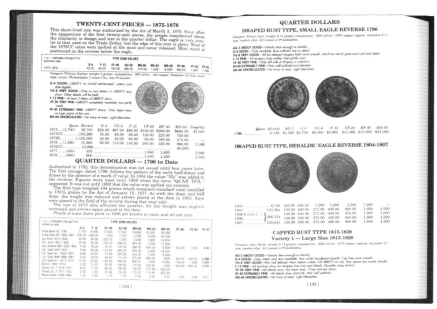

Differences between the quarter dollar listings in the 1997 Red Book and those of a decade earlier include the use of color images and the addition of a table of type coin values.

sands of illustrations needed for such a project may take several years, but the end results will be well worth the effort." It would in fact take a number of years before all of the black-and-white images were replaced with color ones.

Another 16 pages were added, in part to accommodate photos of many of the modern commemorative coins. The essay section was also reinstated. This edition's essay was a six-page feature that discussed and illustrated the Hard Times tokens of the Jacksonian era.

The coin varieties continued to be updated. In the one-cent category, the 1943-D boldly double mintmark was now illustrated, along with the newly discovered 1995 Doubled-Die cent. In addition, an illustration of the doubling for the 1943-P Washington quarter was added. The colonial section's coverage of Massachusetts silver coins had been expanded, and varieties for other state coins had been added. Listings for fractional gold pieces had also been greatly increased.

Yet the Morgan dollars continued to disappoint. The 1895-P Proof and the 1903-O dollars did not budge from their prior year's listings. Once again, this was the ideal time to buy, if any inventory could have been found.

Perhaps as a result of the added pages and color photographs, the Red Book's price rose to $11.95. This year also saw the release of a special anniversary edition; see chapter 5 for details.

Spiralbound Edition

The 50th anniversary of the *Guide Book* introduced an innovation: a new softcover format with a silvertone spiral binding. This was a very welcome change, since this format gave readers more freedom in using their copies for reference. The edition could be folded open at any page without damage to the book, making it much more convenient to use than the hardcover. A Whitman press release described it as an "economy version," noting that it was "priced somewhat lower than the library [i.e., hardback] edition and is bound with a colorful card cover." An additional advantage to the new spiralbound book, according to the press release, was that it was "less bulky and easier to carry" than the regular hardback. To keep the price of this version low, all photographs were rendered in black-and-white; the new color images were reserved for the hardback.

The "colorful card cover" of the spiralbound edition differed from the softcover design of the previous year. The new edition's cover maintained the use of type coin photos, but reconfigured them and added the 50th anniversary logo. In addition, the map of the United States was now overlaid with the design of the American flag, creating a patriotic flavor.

Released at $8.95, or $3 less than the hardcover edition (but an increase of $1 over the price of the previous year's softcover), the spiralbound Red Book was an instant hit with collectors. Today copies of this edition may be obtained with ease, although as a 50th anniversary issue it is very popular and sells for more than usual. Wait to obtain a copy that is New or nearly New for your collection.

Test copies also exist for the 1997 Red Book; see chapter 8 for details.

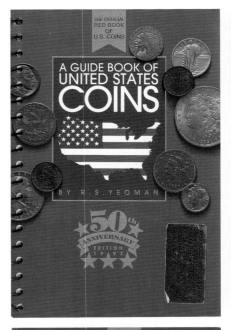

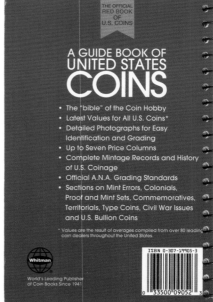

From the August 1997 *Numismatist*. The Red Book's parent company has changed from Western Publishing to Golden Books.

THE 51ST EDITION (1998)

The Year Was 1997, and . . .

The final Prestige Proof set, with the Botanic Garden commemorative dollar, was released. Sales were slow, and totaled only 80,000. With the authorization of secretary of the Treasury Robert Rubin, the Mint produced America's first platinum coins: bullion pieces in 1/10, 1/4, 1/2, and one-ounce weights. The sale of silver Proof sets nearly hit a modern low with only 741,678 sets sold. Today the dime, quarter, and half dollar are considered key dates for collectors. President Clinton signed the 50 States Commemorative Coin Program Act into law on December 1; the state quarters would be released starting in 1999, in the order in which the states joined the Union.

Inside the Red Book

The year of the 51st edition, 1998, was the start of the second half century of publication for the *Guide Book*. In honor of the occasion, the editors redesigned the entire cover. Like the silver medal that was released in tandem with this edition, the cover replicated the 1848 "CAL." quarter eagle, which had been issued with the first California gold to arrive at the Philadelphia Mint. The spine was also redesigned: the font was changed, and Whitman's emblem was included. In addition, inside the book the use of color was greatly extended, with many more color photos included, and some of the contents of the title page rendered in red or blue.

This edition included newly discovered varieties, such as the 1914, 4 Over 3 Buffalo nickel. This variety had recently made headlines in the numismatic press and was hotly desired. No illustration was included. An excellent color microphoto of the 1939 Doubled-Die Reverse Jefferson nickel was also added. The 1955-D, D Over S Jefferson had already been pictured in earlier editions, but the editors chose to update it this year with a clearer picture. Interestingly, the new photo is of a later die state than the one

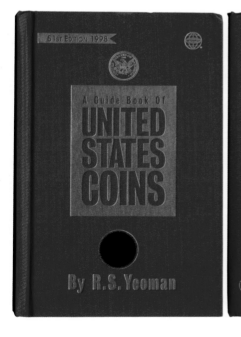

Values of the 51st Edition

Year/Edition	Issue Price	New
1998 (51st ed.), Hardcover	$11.95	$3
1998 (51st ed.), Softcover	8.95	2

Dollar Price Performance

Year	VF-20	MS-60	Proof-63
1895-P	—	—	$20,000
1903-O	$125	$160	Not applicable

that was originally used. In the half dime section, an excellent photograph of the 1861, 1 Over 0 was added; and in the Liberty Seated quarters, the 1854-O, Huge O was shown. This was the first time that either of these varieties had been illustrated.

Next, let's look at the popular Morgan dollar collection. The 1895-P Proof dollar showed an increase reminiscent of its 1990 value of $20,000. This was an 11 percent ($2,000) increase. However, the 1903-O stayed quiet without any movement at all.

Softcover Edition

In a reversal, Whitman decided to release a softcover once again, rather than a spiral-bound edition. This time the cover design was simplified, much like the cover for the hardbound edition. Gone were the pictures of the type coins, and a classier look was introduced—for what would turn out to be only one year. This one-off design introduces some visual themes that would be carried over, in modified form, to future Red Book covers, such as the emphasis on the book's title as the prominent visual element. The faintly screened-in background of the American flag, placed at a dynamic angle, paved the way for the distinctive horizontal stripes that would provide the background starting with the next edition. Another significant change lay beneath the cover: color coin photographs had replaced some of the black-and-white ones, making the softcover edition more similar to its hardbound counterpart.

This book appears to be considerably more difficult to obtain than its low current value would imply. Perhaps the reason for the low selling prices for many of these editions is the lack of a current collector base for them. As they increase in popularity, the prices will probably rise in accordance with demand.

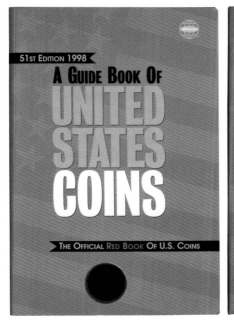

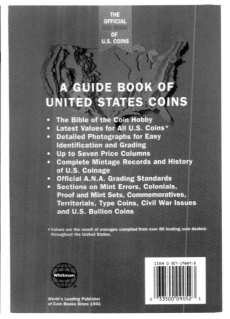

From the October 1998 *Numismatist.* The spiralbound Red Book makes its print-ad debut—but its distinctive binding isn't shown.

THE 52ND EDITION (1999)

The Year Was 1998, and . . .

This was the final year of the eagle reverse of the George Washington quarter. A remarkable chapter in coin-collecting history opened when troubled casino mogul Ted Binion died under mysterious circumstances and was found to have left a concrete bunker filled with silver bullion and coins, including an estimated 100,000 silver dollars. In November 2001 Spectrum Numismatics would purchase the collection for $3,000,000 and go on to sell them slabbed by NGC with a "Binion Hoard" notation. The John F. Kennedy half dollar was issued in a matte finish with the Robert F. Kennedy commemorative dollar. Today the former coin is the key to the set of Kennedy half dollars. The Dollar Coin Advisory Committee successfully recommended that the new design of the dollar coin portray Sacagawea, the young Shoshone woman who famously guided the Lewis and Clark Expedition.

Inside the Red Book

For the 52nd edition, there were several important changes to the *Guide Book*'s layout. The cover was redesigned to reflect the modern look that the interior had adopted, with a bigger, bolder presentation of the title and edition number. The spine was changed to mimic the new look of the cover, and the length was expanded by another eight pages (for a total of 336). Although some of the added pages were used for the addition of current coins and commemorative issues, the section on the coinage for the Philippines was expanded and became much more comprehensive. For the first time, each type was listed by date and mintage, and included values for up to four grades. These revisions showed that the collectible status of these coins was finally being recognized.

In the regular series of U.S. coins, one notable variety was recognized for the first time. The 1795 Flowing Hair silver dollar, with silver plug, was added to the listings. A color photo was included.

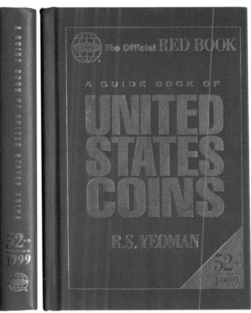

Values of the 52nd Edition

Year/Edition	Issue Price	New
1999 (52nd ed.), Hardcover	$11.95	$4
1999 (52nd ed.), Spiralbound	8.95	4

Dollar Price Performance

Year	VF-20	MS-60	Proof-63
1895-P	—	—	$20,000
1903-O	$125	$160	Not applicable

The year of 1999 would be the first year that the 50 State Quarters® Program was in effect, and everything would change for dealers and collectors alike as millions of new collectors joined the hobby community. However, since the 1999 edition of the Red Book was actually finalized and released in 1998, prior to the flood of new collectors, many valuations remained constant. There were no changes for the values of the studied Morgan dollars this year.

Spiralbound Edition

The spiralbound format returned for the 52nd edition; however, this time the wire coil was white instead of silvertone. The cover boasted a complete redesign: gone was the map design, and the dominant motif was now the title itself. Replacing the previous edition's scattering of coins, three type coins were neatly aligned beneath the title—the Buffalo nickel, the Braided Hair large cent, and the Standing Liberty quarter. A subtle tonal background of broad stripes was reminiscent of the American flag, and a thin circular motif behind the title echoed the coins. The top of the cover is boldly emblazoned with the legend "The Official Red Book." This design format would be carried over for the next several years, with the coin types sometimes changing.

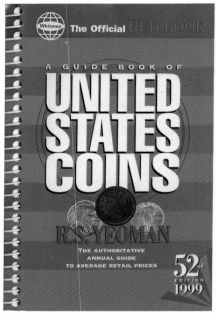

Unlike the earlier spiralbound edition, released in 1996, the 52nd-edition spiralbound Red Book utilized color photographs, as did the previous year's softcover edition. Although the softcover and spiralbound editions had started out as economical versions of the Red Book, they were quickly taking on the attributes of standard editions.

This edition has long been considered to be very common, but a recent search over the course of several months showed only three copies available at Internet auction sites, two of which were for copies described as "used." When I finally located a New copy, I purchased it for over $4, an extremely reasonable price. If the collector is able to purchase a copy in New condition, my recommendation is to grab it at any reasonable price. The seller might not be aware of how difficult it is to obtain a copy.

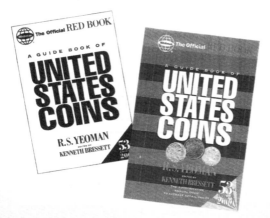

From the November 1999 *Numismatist*. Editor Kenneth Bressett's name has been added to the Red Book cover, and St. Martin's Press is now the parent company.

THE 53RD EDITION (2000)

The Year Was 1999, and . . .

The initial year of the 50 State Quarters® Program started with the release of the Delaware quarter. The greatest coin boom in collecting history soon commenced; surveys by the Mint would later find that almost half of the American population was collecting the quarters. The Susan B. Anthony dollar design was brought back from the dead with a short production run— according to some accounts, in order to satisfy the demand of the Federal Reserve, which reportedly had almost used up its stock. A new record selling price for a single coin was set when an 1804 silver dollar in Proof-68 sold for $4,140,000. The record would stand until the 2002 sale of the 1933 double eagle. Laura Gardin Fraser's 1932 design for the Washington quarter, which had controversially been rejected in favor of John Flanagan's design, finally saw the light of day as a commemorative $5 piece marking the bicentennial of Washington's death. On July 23, a dozen specially minted 22-karat Sacagawea dollars traveled into space aboard the *Columbia* space shuttle.

Inside the Red Book

One of the most significant changes to this edition of the Red Book was apparent to readers before they even opened the book: the addition of editor Kenneth Bressett's name to the cover, a decidedly tardy acknowledgment of his position as helmsman of the book ever since Yeoman's retirement. Inside the book, a section titled "Statehood Quarters" was added to the quarter dollar listings. Since the book was published in 1999, there were no photos or values for the new quarters. Apart from this section, no interesting new varieties were added to the listings, although the editor continued to painstakingly update the prices for all listed coins. More color photographs replaced black-and-white type coin photos.

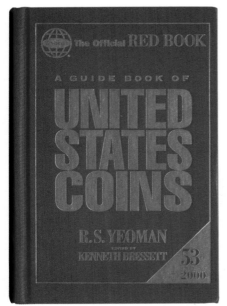

Values of the 53rd Edition

Year/Edition	Issue Price	New
2000 (53rd ed.), Hardcover	$12.95	$2
2000 (53rd ed.), Spiralbound	8.95	2

Dollar Price Performance

Year	VF-20	MS-60	Proof-63
1895-P	—	—	$22,000
1903-O	$125	$160	Not applicable

The Morgan dollars increased in value. The 1895-P Proof dollar jumped $2,000 in Proof-63, which was a 10 percent increase. It is unlikely that this increase was due to the new state quarters program, since most new collectors would be unlikely to start at the top of a series, as with the 1895 dollar. The other dates were relatively quiet, with little change noted.

Spiralbound Edition

The spiralbound version of the 53rd-edition *Guide Book* did not make any drastic alterations to the edition of the year before, aside from the addition of Kenneth Bressett's name to the front. One subtle design change is evident: the circular, coinlike outline that previously provided a backdrop for the title was eliminated, continuing the general tendency toward a more streamlined design.

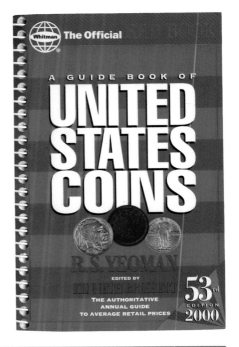

Cropped stock photos commonly used on the Internet give the impression that the edition was available in softcover format. However, none were released (or produced) in that style for this year.

The edition is not considered to be particularly difficult to obtain. A short wait will make a nice New copy available for your collection.

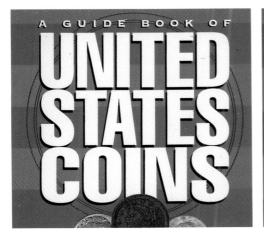
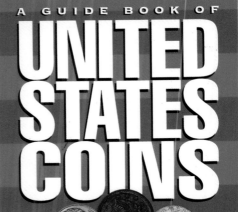

Subtle design changes distinguish the covers of the 52nd and 53rd editions of the spiralbound Red Book: the circular motifs of the 1999 edition (left) have vanished in the 2000 edition (right), continuing the evolution toward a cleaner, bolder look.

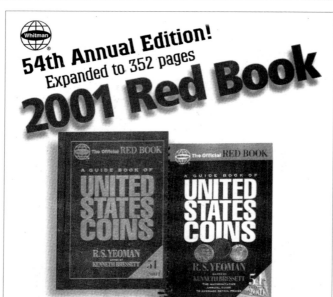

From the October 2000 issue of *Coins* magazine. The Red Book's new length (352 pages) is touted, as is the inclusion of listings for the new state quarters and Sacagawea dollars.

THE 54TH EDITION (2001)

The Year Was 2000, and . . .

The Sacagawea "golden" dollar coin was released. Some in the general public misunderstood the publicity and believed that there was gold in the coins, but soon the coins proved to be as unpopular as the Susan B. Anthony dollars. Genuine gold seized the spotlight when coins and ingots recovered from the wrecked SS *Central America* were displayed for the first time, and the public was able to purchase them at auction. Jay W. Johnson became the new Mint director, but he would hold the office for little more than a year before resigning. A Philadelphia Mint coin-press operator was convicted of stealing misstruck coins from the Mint and selling them to collectors; he was proved to have made almost $80,000 from his nefarious activities. The first bimetallic issue to emerge from the U.S. Mint, a gold-and-platinum $10 coin, marked the bicentennial of the Library of Congress; only 7,261 pieces were sold.

Inside the Red Book

The 54th edition was expanded by 16 pages, for a total page count of 352. Most of the added pages were dedicated to formatting changes. In the bullion section, for example, the previously six-page listing was now spread out to extend over an additional four, and the gold bullion listings had been rearranged to progress from lowest denomination to highest (the reverse of their former order). Other sections were also expanded to provide space for future issues. Four and a half pages were given to the state quarters section. Each of the 1999 state quarters was pictured, and all the quarters through the projected end of the program in 2008 were included in the listing. The new Sacagawea dollar made its first appearance in the Red Book, with a listing that included a color photograph and description of the design, along with a blank page for future updates.

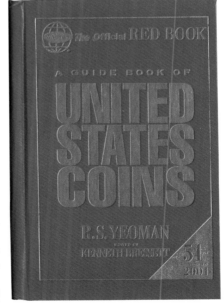

Values of the 54th Edition

Year/Edition	Issue Price	New
2001 (54th ed.), Hardcover	$13.95	$2
2001 (54th ed.), Spiralbound	9.95	2

Dollar Price Performance

Year	VF-20	MS-60	Proof-63
1895-P	—	—	$22,000
1903-O	$125	$200	Not applicable

Aside from these, there were no new varieties added, but the process of upgrading the book's photographs continued with the replacement of a number of black-and-white images with color ones. Additional photographs now appeared in the modern commemoratives section, illustrating for the first time the Franklin D. Roosevelt gold $5 coin and the Robert Kennedy half dollar. Elsewhere in the commemoratives listings, an image had actually been *removed*—the redundant image of the Alabama centennial half dollar obverse. Previously this listing was illustrated with two obverse images, intended to show the "2X2" and "No 2X2" varieties, but in the 1999 and 2000 editions the illustrations of both obverses were actually the same (2X2). The 2001 edition corrected the gaffe by illustrating only the 2X2 obverse.

The annual price adjustments reflect the pervasive impact that the state quarters program was having on the traditional Washington quarter with Eagle reverse: its value in Very Fine condition increased, and the lower-grade Uncirculated values increased as well, evidently affected by the sudden popularity of collecting high-grade coins.

The effect of the state quarters program was being felt throughout many other series as well. Even the Morgan dollars, particularly those in Uncirculated condition, were affected. The 1895-P Proof dollar remained stable, after the previous year's increase of 10 percent. However, the other Uncirculated dollars were awakening from their slumber. The price of the 1903-O changed for the first time since 1993 (when it had decreased in value). Its value in Uncirculated condition rose $40 to $200.

Spiralbound Edition

The cover for the spiralbound version of the 54th edition continued the style that had been established two editions before. The only evident change is in the color of the metal coil binding, which was now black. As noted regarding the previous edition, the cropped stock photos for the 54th-edition spiralbound issue may be deceiving, giving the impression that a soft-cover version was produced. In addition, auction or sale postings for these books often say "paper" or "soft cover," forgetting to mention that it is a spiralbound edition.

These are not scarce. If collectors take their time, a nice New copy can be easily obtained, and for little more than the price of a used one.

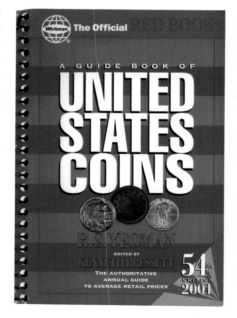

THE 55TH EDITION (2002)

The Year Was 2001, and . . .

The American Buffalo commemorative silver dollar was released to unprecedented demand. In spite of a mintage of half a million, the issue sold out—and continued to increase in value. President George W. Bush appointed Henrietta Holsman Fore 37th director of the Mint. In her confirmation testimony, she stated, "I will have a challenge to encourage and maintain the enthusiasm of the coin collecting community." This year saw the death of former chief engraver Frank Gasparro, whose designs included the Lincoln Memorial reverse on the cent. With literally billions of these coins having been produced, Gasparro once commented, "I've been called the world's richest artist."

Inside the Red Book

Few changes distinguished the 2002 edition from the previous year's—too few, indeed, for some readers. Although the mintage figures for the 2000 state quarters had been added, the illustrations in the state quarter listings had not been updated, in what a customer review at the online retailer Amazon.com called "a glaring omission." In fact, not until the 2004 edition would the illustrations of the state quarters include issues later than 1999. However, in other areas the Red Book continued to improve with age. The two-page section on California gold ingot bars had been almost entirely rewritten, and the old black-and-white images of select ingots had been replaced with a large color photograph of a selection of pieces recovered from the SS *Central America*. The process of replacing black-and-white images with color photographs continued, with new color images particularly prominent in the gold coin listings. Other varieties that had previously lacked illustrations now boasted photographs, such as the Open Wreath reverse variety of the 1849 gold dollar and the Jackie Robinson commemorative issues.

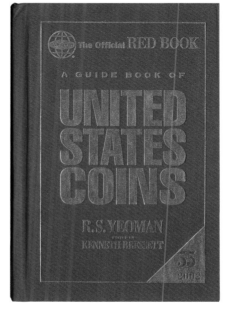

Values of the 55th Edition

Year/Edition	Issue Price	VF	New
2002 (55th ed.), Hardcover	$14.95		$2
2002 (55th ed.), Spiralbound	10.95		2
Special ANA cover	100.00	$82.50	130
SS *Central America* cover		35.00	40

Note: See chapter 5 for discussion of the ANA and SS *Central America* special editions.

Dollar Price Performance

Year	VF-20	MS-60	Proof-63
1895-P	—	—	$24,000
1903-O	$130	$235	Not applicable

There were no new additions to the variety listings in this year's edition, but the new *Guide Book* reflected increases in the values of many coins. The "*Guide Book* as a Collectible" section—one of the only sources of pricing information for these books—also included important information. Although the prices for regular editions remained steady, with little or no change, the special editions (1987 ANA, 1992 ANA, and 1997 50th Anniversary) were in high demand. According to this section, they all increased in value. Collecting the series was becoming increasingly popular.

The 2002 edition came in for comment in Mike Thorne's *COINage* essay "Coin Collecting in 1952: Those Were the Good Old Days!"—a look back at the changes in the hobby over the previous 50 years. Thorne observed,

> A collector in the 1950s would be amazed at what's between the covers of today's Red Book. For one thing, most of the coin photos are in color today, which adds a dimension to the presentation that just didn't exist a half century ago. Also, the 55th edition of the Red Book has at least twice the number of pages as the 5th edition [actually only 96 pages more], both because of all the coins that have been made in the last 50 years and because of the added information contained in the current edition.

The Morgan dollar series began to benefit from the collecting boom. The 1895-P Proof dollar saw another $2,000 boost in value. Although the value of the 1903-O in Very Fine condition increased by only $5, this increase was its first since 1993. In Uncirculated condition, 1903-O was listed for $235, an 18 percent growth in value.

Also released this year were two special-edition Red Books: the SS *Central America* edition and the ANA "Target 2001" fundraising edition. See chapter 5 for detailed discussion of these.

Spiralbound Edition

As in the previous three years, the Red Book was released in a spiralbound version. The cover showed very little change from its predecessor, aside from the rearrangement of the "Official Red Book" legend and Whitman logo to give them more prominence. The only other change is a gold burst bearing the message "New! Over 200 Full-Color Coin Photos." This edition is not particularly difficult to locate. Copies in New condition are still available at reasonable prices; just watch that shipping cost!

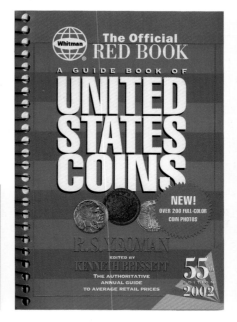

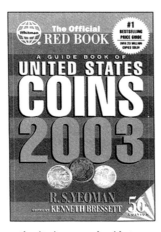
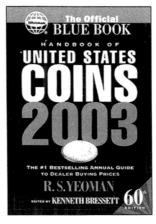
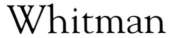
From the August 2002 *Numismatist*. The Red Book shares ad space with its sister publication, the Blue Book. After several changes of name and ownership, the publisher is now Whitman Publishing.

THE 56TH EDITION (2003)

The Year Was 2002, and . . .

The Capitol Visitor Center commemorative series was released. Due to lack of collector interest, the $5 gold commemorative had a distribution of only 6,761 in Uncirculated, one of the lowest for the modern commemorative program. Numismatic auction records worldwide were broken when a 1933 double eagle sold for over $7.5 million at a Stack's/Sotheby's auction. Privately struck fantasy state quarters began to appear, many boasting rude designs. The American Council of the Blind filed a lawsuit against the U.S. Treasury requiring that paper money incorporate features (such as Braille) to facilitate its use by those with impaired vision.

Inside the Red Book

A striking change in the design of the Red Book took place with this edition: the book's spine—not just its front cover—was emblazoned with the legend "The Official Red Book." Now the book's familiar name was visible even when it was tucked away on a shelf.

The discovery of the new "Wide AM" variety of the Lincoln cents of 1998, 1999, and 2000 had made news. (On these coins, the first two letters in "AMERICA" were spread apart; on the "Close AM" variety, these letters touched.) These were added to the *Guide Book*, both reflecting and increasing their acceptance as popular varieties. Prices rose accordingly. Other areas of the new edition's listings, however, had not been brought up to date as thoroughly. The listings for the state quarters still did not contain images of the post-1999 releases, an omission that baffled and irritated some readers. Likewise, illustrations of the modern commemorative coins still ceased with the 1998 Robert Kennedy dollar. The presence of blank pages at the end of these sections made the lack of up-to-date illustrations all the more puzzling.

A rising tide continued to lift all areas of the coin market. This even extended to the values for old editions of the *Guide Book*. All series' key-date values were increasing at a

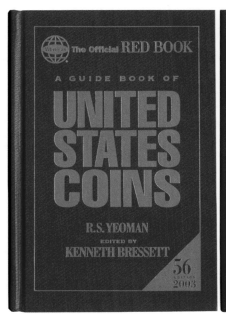

greater rate than they had experienced since the boom market of the late 1970s. The number of collectors is estimated to have increased by the millions, and they were actively exploring all areas of the coin market.

Values of the 56th Edition

Year/Edition	Issue Price	New
2003 (56th ed.), Hardcover	$15.95	$2
2003 (56th ed.), Spiralbound	11.95	2
2003 (56th ed.), Softcover	11.95	2

Dollar Price Performance

Year	VF-20	MS-60	Proof-63
1895-P	—	—	$24,000
1903-O	$140	$250	Not applicable

In the appendix on collecting Red Books, values showed increases that were equal to, if not better than, those shown by the key-date coins. New copies of the first printing of the first edition increased in value from the previous year's $500 to $750—a 50 percent increase. The special editions also increased respectively in price. The 1987 *Guide Book* commemorating the 95th anniversary of the American Numismatic Association rose from $135 to $200, a 48 percent increase—and still a good buy, if a copy could be found.

The Morgan dollars were finally back in the headlines. The 1895-P Proof dollar remained steady at $24,000, a very respectable value. The 1903-O in Uncirculated condition increased $50 to $250, for a 25 percent increase. There were additional modest increases for coins in lower grades.

Softcover and Spiralbound Editions

The 56th-edition Red Book was the first to be issued in both spiralbound and softcover versions. Except for the binding, there is no difference between the two, but both are an integral part of any complete *Guide Book* collection.

The cover design for both these formats had a distinct difference from its predecessors, as it began the trend of prominently featuring the edition's date. The words "United States" had been shrunken to give pride of place to the word "Coins" and the year, 2003, which two elements dominated the cover. Also new was the proclamation "#1 Bestselling Price Guide / Over 20 Million copies sold!" This was the first time since R.S. Yeoman's 1984-edition essay "The Red Book Story" that some idea of the book's printing quantity had been released. This averaged more than 350,000 copies sold per year over the 56-year history of the Red Book! Without exaggeration, this was a monumental feat and proves the enormous continuing popularity of the Red Book.

Both softcover and spiralbound formats were released with a cover price of $11.95. Today it appears, based upon Internet auction appearances, that the softcover is the scarcer of the two. Even so, it is apparent that both are available for the collector and may be obtained at a reasonable price.

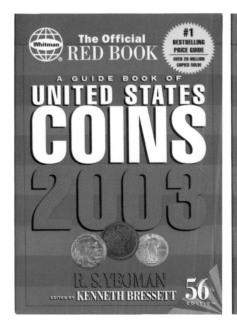

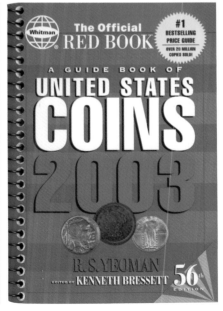

THE 57TH EDITION (2004)

The Year Was 2003, and . . .

The traditional design of the Jefferson nickel entered its final year before being replaced with commemorative designs. The American 5-cent Coin Design Continuity Act was passed in response to concern that the proposed new nickel designs would mean the permanent removal of Monticello from the coin's reverse. The act permitted the Mint to launch the commemorative Westward Journey Nickel Series™, which would commemorate the Louisiana Purchase and the Lewis and Clark Expedition, but mandated that Monticello return to the nickel starting in 2006. The act also established the Citizens Coinage Advisory Committee. The Artistic Infusion Program was launched to create a pool of artists outside the Mint who could provide new coin designs for particular projects. The city of San Francisco gave the historic mint building called the "Granite Lady" to the San Francisco Museum and Historical Society, which made plans to open it to the public in 2012 as a museum and visitors' center.

Inside the Red Book

For the 57th edition, the Red Book team revamped content, primarily in the state quarters section, which had finally been brought up to date. Now the listings included photographs of the reverse for each state's coin through the 2002 releases. Similarly, the illustrations in the commemorative section had been updated with a plethora of new photographs. There was also a new section, "United States Pattern Pieces," which replaced the section on Hard Times tokens. The new content consisted of an excellent essay on pattern pieces—that is, test pieces made by the Mint not for circulation but to try out new coin possibilities—as well as illustrations and prices for some of the popular patterns. Some readers were startled by the introduction of small advertisements for Whitman products scattered throughout the book, helping to fill up formerly blank spaces of a half or quarter page.

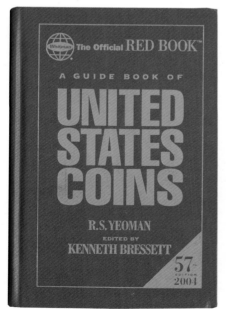

Values of the 57th Edition

Year/Edition	Issue Price	New
2004 (57th ed.), Hardcover	$15.95	
2004 (57th ed.), Spiralbound	12.95	
2004 (57th ed.), Softcover	11.95	

Dollar Price Performance

Year	VF-20	MS-60	Proof-63
1895-P	—	—	$25,000
1903-O	$175	$325	Not applicable

The coin market of 2003 to 2004 was extremely active. Values for many key dates were quickly increasing, as collectors were ready, willing, and able to spend large sums of cash for desirable coins. The available supply of these key dates was drying up, and obtaining good-quality, original pieces at any reasonable price became difficult. Dealers demanded prices that reflected anticipated price increases, forcing costs even higher.

The contributors concentrated on keeping values current with the market, and the addition of new varieties was placed on the back burner. The key-date Washington quarters, the 1932-D and 1932-S, increased another 25 percent in value. They were each worth $75. One had only to look back as far as 1998 to see a time when every dealer had multiple pieces in stock and couldn't give them away! The state quarters were having an immense effect on the market.

The Morgan dollars were in full swing. Prices showed impressive gains in all areas. The 1895-P Proof grew $1,000 in value. The 1903-O showed increases in all grades: Very Fine condition increased 25 percent and Uncirculated pieces increased 50 percent. This was the highest value in Uncirculated condition since the release of the Treasury hoard in the 1960s.

Softcover and Spiralbound Editions

Once again, the Red Book was produced in both softcover and spiralbound editions. The blazing notation "Over 20 Million copies Sold!" was continued on the cover. There is one notable change to the cover design: the Standing Liberty quarter design was replaced by a Delaware state quarter.

For the first time, however, collectors had to consider a price difference when choosing between the softcover and the spiralbound edition, which now cost $1 more than its counterpart. For collectors there was no doubt that the spiral format was well worth the additional cost, since it could be kept in a nicer condition throughout its use. Today both formats of this edition are readily available, and neither should be priced at a premium.

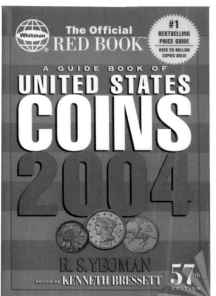
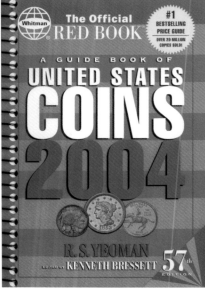

THE 58TH EDITION (2005)

The Year Was 2004, and . . .

The Westward Journey Nickel Series began with the release of two commemorative reverse designs for the Jefferson nickel. At the Smithsonian Institution, the "History of Money and Medals" exhibition closed after 40 years on display.

Inside the Red Book

The vast array of changes to the 58th edition shows that Kenneth Bressett and the *Guide Book* staff continued to work to improve the reference and keep it fresh. "Special consultants" were now credited on the contributor page: Q. David Bowers, Jeff Garrett, Philip Bressett, Tom Hallenbeck, and Robert Rhue. A whopping 32 additional pages had been added, bringing the total to 384. Despite this expansion, the book was actually thinner than the previous 352-page edition, thanks to thinner paper.

Cosmetic alterations included the replacement on the spine of the small title type with a significantly larger one. Between the covers, a new typeface gave an airier appearance to the text; in charts and grading guides, the old serifed typeface had been replaced with a sleeker sans serif font. The substitution made one online reviewer grouse, "It's a smaller and thinner typeface. . . . I think I'll take out my loupe just to look up a coin!" Future editions would continue to experiment with different fonts, type sizes, and layouts in the ongoing struggle to balance legibility with space constraints—a juggling act made more difficult as new coin series and commemorative issues swelled the listings.

Moving on to the content itself, four new sections made their debut: "Coins From Treasures and Hoards," by Q. David Bowers; "Great Collectors and Collections of the Past," by Ron Guth and Jeff Garrett; a glossary of numismatic terms; and "Top 250 Coin Prices Realized (from auctions since 1994)." The "Treasures and Hoards" appendix would be relocated in future editions to the front of the book. The "Great Collectors" section was short-lived, however, vanishing after the 2007 Red Book. The other two new elements, the glossary and auction record list, would continue to appear in future editions, with updates as necessary.

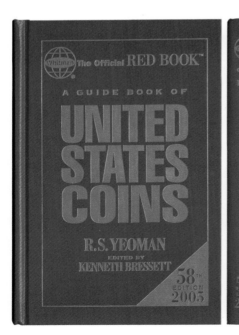

Values of the 58th Edition

Year/Edition	Issue Price	New
2005 (58th ed.), Hardcover	$15.95	
2005 (58th ed.), Spiralbound	12.95	
2005 (58th ed.), Softcover	11.95	
Leather Limited Edition	69.95	$90
FUN special edition		120

Note: See chapter 5 for discussion of the leather Limited Edition and FUN special edition.

Dollar Price Performance

Year	VF-20	MS-60	Proof-63
1895-P	—	—	$35,000
1903-O	$200	$425	Not applicable

Further changes were noted by online reviewer Jan Nedelka, who enthused:

> The introduction has been improved with a summary of abbreviations used throughout the book. An additional column of grades has been added to the early coinage, which is nice. . . . The hard times tokens are back, and . . . a few new notes from Q. David Bowers really enhance the sense of what numismatics is about. . . . Overall, this is an excellent edition. Meaningful additions were made and existing materials enhanced.[24]

In the "*Guide Book* as a Collectible" section, values for all early and special-edition Red Books showed considerable increases. The section included three typos. First, prices for the 1992 ANA special edition shifted to the left, and no price was given for the book in new condition. Next, the 1995 softbound edition was valued at $800 in both Very Good and Fine conditions, but at $3 in new condition. Finally, the values for the SS *Central America* edition were also shifted one column to the left.

Let's turn to the Morgan dollars. The 1895-P Proof grew by $10,000—an increase of 40 percent! The 1903-O rose from $175 to $200 in Very Fine condition and from $325 to $425 in Uncirculated (increases of 14 percent and 31 percent, respectively).

A new innovation was introduced for the 2005 Red Book: the leather-bound Limited Edition. Also released was a special edition honoring Florida United Numismatists, Inc. (FUN). See chapter 5 for a full discussion of Limited Editions and special editions.

Softcover and Spiralbound Editions

Both a softcover and a spiralbound version were issued again this year. The cover again featured the Delaware state quarter, this time moved to the center and flanked by the Lincoln cent and the Peace Medal reverse from the Westward Journey nickel series. Copies are readily available; however, perhaps because the books are more contemporary (and their value listings thus more timely), prices tend to be much higher than for earlier editions. Some patience may be necessary for a more reasonable price.

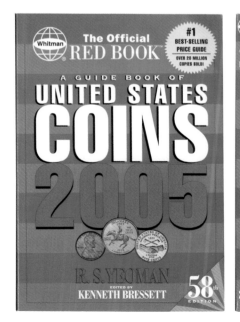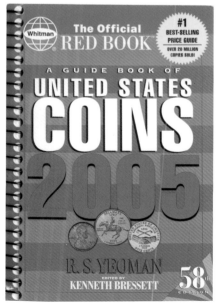

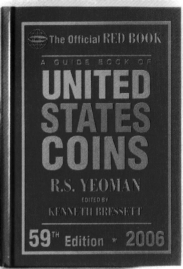
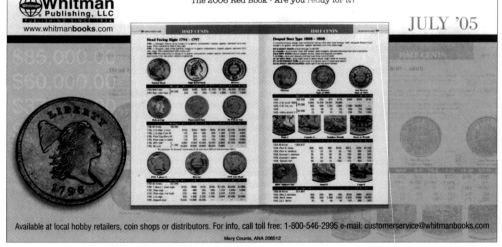
From the June 2005 *Numismatist*. This bold advertisement heralds the dramatic overhaul—or "red"esign—that took place with the 59th edition.

The 59th Edition (2006)

The Year Was 2005, and . . .

A redesigned portrait of Thomas Jefferson made its appearance on the nickel obverse. The two commemorative reverses in the Westward Journey Nickel Series featured an American bison and an ocean view inspired by William Clark's journal entry of November 7, 1805. Starting in this year, Uncirculated Mint sets were made with a satin finish that differed from the finish on standard Uncirculated coins.

Inside the Red Book

Although the 2005 *Guide Book* had contained some wonderful additions and changes, the 2006 edition seemed determined to outshine it. In late March and early April 2005, editor Kenneth Bressett, along with Whitman's new publisher Dennis Tucker, editorial director Diana Plattner, and Q. David Bowers, mapped a redesign of the Red Book's information architecture in a sweeping 12-page plan. Most of the changes were subtle; some were dramatic. All were designed to improve the reader's experience, making the book easier to use and more visually attractive.

With an additional 32 pages (which brought the page count to 416), the 59th edition exceeded 400 pages for the first time. The most readily obvious changes to the edition were in the layout and design. The bold new header bars and column shading in the value tables made these easier to use and provided strong visual separation between issues. The newly designed pages included the innovative addition of color-coded borders at the top of each page. Each section of the book was designated a different color, making it faster and easier for the reader to browse through and locate the different denominations. The new heading "Welcome to Numismatics" now introduced the overview text, as well as sections that had been moved from other areas of the book. These included the brief feature on the Spanish milled dollar, which had appeared close to the front of the book ever

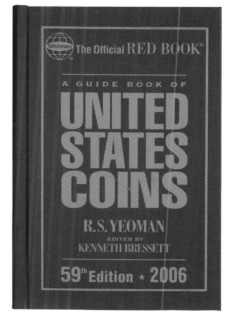

Values of the 59th Edition

Year/Edition	Issue Price	New
2006 (59th ed.), Hardcover	$16.95	
2006 (59th ed.), Spiralbound	14.95	
2006 (59th ed.), Softcover	12.95	
Leather Limited Edition	69.95	$80

Note: See chapter 5 for discussion of the leather Limited Edition.

Dollar Price Performance

Year	VF-20	MS-60	Proof-63
1895-P	—	—	$44,000
1903-O	$300	$425	Not applicable

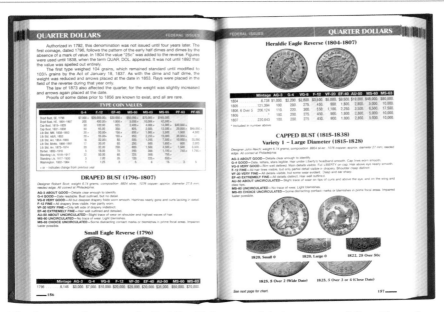

The dramatic changes to the Red Book's layout and design are especially evident when the quarter dollar listings are compared to those illustrated from previous editions.

since the first edition, and "Coins From Treasures and Hoards: A Key to Understanding Rarity & Value," by Q. David Bowers. The latter section had been updated with the latest news on the SS *Republic*. The section on pre-federal releases had been rearranged: before, all of the front-of-the-book material (from Sommers Islands "Hogge" money to post-Revolution Washington tokens and 1792 patterns) was grouped into 10 separate categories ("The British Colonies in America" to "First United States Mint Issues"). In the 2006 Red Book, these coins and tokens were arranged into a single pre-federal section, divided into colonial and post-colonial subsections. Continental currency, Nova Constellatio patterns, Fugio cents, and 1792 proposed coinage were grouped under their own heading of "Contract Issues and Patterns."

The typeface of the text portions was changed to a new sans serif font, giving the book a more streamlined, modern appearance. A particularly welcome addition to the book's organization was the table of contents; this seemingly basic component had not appeared in any previous Red Book! Among the list of "special consultants," Mary Sauvain appears on the list for the first time. Also for the first time, Q. David Bowers and Jeff Garrett were identified by their special roles as editorial assistants to Kenneth Bressett: Bowers as research editor, and Garrett as valuations editor.

As far as the new edition's contents, one new section was a consolidated bibliography, which brought together in one place the listings that had previously been divided across the different type categories. Nearly every coin was illustrated with a clear color photo, including some wonderfully toned coins like the Liberty Seated and Barber quarters. Also, the state quarters section was completely redesigned and included photographs that were greatly improved; the newest issues in both this series and the Westward Journey nickels had been added. A new footnote in the Indian Head cent section acknowledged the "bold N" and "shallow N" varieties. The commemorative section, which had been arranged alphabetically ever since the 16th edition, had been revamped to list the issues in chronological order. As the Whitman press release explained, "Back in 1946, when the first edition . . . was published, the series was small. Now it includes hundreds of different types and varieties, growing by the year. Recognizing this, we have rearranged the Red Book's listings from alphabetical to chronological." The rearrangement also eliminated the division between silver and gold issues in the classic commemorative period, a change that must have gladdened the heart of Daniel Byrns (see his criticism of the Red Book in chapter 2). An "Alphabetical Reference to Dates" helped readers look up their coins by either system. Within the reorganized listings was a further tweak that even the sharpest-eyed of readers might have missed: in the description of the 1935 Hudson, New York, Sesquicentennial half dollar, the name of the explorer who was the river's namesake was now given as Henry Hudson—the spelling historical documents show that he preferred—rather than Hendrik Hudson.

The fully developed statehood-quarters program had awakened the collecting public, and millions of new collectors joined the hunt for better coins. Perhaps as a consequence, the Morgan dollars were blazing new territory in value. The series was described in a survey as the most collected series of U.S. coins, and the values suggested the same. With an increase of $9,000 (26 percent) to $44,000, the 1895-P Proof dollar was without comparison, and demand for the legendary coin was undiminished despite the high cost. The 1903-O, with an increase of $100 in Very Fine condition, also demanded attention. The price of the Uncirculated piece held steady at $425.

It should be noted that for this edition, the title of the appendix on collecting Red Books changed from "The *Guide Book* as a Collectible" to "The Red Book as a Collectible." Like the addition of the logo "The Official Red Book" to the cover of the 1999 edition, the change showed that Whitman was embracing the long-used nickname.

Readers welcomed the renovated 59th edition with enthusiasm. "This is the best edition yet," states one online review posted at Amazon.com. "The editors of the Red Book hit the ball out of the park with this edition," marvels another. A reviewer writing under the moniker "Avid Reader" asserts, "Like a fine wine, it [the Red Book] continues to improve with age," and explains why the decades-old reference continues to be relevant:

> There are many books that list coin prices. There are numerous web sites that also list prices—some, such as PCGS, update them on a weekly basis. There are still more magazines, books and websites that deal with the history and minutiae of coins but there is no single repository of knowledge containing all three like this tremendous book. . . .
>
> This year, the photography has improved greatly (it was already spectacular). The whole book was updated as it is every year and this is perhaps its greatest strength: It is necessarily a work in progress, noting new errors, old finds, historical discoveries, trends, etc.[25]

Similarly, a lengthy review by Mike Thorne in *Coins* magazine observes that "the Red Book has come a long way," and enthuses over the improvements to the new edition. In addition to approving of the new placement of the sections on modern proof sets and bullion coins, Thorne writes that "the new layout of [coin] values looks nicer than in previous years," and the new tinting of the grade columns made it "easier to spot" specific columns. He closes his remarks with a powerful endorsement of the book's value:

> Is the new Red Book worth a couple of bucks more than last year's? You bet it is. I know this venerable value guide has lots of competition, because I've favorably

reviewed some of its competitors. . . . I would have to say that competition has been beneficial to this year's Red Book, as it's in many ways superior to its predecessor.[26]

The entire market was on fire. Collectors placed unprecedented demands on the limited supply of coins and coin-related memorabilia, like the *Guide Book*. The 59th edition, in fact, sold out in February—earlier than usual, according to Whitman Publishing's president, Mary Counts. There were considerable increases in prices, particularly for early Red Books and special editions. Books signed by R.S. Yeoman or Ken Bressett sold for two to three times what they had sold for just one year previous. Many books sold for even more than their listed value. The 1987 ANA special edition, for example, was listed for $500 in new condition. Yet a copy on the auction block would likely sell for more than $1,000, especially since a like copy had not appeared in more than a year. A signed copy would probably fetch nearly double that amount.

Softcover and Spiralbound Editions

The 59th edition's softcover and spiralbound formats presented another change to the cover design. From left to right, the coins depicted were the 2005 American Bison nickel, a Walking Liberty half dollar, and an Indian Head cent. Another notable change was to the publication notation, which now read, "Over 21 Million copies sold!" The design of the title was also tweaked to reduce the size difference between "United States" and "Coins"; both of these elements now retreated out of the way of the giant date of the edition. The spine of the softcover format also featured the addition of a gold band at the bottom.

Copies of both formats in this edition are readily available; and once again, the prices are higher than for their older, scarcer counterparts. Don't settle for a used copy; New examples are readily available for a modest premium.

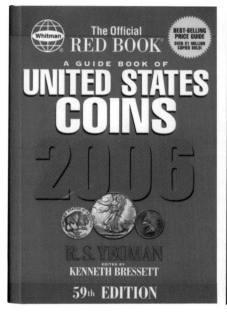

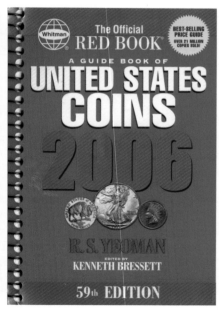

THE 60TH EDITION (2007)

The Year Was 2006, and . . .

American Buffalo gold bullion pieces became an instant hit. Bearing the design of James Earl Fraser's famous Buffalo nickel, they carried a face value of $50 and were the first 24-karat gold issue of the Mint. The Jefferson nickel featured another redesigned portrait, marking the first time that a president was shown in a forward-facing view on a U.S. circulating coin. Two different commemorative silver dollars were released in honor of Benjamin Franklin, and the historic San Francisco mint building, the "Granite Lady," was featured on a commemorative silver dollar and gold half eagle. Representative Jim Kolbe brought a bill before Congress that sought to abolish the cent, whose production cost now exceeded its face value. Edmund C. Moy was sworn in as the 38th director of the U.S. Mint.

Inside the Red Book

It was to great anticipation that the 60th edition of the *Guide Book* was released in early 2006. As part of the 60th anniversary celebration, the new Red Book's release date was pushed up to coincide with the American Numismatic Association's National Money Show in April. For 2006, this annual event took place in Atlanta—the perfect place for Whitman Publishing, based in Atlanta since 2003, to unveil the new edition of its cornerstone publication.

As part of the anniversary celebration, Whitman created two free offers for Red Book buyers. Each book contained a special mail-in page between pages 384 and 385. There were two versions: one offered a Lewis and Clark Westward Journey nickel set in a plastic case, and the other offered a Westward Journey nickel folder. Both premiums were valued at five dollars. All readers had to do was remove the postage-paid card from the book and mail it in by April 9, 2007. (Of course, this was not easy for most purists, who

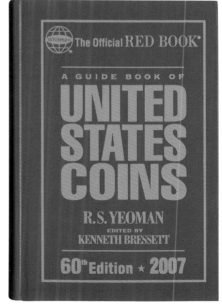

Values of the 60th Edition

Year/Edition	Issue Price	New
2007 (60th ed.), Hardcover	$16.95	
2007 (60th ed.), Spiralbound	14.95	
2007 (60th ed.), Softcover	12.95	
Leather Limited Edition	69.95	$75
Special ANA cover		100
Michigan special edition		100
1947 Tribute Edition, Hardcover	17.95	18
1947 Tribute Edition, Leather Limited Edition	49.95	110

Note: See chapter 5 for discussion of the Limited Editions and special editions.

Dollar Price Performance

Year	VF-20	MS-60	Proof-63
1895-P	—	—	$47,500
1903-O	$340	$475	Not applicable

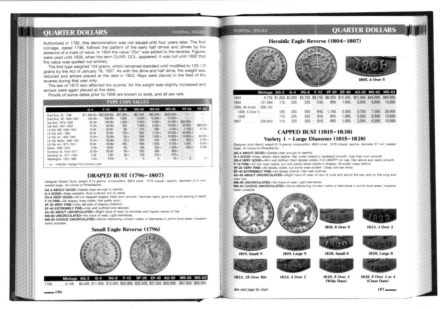

The layout of the 60th edition is much like that of the previous one, but more micropho-tographs have been added, as have higher-quality images of the 1796 quarter dollar.

are loath to remove pages from their perfect set of books.) To further mark the momen-tous anniversary, Whitman released a special replica of the first-edition Red Book. Chapter 5 discusses this Tribute Edition in detail.

Among significant changes to the book itself, the Civil War tokens listings had been expanded to three times their former size, reflecting the growing popularity of these pieces. The Extra Leaf High and Extra Leaf Low varieties of the 2004-D Wisconsin state quarter were featured for the first time, with descriptions and photographs.

The coin market continued to exceed expectations as values again increased. There was unprecedented demand for all nice original coins. The Morgan dollars were no exception. The 1895-P Proof increased in value another $3,500 (8 percent), to a price that was still considered an excellent value. (However, as one might expect, this coin became increasingly hard to find.) The 1903-O increased 13 percent and 12 percent in Very Fine and Uncirculated conditions, respectively.

In the appendix on collectible Red Books, the values given were conservative. For example, the 1987 ANA special edition was priced at $750, while a copy would most likely sell for at least $1,000 at auction. There was a very strong demand for signed copies of this book, and the sale of one would probably surpass even the value of a Very Fine first-edition, first-printing *Guide Book*. Similarly, a Very Fine copy of the second edition was listed at $250, while the fifth edition was valued at $350. Both these books would probably sell for significantly more money. The values of other books seem more on target: the 1991 ANA special edition, for example, was listed at $250, and sales hov-ered right around that value.

Readers greeted the 60th anniversary edition with warm praise. "I have had earlier editions of this book," wrote one Amazon.com reviewer, "[but] this latest edition is greatly improved with better pictures and expanded coverage." The California Book-watch offered a succinct but firmly positive review, asserting that the new edition "assures the classic coin collector's reference remains a hit. . . . Over 700 new color photos and updated mintages and values based on auction records keep the reference alive and well—and more useful than weightier titles meant as desk references alone."

The 60th anniversary *Guide Book* was also released in numerous special editions and Limited Editions. See chapter 5 for details on these issues.

Softcover and Spiralbound Editions

For the 60th edition, the cover was updated once again for the softcover and spiralbound issues. The 2006 Jefferson nickel with redesigned obverse was displayed to the left; in the center was Augustus Saint-Gaudens's gold $10 coin; and on the right was the Winged Liberty or "Mercury" dime. This would prove to be the last year that a softcover edition of the Red Book was released, but Whitman Publishing would continue to introduce alternate formats of the Red Book, starting with the covered coil binding (see the following entries).

As recent as the 2007 edition is, there is no question that it is readily available; however, most sellers are still demanding a higher price for their inventory. There is no reason to settle for a used copy, since ones in New condition are easily obtained.

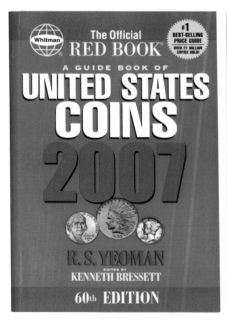
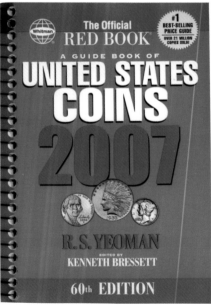

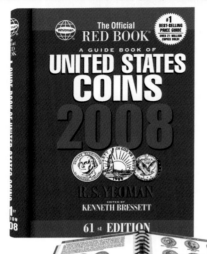
From the Whitman archives. The new Red Book format with covered coil binding takes center stage in this ad for the 61st edition.

THE 61ST EDITION (2008)

The Year Was 2007, and . . .

The first issue in the presidential dollar program, the George Washington dollar, was released on February 15 to coincide with Presidents' Day. Later this year, Martha Washington appeared on the premier coin of the First Spouse bullion series. Commemorative coins honored the 50th anniversary of the historic desegregation of Little Rock Central High School and the 400th anniversary of the founding of Jamestown.

Inside the Red Book

The 2008 *Guide Book* was released amid great fanfare. Numerous changes were evident in this edition, starting with the many new coins that had been released during the previous year. The 2007 state quarters, as well as the new commemorative coins, were given listings and photos.

Several sections were expanded: regular issues were given four more pages; bullion was given three more pages; and the commemorative section grew one more page. A new feature on the Libertas Americana medal was added, as well as new grade listings in the colonial and pre-federal section. One of the most dramatic changes was updated mintage figures from two sources: in the Lincoln cents section, new research by noted numismatist Roger Burdette led to revised mintages, and the commemorative section contained newly updated data from the U.S. Mint, which in some cases revised mintages from many years before. The small cents section now contained individual value listings for the Indian Head cents in Bold N and Shallow N varieties.

The 61st edition also contained a listing that has come to be considered an error, although it merely reflected the information available at the time of the book's preparation. At the time of the 2008 edition's writing in 2007, there was talk of Congress requesting that the new presidential dollars be released in silver as well as in their circulation composition. It appeared that this proposal was going to be approved, so the 2008 listings included silver Proof presidential dollars. Subsequently, however, silver coinage legislation

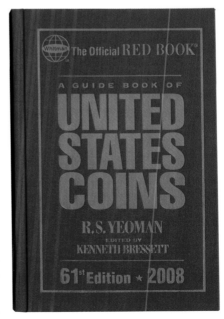

Values of the 61st Edition

Year/Edition	Issue Price	New
2008 (61st ed.), Hardcover	$16.95	
2008 (61st ed.), Spiralbound	14.95	
2008 (61st ed.), Spiralbound Hardcover	19.95	
Leather Limited Edition	69.95	$70
Leather Limited Edition, NLG		800
Special ANA edition		40
Stack's Rare Coins edition		30

Dollar Price Performance

Year	VF-20	MS-63	Proof-63
1895-P	—	—	$55,000
1903-O	$360	$550	Not applicable

was not formally proposed and the coins were never minted. All issues of the 2008 edition included this listing.

Although the coin market was still strong, the great price increases of recent years had calmed. Nevertheless, our look at the values of the Morgan dollars shows that the 1895-P, never one to disappoint, increased by $7,500 (an increase of nearly 16 percent). The 1903-O also showed some growth, increasing by $20 in Very Fine condition and $75 in Uncirculated condition.

Included with this edition was another mail-in card with the offer of a free Whitman product. This year there were three possible offers: a presidential dollar coin and case; a presidential dollars folder; and a copy of *The Expert's Guide to Collecting and Investing in Rare Coins* by Q. David Bowers—a particularly fine giveaway, since its retail price was higher than the cover price of the Red Book itself.

Spiralbound Editions

In a very nice innovation, the softcover edition was discontinued this year and replaced with a hardcover spiralbound edition, on which the coil binding was hidden. Although it was priced slightly higher than the regular spiralbound and hardcover editions, the new format was a terrific addition to the collection. This version gave the ease of use of a spiral edition with the look and feel of a hardcover. The innovative cover also made it possible to identify the book when it was on the shelf, unlike the standard spiralbound.

This year the book's designers updated the cover of the spiralbound editions to display the first presidential dollar, the newly released Washington dollar. It appears on the right, accompanied by the 1986 Statue of Liberty commemorative half dollar, in the center, and the reverse of the Standing Liberty quarter on the left.

The free offers that were included in the regular edition of the *Guide Book* were also available in the spiralbound format, which meant that collectors who did not wish to remove the page from their hardcover copy had a less expensive way to get the free offer than by purchasing a duplicate.

Copies are readily available and easily found.

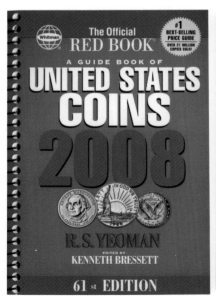
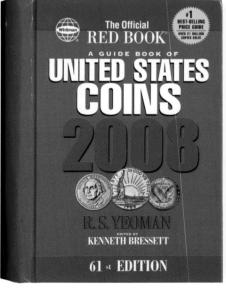

From the Whitman archives. Now four different versions of the "one-volume library" of U.S. coins are featured.

THE 62ND EDITION (2009)

The Year Was 2008, and . . .

The 50 State Quarters® Program ended, and a new program authorized the release of quarters honoring the District of Columbia and the five U.S. territories: the Commonwealth of Puerto Rico, Guam, American Samoa, the U.S. Virgin Islands, and the Commonwealth of the Northern Mariana Islands.

Inside the Red Book

The 2009 *Guide Book* was released in April 2008. I was present when boxes of the new books were opened at a local coin show, and at one point, there was actually a line of people waiting to purchase a copy. Some, like myself, waited to buy both a hardcover and a spiral edition.

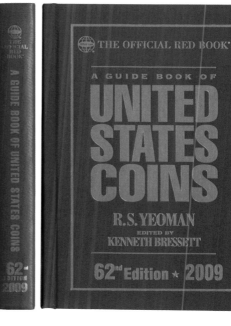

Dollar Price Performance

Year	VF-20	MS-63	Proof-63
1895-P	—	—	$52,500
1903-O	$360	$550	Not applicable

Changes were numerous in this edition, which had grown another 16 pages (to 432). Kenneth Bressett said in the press release, "a number of new features have been added to expand the book's usefulness as a reference to mainstream U.S. numismatic prices." These new features included a three-page illustrated appendix on American Arts medals; a section on Puerto Rican coins (which had not appeared in the Red Book since the 25th edition); expanded information on Hawaiian plantation tokens, Special Mint Sets, and rare pattern coins; and descriptions of planned future issues, such as the 2009 Lincoln cent redesign and upcoming Native American dollars. The quarter listings contained updates for state quarters and noted the passage of legislation to release quarters for Washington, D.C., and U.S. territories. Also included were value listings for the Wisconsin 2004-D Extra Leaf High and Extra Leaf Low varieties. Coverage of pre-federal and colonial coins was expanded, and the auction record appendix was updated to reflect sales through the March 2008 Baltimore Coin and Currency Convention. Valuations editor Jeff Garrett also pointed out that the new edition had "many improved color photographs that should please beginners as well as advanced collectors."

Personally, when a new edition of the *Guide Book* comes out I instantly flip to the appendix to check the new prices on past Red Books. This year saw a change in the section on Red Books as collectibles: for the first time, values were given for some early editions of the Blue Book as well. The values for some of the listed editions seemed to be quite low—many Blue Book collectors would be happy to find the listed prices. The seventh edition in New, for example, is listed for $20; however, many copies have sold in New condition for multiples of that price. Future editions will endeavor to provide a more complete listing, including valuations for the variants mentioned in the narrative, such as the fourth-edition overprint. (See the appendix for more discussion of collectible Blue Books.)

A free offer also came with this edition: a Whitman coin folder for the complete state quarter set, including the newly authorized releases for the District of Columbia and the U.S. territories.

Spiralbound Editions

The 2009 spiralbound edition was issued in two versions: the traditional open coil binding, and the covered coil binding that had been introduced the previous year. The publisher made only small changes to the overall cover design, moving the logo "The Official Red Book" into the top border and rendering it in all capital letters to formalize the registration. The three cover coin images were also replaced. On the left was an 1803 large cent; a 1921 Peace dollar was in the center; and the Heraldic Eagle reverse of the $10 gold coin (1797 to 1804) was on the right.

Once again the free-offer card was available in the spiralbound editions as well as the standard hardcover.

Journal Edition

Whitman Publishing introduced a new format for the 2009 Red Book: the Journal Edition. Designed as an interactive, truly hands-on reference, this book came in a three-ring binder to allow buyers to add, remove, or rearrange pages. Color-coded tabbed dividers separated the main sections of the book, allowing for quick reference, and blank pages were added at the end of the sections for the reader's notes. The cover design closely resembled that year's spiralbound hardcover edition, with a few exceptions: the Journal Edition added gold foil stamping to the cover date and spine, the identifying phrase "Journal Edition" under the cover date, and a gold foil burst emblem on the front that proclaimed, "New / with extra pages for your notes!" Measuring 8 inches by 10-3/4 inches, it was the largest-format *Guide Book* yet produced. The Journal Edition was released at an issue price of $29.95.

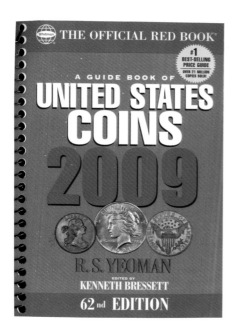
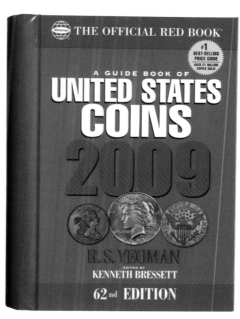
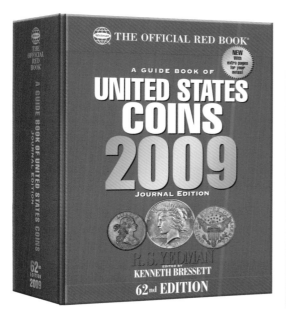
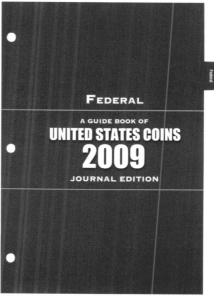

5

RED BOOK
SPECIAL EDITIONS AND
LIMITED EDITIONS

Several different varieties of the *Guide Book* have been released. These varieties are known as special editions, Limited Editions, and authorized editions. In the years when one of these versions was published, the regular Red Book was published as well. As a result, collectors can choose among several different sets of collections. You can decide, for example, to collect regular editions from every year without having to buy any of the other *Guide Book* varieties. Personally, I find these varieties just as intriguing.

The first special-edition *Guide Book* was a 40th edition (1987) published in 1986. From that point forward, one would be printed every few years. The books designated special editions have had their covers, as originally printed and bound, specially prepared and designed for a particular event. The interiors of these books are identical to those of the regular editions, except where noted.

Another variation of the Red Book is the leather edition, introduced in 2005. Called Limited Editions, these books are larger than the standard dimensions, with leather covers, hubbed spine, silk ribbon page markers, and gilt edges. There have also been a number of authorized editions released. Authorized editions will be discussed in chapter 6, while the special editions and Limited Editions will be explored within this chapter. All three varieties are now collected as separate sets.

SPECIAL EDITIONS

If you don't want to take on the challenge of collecting a set of regular-edition Red Books, you may want to consider completing a set of special editions. It is still a great and challenging collection, because some are difficult to find, particularly in Very Fine or New condition. The cover dates of these editions, followed by the occasions for which they were produced, are as follows:

1987: 90th anniversary of the ANA

1992: 100th anniversary of the ANA

1997: 50th anniversary of the Red Book

2002: ANA "Target 2001" building campaign

2002: SS *Central America* recovery

2005: 50th anniversary of FUN

2007: 115th anniversary of the ANA

2007: 50th anniversary of the Michigan State Numismatic Society

2007: 1947 Tribute Edition for Red Book 60th anniversary

2008: ANA World's Fair of Money

2008: Stack's Rare Coins

In addition to those listed here, three leather Limited Editions were released as special editions:

> 2007: 1947 Tribute Edition, leather Limited Edition
>
> 2008: Numismatic Literary Guild leather Limited Edition
>
> 2008: ANS Limited Edition

These are included in the category of Limited Editions.

The 1995 *Guide Book* introduced a pricing guide for past Red Book editions, and this section has been continued through the present. In these listings, special editions are included with the regular editions. Not surprisingly, the value of these books has followed the coin market in general. In this chapter we will provide charts showing the performance of special editions as reported over the years in the Red Book. These show that the greatest price increases have been in recent years, when the coin market has experienced its greatest growth. The values listed for new books are shown in the 2009 *Guide Book*, in the section entitled "Collectible Red and Blue Books." The values for signed Red Books are estimated, because the *Guide Book* does not include listings for signed copies.

The recent increases in price directly correlate with the explosion in coin prices that occurred after the 1999 introduction of the state quarters. As often happens with hobbies, people became interested in one aspect of the pastime and gradually migrated to its other areas. It is a natural progression to move from the state quarters to earlier Washington quarters to other segments of the hobby, including early coin books.

1987: ANA 95th Anniversary Edition

The first special-edition Red Book was produced in 1987 to celebrate the 95th anniversary of the ANA. For the ANA special edition, the 40th anniversary design that appeared on that year's regular edition was replaced with a different emblem. It bore the legend "95th Anniversary Convention Milwaukee 1986" and showed the names and likenesses

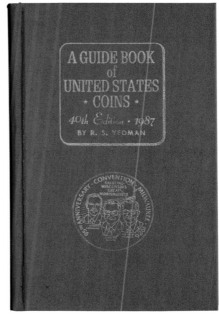

Pricing History of the 1987 ANA Special Edition

Red Book Edition	Value, New	Value, Signed
1995–2001	$100	
2002	130	
2003	200	
2004	275	
2005	275	
2006	500	
2007	750	Yeoman: $1,000 Bressett: $950
2008	775	Yeoman: $1,000+ Bressett: $950+
2009	1,000	Yeoman: $1,500 Yeoman, Krause, and Bressett: $2,500 to $3,500

of Henry O. Granberg, Chester Krause, and R.S. Yeoman above the legend "Saluting Wisconsin's Great Numismatists." The special edition, unlike the regular one, did not include the cover sticker with the silver-round offer.

The book had an estimated printing of 500 copies and was given as a dinner favor to those who attended the banquet at the 1986 ANA convention in Milwaukee, Wisconsin. Those present were the only recipients of the book. This special edition is highly desirable. It is one of the most coveted editions, and some collectors consider it even more desirable and difficult to locate than a first-edition Red Book (of either printing). It is usually found in excellent condition because most of the recipients took very good care of their copies. Still, some recipients simply used it as a reference, and there are copies that show considerable wear.

We can hypothesize explanations for the continued scarcity of this issue. Recipients may want to keep their copies, or they may have forgotten that they own them, so that their copies are sitting on shelves gathering dust. It is also possible that owners have seen the rapid price increase in recent years and are waiting to see how high the value will go.

A medal replicating the Red Book's special cover emblem was also created for the ANA's 95th anniversary. Collectors can add interest to a display of their 1987 ANA edition with thematically related items like this one. (Actual size 31.5 mm)

Regardless of the reason, there is not much auction history available for this book. Only one copy has been sold on eBay during the past few years. This copy, in good condition and without the signature of the editor, sold in March 2005 for $540. However, eBay may not be the best venue for selling this very scarce edition. While eBay sellers may realize high prices for some copies of the *Guide Book*, the truly scarce copies are unable to realize their full potential through this venue. Further pricing information is scarce since there are few auction records for this particular issue, but in 2005 numismatic book dealer Fred Lake reported that some copies had sold for as much as $1,000.[27] Thus, it seems likely that the book could exceed prices of $500 in Very Fine and $1,000 in New.

This edition is usually found without R.S. Yeoman's signature. It is estimated that no more than a dozen (and quite possibly fewer) were signed by Yeoman, and these are highly sought after—especially if also signed by Chester Krause. (Henry Granberg, the third member of the honored trio, was deceased.) An edition with R.S. Yeoman's signature, for example, would probably have an asking price of between $1,500 and $2,000—or possibly more—and would sell very quickly. Naturally, copies with signatures in addition to Yeoman's and Krause's, such as that of Ken Bressett or other contributors, would realize even more than that. Good luck in your search.

1992: ANA 100th Anniversary Edition

The second special edition again honored the ANA. This time, the book celebrated the association's 100th anniversary. The year's regular edition displayed a central device that showed a Barber Liberty head (as used on the silver coinage of the dime, quarter, and half dollar, from 1892 to 1916). For the special edition, the Barber coin design was removed and replaced with a legend that read, "American Numismatic Association, Celebrating 100 Years." At the bottom was printed "1891–1991" along with the notation "August 13–18, 1991, Chicago, Illinois." Like the 1987 special edition, the 1992 version was released without the special-offer sticker that had come on the regular edition.

The 1992 special-edition Red Books were given as favors at an ANA banquet held in Chicago, Illinois on August 17, 1991. It is believed that about 600 books were printed. There were not enough copies for every guest, and a number of them (approximately 50) were disappointed not to receive a book. But this issue is not nearly as scarce or hard to find as the 1987 issue, and is available for more reasonable prices. Perhaps the novelty of the special cover had worn off, or perhaps there were enough available for the aftermarket. It is also possible that many attendees, aware of what they had, decided to realize a quick profit. Currently valued at $250, this edition is occasionally seen on eBay and usually generates a lot of interest and fierce bidding. Copies in New condition sell for between $200 and $250.

Yeoman passed away in 1988, so any copies of this edition with his signature are forgeries. Copies signed by Bressett, or by other contributors or popular dealers who attended the show, sell for about $100 more than unsigned ones.

The pricing of this special edition, like the earlier one, has moved in a straight upward direction. In this case, however, the price movements are slower and less dramatic. This may be due to its greater availability. It remains to be seen whether this issue is as widely available as the pricing pattern presently indicates.

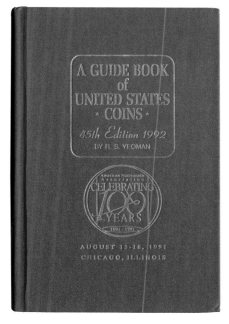

Pricing History of the 1992 ANA Special Edition

Red Book Edition	Value, New	Value, Signed by Bressett
1995–2001	$75	
2002	150	
2003	150	
2004	150	
2005	150	
2006	150	
2007	250	$350
2008	255	350
2009	275	375

1997: Red Book 50th Anniversary Edition

In recognition of the 50th anniversary of the first edition of the Red Book (which was dated 1947, with a copyright date of 1946), Whitman decided to produce a special cover. The original selling price for this edition was $24.95, with a limited run of 1,200 copies. Each book had a special maroon cover in the design of the original 1947 edition, and was hand-numbered on a special bound-in insert page of heavy paper stock.

The edition was offered for sale through retail outfits, but was also given away at an ANA banquet as a table favor. Those who received the book in that manner were truly fortunate, and probably received the lowest-numbered copies. Usually, those offered for sale are numbered in the 500 range and up (of the 1,200 printed).

The value of this special edition has increased rapidly since its publication. The first one that I was able to find was at the ANA New York City convention in August 2002 and had an asking price of $60. The chart shows how the book's valuation has changed.

As the chart illustrates, the value of the 1997 special edition moved upward until reaching the current New price of $125. This edition, with almost double the production of the two earlier ANA editions, has not shown the same leaps in price that the earlier editions show. However, it also appears that current owners of the books are not yet willing to part with them. A review of Internet sales shows that only around eight are sold in any given year, although this does vary, and the number is decreasing. Often months will go by without any being offered. Only when more copies become available on the market will we know if the pricing chart is accurate.

In Celebration of the 50th Anniversary of *A Guide Book of United States Coins* by R.S. Yeoman, popularly known as the *Red Book*, this copy is No. **986** of a special limited edition of 1,200 produced for the occasion.

However, the individual, handwritten numbering of these books makes them particularly novel. As opposed to books of the earlier editions, each of these volumes is unique, and it seems likely that lower-numbered books will soon be assigned a higher value than those with higher numbers. It is also possible that copies with special numbers—such as 10, 250, 500, 1,000, and 1,200—will become popular. Only time will tell.

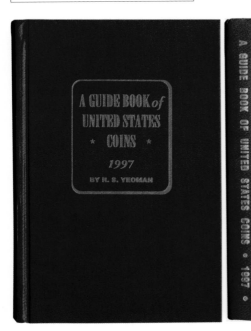

Pricing History of the 1997 Red Book 50th Anniversary Special Edition

Red Book Edition	Value, New	Value, Signed by Bressett
1998–2001	$75	
2002	80	
2003	120	
2004	120	
2005	120	
2006	120	
2007	120	$175–195
2008	125	175–195
2009	125	175–195

2002: ANA "Target 2001" Edition

In 2001, the American Numismatic Association was again the beneficiary of the printing of a special-edition *Guide Book*. This 2002 edition was created as a fundraiser for the ANA, which was planning a building renovation. Only 500 of these were produced, and each was signed by Kenneth Bressett. The special cover bore the legend "Target 2001: Building for a New Century." The original press release from the ANA read,

> To help the ANA in its fund-raising effort, St. Martin's Press has donated 500 copies of its 2002 edition of *A Guide Book of United States Coins* (popularly known as the "Red Book") to the Association. These special-issue reference books, signed by Editor Kenneth Bressett and bearing the "Target 2001" building renovation fund logo, will be sold by the ANA for $100 each. The $50,000 raised from the sale of the books will go to the "ANA Target 2001" building fund. Previous special-issue "Red Books" have become collector items, with values far exceeding their original issue price.

The Red Book's support of the ANA's renovation efforts was particularly fitting because, as David Crenshaw points out, it was Yeoman who, in the early 1960s, brought about Whitman's donation to the ANA National Headquarters Building Fund. However, the books were not heavily promoted and not all copies were sold. Remaining issues were sold as a lot to one book dealer, who has since parceled them out carefully for sale through Internet auctions.

This book is different from the preceding special editions. Previously, the cover simply added the ANA design to the bottom of the book's logo. For this edition, the entire cover was redesigned. This was not a surprise; after all, the regular cover had also undergone a dramatic change since the initial two special editions. The standard Red Book cover was now almost entirely filled by the words of its title, which mandated a complete change to the cover in order to accommodate the ANA design. The design reads 2001, the release date of the book, even though the *Guide Book* is dated 2002.

Pricing History of the 2002 ANA Special Edition

Red Book Edition	Value, New
2003	$125
2004	125
2005	125
2006	125
2007	125
2008	130
2009	130

Note: There is no added value for Bressett's signature because all copies are reported to have been signed by him prior to presentation. Therefore, it would actually be much more rare to find one of these books *without* his signature. However, none are known to exist.

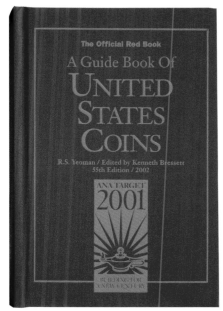

As illustrated in the pricing chart, the valuation of this edition has been static since its release. This is probably because the book is relatively available when compared to the other special editions.

There have been reports that the special-edition printings were actually in much larger numbers than what collectors guessed. This, however, cannot be verified, and is not necessarily true. It is now generally believed that there were 600 copies of this edition printed, not 500, just as there were 600 copies of the 1992 ANA edition. Why, then, has the valuation of the 2002 special edition been so static? There is currently no definite answer. The only acceptable possibility is that the books were given to recipients who quickly resold them on the secondary market, making them more immediately available on the collector's market. Of all editions, this one appears to be the best value and, as the ignored issue, probably has the best chance for future appreciation.

2002: SS *Central America* Edition

The year 2002 is famous for collectors of the *Guide Book* because it was the first edition year for which two special editions were published. In commemoration of the finding and sale of the treasure of the SS *Central America*, the publisher authorized another special edition. Reading "Special Edition 2002" on its spine and "SS *Central America* Special Edition" on its cover, this Red Book was the first to have different notations on its spine and cover.

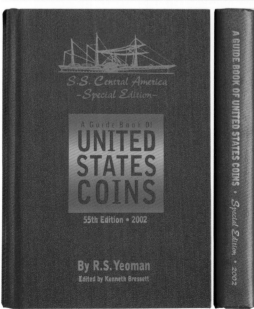

Pricing History of the 2002 SS *Central America* Special Edition

Red Book Edition	Value, New	Value, Signed
2003	$150	
2004	150	
2005	150	
2006	50	
2007	40	Evans: $50–55 Bressett: $75–80
2008	40	Evans: $50–55 Bressett: $75–80
2009	40	Evans: $50–55 Bressett: $75–80

The SS *Central America*, sometimes called the Ship of Gold, sailed from the Panama Canal on September 3, 1857, with 435 passengers. The gold coins and ingots on board were, at the time, valued at an estimated $26 million. On September 11, the ship encountered what was recorded to be one of the strongest hurricanes ever experienced. The ship sank in 7,200 feet of water, taking with it all the lives, and treasures, on board. The financial markets reacted violently to this loss, contributing to the Panic of 1857.

In 1985, Tommy Thompson and the Columbus-America Discovery Group succeeded in locating the wreck and began to salvage the treasure. Starting in 2000, the group sold the treasure for a total that is estimated to have exceeded $100 million. A discussion of this ship, its treasure, and its recovery later appeared in the 58th (2005) edition of the *Guide Book*, pages 367 to 368. For further reading, a complete account of the ship and its fate is available in *A California Gold Rush History* by Q. David Bowers.

No one knows the total number of special editions printed in honor of the ship. Initially, the book was considered very scarce and copies sold for in excess of $200. However, there is apparently an ample supply, and copies can now be obtained without difficulty. They have even been offered in full original cartons, at $240 for a box of 24.

There are copies that have been signed by the mission's chief scientist, Bob Evans. However, these are not scarce and generally sell for a premium of only $10 to $15 over an unsigned copy. Copies with Ken Bressett's signature, on the other hand, are very scarce, and would probably sell for more than twice the normal price.

2005: FUN 50th Anniversary Edition

In 2005, Whitman honored the 50th anniversary of Florida United Numismatists, Inc. (FUN). A special Red Book cover was designed and printed to celebrate this nonprofit group, originally organized in 1955. The redesigned cover has the usual title, reduced in size. Under this is a circle that contains a silhouette of the state of Florida. The legend "Florida United Numismatics, Inc. January 13–16, 2005" is printed on the circle,

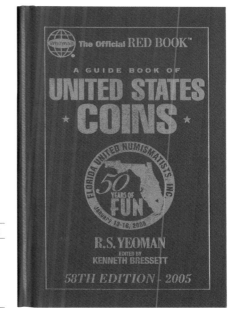

Pricing History of the 2005 FUN Special Edition

Red Book Edition	Value, New	Value, Signed by Bressett
2006	$100	
2007	75	$200
2008	110	200
2009	120	200–220

and the center of the design reads, "50 Years of FUN." Besides the ANA, this organization was the first to be so honored.

Approximately 1,100 copies are said to have been given out, with most going to attendees of the FUN convention's Saturday night banquet and the remainder distributed to various FUN member clubs around Florida. With that many distributed, it would seem logical that the book would be widely available. However, the opposite is true. Many of the recipients have kept their copies, and few books have entered the secondary market. To date, there have only been a few sales noted on Internet sites. Sales are so infrequent that it is difficult to properly determine this edition's actual value.

The drop in value shown in 2007 is inexplicable, as every sale recorded to date has been for at least $100. In 2005, FUN vice president Bob Hurst reported that copies had sold for more than $200.[28] The decrease in listed value is most likely due to the difficulty of establishing a fair market price. In addition, the book is very new, and many collectors may not be aware of its existence (although it has been listed in the

Guide Book since the 2006 edition). To date, the only sale of a 2005 special edition with Ken Bressett's signature was on eBay in May 2006 for more than $200. This is one edition that is certainly worth watching, and it will probably escalate in price as more become available on the market.

The ticket to the FUN banquet also served as a coupon, entitling the bearer to the special-edition Red Book.

2007: ANA 116th Anniversary Edition

In 2006, another special-edition *Guide Book* was issued for the ANA. With a 2007 cover date, it honored the ANA's 116 years of existence. Only 500 were printed and released,

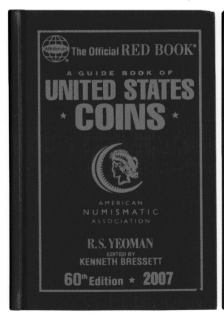

Pricing History of the 2007 ANA Special Edition

Red Book Edition	Value, New	Value, Signed by Bressett
2008	$100	$125
2009	100	125

each with a special bookplate that honored August 20, 2006, as Membership Appreciation Day. Each bookplate was hand numbered and signed by Ken Bressett.

Members who attended a special event that day were given a copy of the book. Additional copies were available for purchase at $50 each. As of this writing, the only books to enter the secondary market have had high serial numbers.

The issue is unique: it was the first edition with a special printing for the event on its back cover and the first edition to have a special notation ("ANA Edition") on its spine. Unfortunately, there was a problem in production. A different preparation process was used for the cover than was used for the regular editions. As a result of this process, any copies whose corners were bumped suffered slight damage to the color on their corners. This effect is common, and perfect copies should be valued higher.

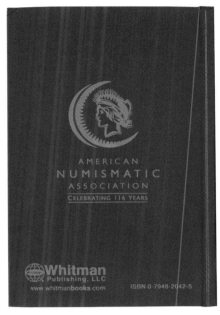

There is little pricing history available yet for the 2007 special edition. Copies are scarce and currently sell for more than $100. Even books with damaged corners bring strong prices. It is advisable to find yourself a copy, with or without this damage, before the prices begin to increase.

2007: MSNS 50th Anniversary Edition

For only the second time, more than one special cover was produced in the same year. There were, in fact, four special editions released for the 2007 edition. One edition

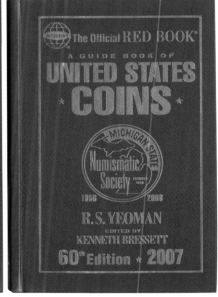

Pricing History of the 2007 MSNS Special Edition

Red Book Edition	Value, New	Value, Signed by Bressett
2008	$100	$125
2009	100	125

honored the Michigan State Numismatic Society (MSNS) on the occasion of its 50th anniversary. The emblem on the cover included a stylized representation of the state of Michigan and a different typeface from that used on the ANA special edition covers.

This issue also had a special spine notation: "MSNS Edition." However, as opposed to the 2007 ANA issue, it did not have a special back cover. There were only about 500 produced, and approximately 50 books were lost during shipping. About 50 were hand signed by Ken Bressett for presentation at the MSNS event.

Members who attended the MSNS 50th anniversary banquet on Saturday, November 25, 2006 (held at the Hyatt Regency Hotel in Dearborn, Michigan), received a copy. The banquet tickets included a stub that read, "Good for one 50th Anniversary Commemorative Red Book / Coupon." A limited number of copies were available to nonattenders for a $20 contribution to the MSNS.

Prices today often exceed $100 per copy, and the book has been priced as high as $200. One copy with Kenneth Bressett's signature was offered on eBay shortly after the event at an asking price of $250.

Each ticket for the MSNS anniversary banquet also served as a coupon that could be exchanged for the special-edition Red Book.

2007: 1947 Tribute Edition, Hardcover

To celebrate the Red Book's 60th anniversary, Whitman released a special 1947 first-edition commemorative reissue. This release was designed to replicate the first printing of the first edition. So thorough was the attention to historical detail that the binding even replicates that of a first edition: sharp-eyed collectors will notice the absence of a head band, a feature not introduced until the 18th edition (see chapter 4).

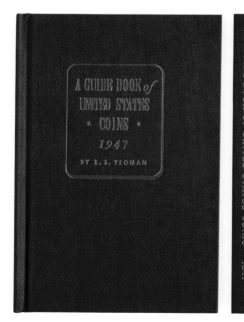

**Pricing History of the 2007
1947 Tribute Edition, Hardcover**

Red Book Edition	Value, New	Value, Signed by Bressett
2008	$18	$50
2009	18	50

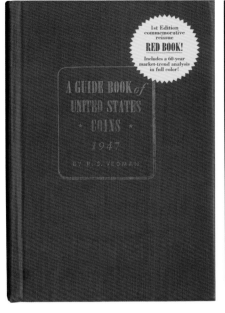  

This was the first Red Book to feature a dustjacket, and this too replicated the look of a used first-edition copy, whose gilt stamping had dimmed somewhat and whose binding showed faint signs of wear. The front of the jacket featured a yellow burst emblem proclaiming, "1st Edition commemorative reissue Red Book! Includes a 60-year market-trend analysis in full color!" The spine of the dustjacket also featured a yellow band that identified the book as a commemorative reissue. The back of the dustjacket contained text describing the book and its contents, and the back flap featured portraits of Yeoman and Bressett by numismatic artist Charles Daughtrey.

Apart from the dustjacket, the only anachronism in the book was the addition of a market-trend analysis. This 32-page discussion was printed in full color (unlike the rest of the book, which replicated the first edition's black-and-white format) and offered a detailed and engaging comparison of the coin-collecting hobby in 1946 and 2006.

Originally offered for sale at $17.95, the commemorative reissue was immediately popular. Wayne Homren of the Numismatic Bibliomania Society gave it an enthusiastic review in the online publication *E-Sylum* and declared it "a fine way to honor the inaugural 1947 edition of Dick Yeo's gift to numismatics." Coin collectors who had not previously been interested in the *Guide Book* suddenly wanted copies, and coin dealers who usually never dealt in books had them available for sale. Just the presence of a copy for sale at a coin show was enough to cause a stir among attendees.

Information on the leather-bound Limited Edition of this issue is found in the next section of this chapter.

2008: ANA World's Fair of Money Edition

The ANA held its 2007 summer convention, the World's Fair of Money, in August in Milwaukee, Wisconsin. To honor the association, Whitman produced a special-edition *Guide Book*, which was given as a favor at the convention's Saturday evening banquet. The cover commemorated the event. For the second time, the back cover was imprinted. It pictured a line-art rendition of the Wisconsin state quarter and stated, "The Red Book Comes Home to Wisconsin ANA World's Fair of Money 2007." The spine was imprinted, "ANA Edition."

Imprinted on the back of the ANA banquet ticket is the notice "Present This Ticket for your 2007 Red Book gift provided by Whitman Publications."

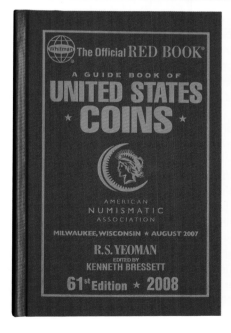

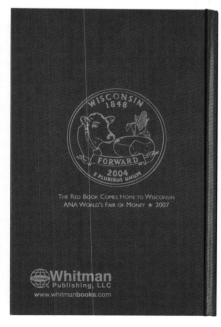

It is estimated that 1,080 books were produced for distribution, and all were either distributed that evening or sold to raise money for the association. They were not individually numbered and signed, although Ken Bressett was kind and patient enough to sign copies for requesting attendees. Copies are currently very scarce, as owners hold onto their books to see what values the edition will bring in the future marketplace. The value of this edition is estimated at $75, and signed copies should sell for an additional $50 or more.

The 2008 ANA special edition is presently valued at $75 in New condition.

2008: Stack's Rare Coins Edition

The year 2007 marked the first time that *three* special-edition Red Books were released: the Milwaukee ANA edition, just described; the Numismatic Literary Guild edition (discussed in the section on leather editions); and the Stack's Rare Coins edition.

Stack's had recently merged with American Numismatic Rarities of Wolfeboro, New Hampshire. In cooperation with Whitman Publishing, the company elected to have 2,000 copies of the 2008 Red Book printed and bound with a special insert. This read, "Your Personal Invitation / Stack's / Visit our world famous showroom in New York City," and listed the company address, phone number, and Web site address. In addition, there was a special three-page full-color inserted advertisement. Some copies had a special unbound insert noting that the book was compliments of Stack's. The books were displayed without fanfare at the 2007 ANA World's Fair of Money, and offered to anyone who walked up and requested a copy. A small number of copies were signed by Ken Bressett at the convention.

I had the opportunity to attend the convention, where I was able to obtain a copy and speak to a number of the attendees who had also obtained them. Most were not aware of the difference in the edition, and had thought that it was just a regular *Guide Book*. Because of this misconception, and because many of the copies were given to young numismatists, who are more likely to keep their books for use as reference, it initially seemed unlikely that many of these books would appear on the secondary market. However, in 2008 a quantity of several hundred of these books was inventoried in Stack's Wolfeboro office.

Signed copies will probably realize many times the listed price. As of this writing none have been auctioned in regular numismatic auctions.

Stack's is pleased to support the programs of the American Numismatic Association. We hope you find this special hardbound edition of the 2008 Red Book a valuable part of your library.

Compliments of your friends at

Stack's

123 West 57th Street • New York, NY 10019
Box 1804 • Wolfeboro, NH 03894
866-811-1804 • 800-566-2580
www.stacks.com • email: auction@stacks.com

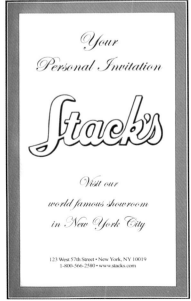

Your Personal Invitation

Stack's

Visit our world famous showroom in New York City

123 West 57th Street • New York, NY 10019
1-800-566-2580 • www.stacks.com

LIMITED EDITIONS

Starting in 2004, with the 2005 edition of the *Guide Book*, Whitman has released leather-bound Limited Editions. A limited run (of 3,000 copies) was printed and released. These Limited Edition Red Books were quite similar to the regular editions.

The major differences between the two versions are as follows.

- The regular editions are 5-1/4 inches wide by 7-3/4 inches high; the Limited Editions are 6-1/2 inches wide by 9-1/4 inches high.
- The cover of the Limited Editions is leather, with a hubbed spine and gold-foil title.
- Each page of the Limited Edition is edged in gold leaf.
- Limited Editions have a silk ribbon page marker.
- The individual pages of the early Limited Editions are printed with a decorative border or banner, which fills the extra page space, allowing the layout of the regular edition to be maintained. (Later Limited Editions have the layouts expanded to fill the page.)
- Each copy of the leather Limited Edition has a special bound page insert that reads, "Certificate of Limited Edition." These pages are each individually numbered (from 1 to 3,000) and hand signed by Kenneth Bressett.
- The Limited Editions are shrink-wrapped in protective plastic.

Some Limited Editions contained minor changes from the regular-edition text. These changes will be described in the individual discussions of each edition.

As noted here, leather Limited Edition books come encased in plastic shrinkwrap. There is some debate as to whether it is preferable to buy a book in its original protective plastic or without it. Most sales are currently being made with the shrinkwrap intact. However, there may be a disadvantage to purchasing the sealed book, because the plastic can appear original but actually be a replacement. Additionally, the effect of heat on the plastic packaging around the leather binding is unknown. Also, the individual serial number of each book can only be seen if the plastic is removed. Whether to buy copies with or without their plastic covering is a decision for the individual collector.

The special features of the leather Limited Edition Red Books are described in this ad from the *Coin World* issue of December 27, 2004.

2005 Leather Limited Edition

The first of the leather Limited Editions, the 2005 edition features a pale gold border around the content of each page, somewhat like an academic diploma. In most other respects the contents of the regular 2005 edition are carried over intact, but there are some changes. An important revision is in the listings for "The *Guide Book* as a Collectible." The 1995 softbound edition in Very Good and Fine, mistakenly priced at $800 in the 2005 regular edition of the *Guide Book*, shows a corrected value of $.80. Interestingly, however, all the other pricing errors have been preserved. For example, the values for the 1983 edition remain shifted two columns to the left. Similarly, the values for the 1992 ANA special edition and the 2002 SS *Central America* special edition are still shifted one column to the left.

The issue price of this edition was $69.95. In New condition it is currently valued at around $85, and it is very likely that the value of this edition will appreciate much further. Most of the 3,000 books printed were sold to *Guide Book* collectors, with not many left for subsequent sale. Those that are sold on the Internet are currently being offered at a premium to the original selling price. As prices increase, more collectors will probably release issues for resale and the book will become more readily available.

At this time, the numbering of these books is not considered important. In the future, however, the serial number may be considered when determining a book's value. Certain numbers in the sequence (such as 11 through 20, 100, 200, 300, 500, 1,000, 2,000, and 3,000) may sell for a premium in the future. The copies numbered 1 through 10 were reserved for the Whitman Publishing archives and company officers and dignitaries.

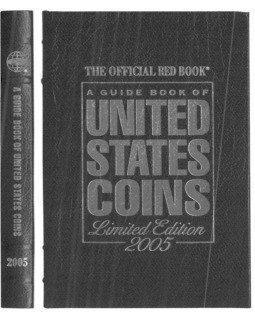

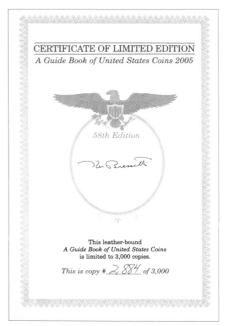

Originally issued at a price of $69.95, the 2005 Limited Edition has a current value of $85.00.

2006 Leather Limited Edition

No changes in the text from the 2006 regular edition to the 2006 Limited Edition have been noted at this time. The pricing errors of the 2005 Limited Edition in the section "The *Guide Book* as a Collectible" are not repeated in either the 2006 regular edition or the 2006 Limited Edition. The page design changed, however: the decorative gold border in the previous leather edition was replaced with a color-coded section banner, in what Wayne Homren of the *E-Sylum* termed "a much handier use of spare ink."

In the first (2005) Limited Edition, each "Certificate of Limited Edition" was signed and hand numbered by Kenneth Bressett. In the 2006 edition the numbering was not done by Bressett, but each copy still carries his signature.

The 2006 Limited Edition maintained its predecessor's issue price of $69.95. For a short time, this edition was available at a discounted price from industry suppliers, but any extra supply has since evaporated. It now carries a value of $80 in New condition. Currently, there is a sufficient number of copies available to col-

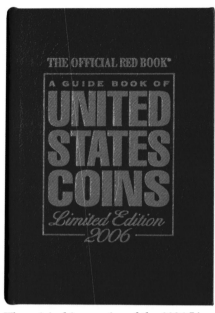

The original issue price of the 2006 Limited Edition was $69.95; its current value in New condition is $80.00.

lectors in the secondary market, although only 3,000 books were published. This availability may be because speculators purchased multiples for later resale. Their future importance and desirability rely on the collection's expansion in the coming years. As the series grows, and the number of collectors with it, the early Limited Editions should increase in popularity and value.

2007 Leather Limited Edition

Collectors of the *Guide Book* were elated when it was announced that production of the Limited Edition books would continue for 2007. This was the third consecutive year that Whitman Publishing released a leather edition. This Limited Edition made its debut in mid-August at the ANA show in Denver, Colorado. Again, only 3,000 copies were released, and by September of that year they had sold out. Although the "Certificate of Limited Edition" was still hand signed by Kenneth Bressett, the identification of each copy was done with a numbering stamp.

A special section was added to the 2007 Limited Edition. The table of contents, which remained on page 6, was followed by an unnumbered, four-page "Tribute to Kenneth Bressett." It included a lithograph drawing of Bressett and R.S. Yeoman by Charles Daughtrey. There was also a biographical sketch of Bressett that described his service to numismatics and to the *Guide Book*. Since the pagination skips this special section and picks up afterward, the added pages are not immediately obvious; the additional content is in the nature of a bonus for collectors of the Limited Edition.

This edition was released at a price of $69.95, unchanged from the previous issues, and is currently valued at around $75 in New condition.

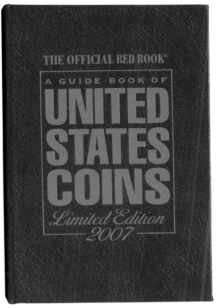

The original issue price of the 2007 Limited Edition was $69.95; its current value is $75 in New condition. The opening page of the "Tribute to Kenneth Bressett," shown here, features art by Charles Daughtrey.

2007: 1947 Tribute Edition, Leather Limited Edition

Whitman Publishing released another Limited Edition for 2007, this one a special edition as well. This was a special reproduction of the original first edition, first printing, of the 1947 *Guide Book.* (For details of the differences between the first and second printings, see chapter 4.) Released in a limited production run of 500, these books replicated the original edition but had a burgundy leather cover. Each was numbered and hand signed by Ken Bressett, and included a special page with a certificate of limited edition. The leatherbound Tribute Edition also came with the 32-page retrospective color section found in the regular hardcover Tribute Edition, which compared the coin-collecting hobby at the time of the Red Book's first appearance to its state in the present day, and included market comparisons.

At an issue price of $49.95—significantly less than that of the regular Limited Edition—the entire press run immediately sold out. Collectors lucky enough to have obtained this edition at or near the issue price will surely be pleased when the time comes to sell. Within a month of the sellout, copies were offered on the Internet for double the issue price, and its current values exceed that amount. Collectors are grateful for the reasonable initial price, which ensured that the purchase would appreciate in value.

2008 Leather Limited Edition

The 2008 Limited Edition *Guide Book* was of the same style as those from the three previous years and had the same print run (3,000 copies). The continued production of this series suggested that it had found an enthusiastic fan base. Released at the same price as other leather Limited Editions, it shows no appreciation yet worth mentioning, although as more time passes this is likely to change.

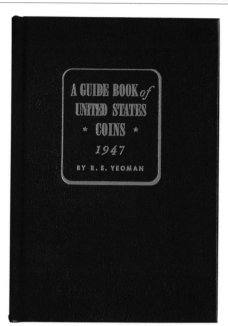
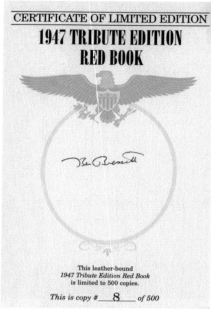

Released at a price of $49.95, the leather-bound Tribute Edition now carries a value of $110 in New condition. Signed copies have no additional value because all copies were signed before release.

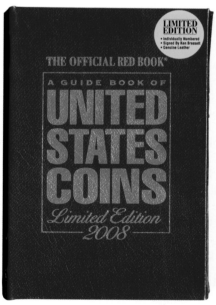
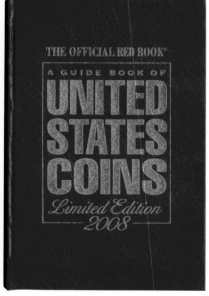

The current value of the 2008 Limited Edition hovers around its issue price of $69.95. This edition is shown here both with and without its shrinkwrap covering.

2008 Numismatic Literary Guild Limited Edition

The year 2007 was the first during which Whitman Publishing produced more than one Limited Edition Red Book. In fact, two special-edition versions of the leather Limited Edition were prepared for the 2008 edition. One of these was produced for the 2007 summer banquet and awards ceremony of the Numismatic Literary Guild (NLG), which took place in Milwaukee at the ANA annual convention. Production was limited to 135 books, of which 10 were reserved for distribution from Whitman Publishing headquarters in Atlanta. The other 125 books were distributed at the banquet—at which there were more attendees than books. (Note: the 2009 Red Book erroneously gives the number of copies prepared as 250.)

The Red Book's relationship with the NLG, a society formed for numismatic writers, editors, and publishers, can be said to extend to its founding in 1968, as R.S. Yeoman was one of the founding members. Its membership includes many of today's most widely read numismatic authors, such as Q. David Bowers, Kenneth Bressett, Roger W. Burdette, Beth Deisher, Bill Fivaz, Jeff Garrett, Barbara Gregory, David Harper, David W. Lange, Clifford Mishler, Eric P. Newman, Ed Reiter, Ed Rochette, Neil Shafer, J.T. Stanton, and Scott Travers.

The back cover had an imprint to commemorate the event, and the books as distributed were sealed in plastic. Subsequent to the NLG event, the first copy available for sale at the ongoing ANA convention had an asking price of $500; it is not known whether it sold for that amount. With a total production of only 135, this book is set to become the scarcest Limited Edition yet and may reach previously unheard-of value.

Only two copies were offered and sold on eBay in the 12 months following the NLG banquet. One had a final realized price of $800, in November 2007. In July 2008, a copy became available at an opening price of $800 and a buy-it-now price of $1,000. In a 2008 auction by Fred Lake, a copy realized a final price of $1,200. At the time of this writing, another numismatic book dealer had one priced at $1,000. Now may be the time to purchase a copy (if the opportunity arises), since increased publicity and interest in this very limited edition may greatly increase the value.

The current estimated value of the 2008 Limited Edition with NLG imprint is $1,000 in New condition.

2008 American Numismatic Society Limited Edition

Whitman Publishing created another 2008 special Limited Edition when it aided the American Numismatic Society by donating a special edition of the leather-bound issue as a banquet gift. The edition of 250 copies incorporated a special bookplate honoring the 150th anniversary of the ANS and the celebratory dinner on January 10, 2008. The event took place at the Waldorf-Astoria in New York City, and the ticket cost of $350 included a copy of the book.

At this time only three copies of the ANS edition have been offered publicly for sale or auction. It appears that most attendees are determined to keep their souvenir of the event. If any more copies appear on the market, the collector would be wise to obtain one, since it does not appear that they will become widely available soon—if ever.

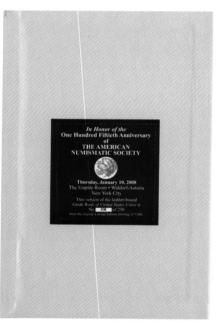

The current estimated value of the 2008 Limited Edition with ANS bookplate is $1,000 in New condition.

6

RED BOOK
AUTHORIZED EDITIONS

As noted in the last chapter, various special-edition Red Books have been prepared and issued by the publisher. Each had a cover distinct from that of the year's regular issue.

The Red Books classified here as "authorized editions" differ in that they are regular volumes of the *Guide Book* whose covers were overprinted, with the permission of Whitman Publishing, with a special designation for a particular event.

As of this writing, it is impossible to say for certain how many authorized editions have been issued. The following list of the best-known authorized editions gives the edition year of each.

> 1970: *Coin World* 10th anniversary overprint
>
> 1985: *Coin World* 25th anniversary overprint
>
> 1991: American Numismatic Association luncheon cruise overprint
>
> 1995: 50th Anniversary of the Milwaukee Numismatic Society overprint

These four are the most widely known, but other overprinted Red Books have surfaced that may also have been authorized by Whitman. In spring of 2008 an eBay auction offered a copy of the 15th edition with an overstamp reading "Souvenir / Century 21 Exposition / Seattle World's Fair / 1962." David T. Alexander has noted the existence of a 27th (1974) edition with an overprint commemorating the Miami Beach International Coin Convention (see his Red Book Recollection on page 8). Charles Davis has reported Red Books with other overprints. Determining the number of authorized-edition Red Books is complicated by the likelihood that *unauthorized* editions—Red Books overprinted without the permission of the publisher, and not officially recognized—have sometimes been created.

Many collectors readily accept the authorized editions as an integral part of the complete *Guide Book* set. Moreover, because these books have not been tracked as scrupulously as those distributed by the publisher, this is an area where a collector may actually be able to discover a "new" edition!

New collectors of authorized editions may find it encouraging that this line consists of so few known types—however, it is not necessarily easy to obtain them. The two *Coin World* editions can often be found fairly easily, but the 1970 *Coin World* is difficult to obtain in Near Mint or New condition. (On the other hand, the 1985 *Coin World* edition is usually available in New condition at a reasonable price.) The 1995 Milwaukee Numismatic Society edition can be rather difficult to find and is considered one of the keys to the set. The 1991 ANA Luncheon Cruise edition is similarly scarce.

At this time, there are no plans for any additional authorized editions. In recent years Whitman Publishing has produced its commemorative or special-occasion editions in house rather than authorizing another party to overprint regular editions.

1970: *COIN WORLD* 10TH ANNIVERSARY OVERPRINT

To commemorate the 10th anniversary of *Coin World*'s publication, a special overprint was authorized for the 1970 *Guide Book*. It appeared at the bottom right corner and read, "Compliments of *Coin World*, the Weekly Newspaper of the Entire Numismatic Field." There was also a special inserted (unbound) sheet that read, "A Birthday Gift for YOU!" and included a description of the anniversary and the book. The books were sent to *Coin World*'s new subscribers (see David Alexander's Red Book Recollection on page 8). An estimated 3,000 were produced, and all were given away.

This edition as a whole is not scarce. However, many of the books were treated as regular copies and used for daily reference rather than being preserved as collectibles. In addition, at the time they were given out, *Guide Book* collecting was not far from its infancy and there was not a rush to keep mint-condition copies. As a result, well-preserved books with full cover gilt and the original insert sheet are quite scarce.

The edition occasionally appears on auction sites and usually sells for about $20 to $25, although copies in Very Fine condition command more. A book that contains the "Happy Birthday" insert is worth a premium, and may sell for $10 to $15 more than its usual price. A copy in New condition with the insert may sell for more than $50.

Copies signed by R.S. Yeoman will sell for a considerable premium over unsigned copies. If you have the opportunity to purchase a book with his signature, grab it. Copies

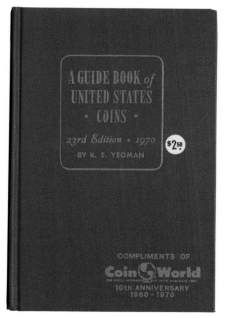

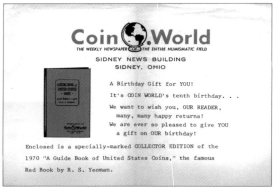

Values of the 1970 *Coin World* Authorized Edition

Condition	Value	Value, Signed by Yeoman
Mint, with full gilt	$45–50	$200
Very Fine	25	100
Fine	15	50
Good	5	—

with additional signatures are worth even more, with the value depending on the signers. See chapter 7 for a copy signed not only by Yeoman but also by other numismatic writers and coin dealers.

1985: *COIN WORLD* 25TH ANNIVERSARY OVERPRINT

Coin World celebrated its silver anniversary with a special *Guide Book* edition. The overprint used for this promotion was simpler than that used for its 10th anniversary; it merely stated, "Compliments of *Coin World*." As was done previously, copies were distributed to new subscribers of the publication. With only 1,500 copies issued, the production was half that of the 1970 authorized edition.

It has been rumored that many of the copies were damaged by water, resulting in very few available copies. The validity of the story is debatable, since the issue is not scarce and is regularly offered for sale. Copies in New condition used to sell for $30 or more. More recently, however, hoards of the edition (including one that included 100 books) have come to light, and pricing for New copies has settled in the vicinity of $20. Books signed by Bressett are valued at $40 to $50.

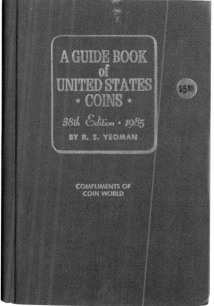

**Values of the 1985 *Coin World*
Authorized Edition**

Condition	Value	Value, Signed by Bressett
Mint, with full gilt	$20–25	$50
Very Fine	10	25
Fine	8	—
Good	5	—

1991: AMERICAN NUMISMATIC ASSOCIATION LUNCHEON CRUISE OVERPRINT

In 1991, the American Numismatic Association decided to promote one of its special events, a luncheon cruise, by issuing an authorized edition of the Red Book. Attendees were fortunate to receive a free "ANA Luncheon Cruise" overprint on a copy of the regular-issue 44th-edition (1991) *Guide Book*. Copies are rarely offered for sale and usually garner large premiums over the regular edition. Yet the listed price is low because most collectors are unfamiliar with this rare edition. It will most likely become more popular in coming years, and its value should increase as well.

The "ANA Centennial Friendship Luncheon Cruise," as it was entitled on the event program, was held on Friday, August 15, 1991, aboard the *Spirit of Chicago* cruise ship. The program cover bore an illustration of the cruise ship against the Chicago skyline. Inside, the menu and program descriptions were accompanied by the gold-embossed ANA 100th anniversary logo (as rendered on the obverse of the ANA medal, shown in chapter 8). The cruise program, if any are still to be found, would enhance a display of either the ANA medal or the Red Book edition authorized for the event.

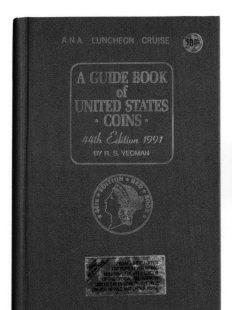

Values of the 1991 ANA Luncheon Cruise Edition

Condition	Value	Value, Signed by Bressett
Mint, with full gilt	$300	$450
Very Fine	250	—
Fine	225	—
Good	200	—

1995: 50TH ANNIVERSARY OF THE MILWAUKEE NUMISMATIC SOCIETY OVERPRINT

In 1994 the Milwaukee Numismatic Society (MNS) celebrated the 60th anniversary of its inception. To commemorate this milestone, a limited number of copies of the 48th-edition Red Book was overprinted as an authorized edition. The MNS logo and "Founded October 29, 1934" appeared on the cover. Additionally, a replica of a Japanese government–issued Philippine 10-peso note, used during the Japanese occupation of the Philippines during World War II, was included in the book. The note was overprinted with the society's logo and an additional legend that read, "50th Anniversary / End of WWII / 1945–1995."

The cover's approved overprint was the idea of Bill Spencer, the coin dealer from Racine, Wisconsin, who was responsible for the minting of the Red Book commemorative silver rounds (see chapter 8). Unfortunately, the logo was printed with an excessive amount of gilt. As a result, it is difficult to decipher the words on most copies. Holding the book at a slight angle makes it easier to read.

The book was distributed at the society's anniversary dinner. The Japanese notes were included in every copy. It is believed that only 300 copies were produced, making the edition very scarce. Auction records are correspondingly uncommon. While this book is not as popular as the special editions, it is just as difficult to obtain as the 1987 ANA special edition. Despite this, it is usually sold for less money, evidently because of collectors' unfamiliarity with its existence.

Kenneth Bressett did not attend the MNS anniversary convention, so any signed editions would have to have been autographed after the fact. They are estimated to be worth at least twice a regular copy's list value.

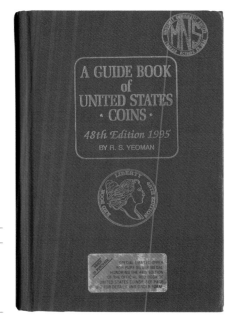

Values of the 1995 Milwaukee Numismatic Society Edition

Condition	Value	Value, Signed by Bressett
Mint, with full gilt and insert	$250	$350
Very Fine	175	275
Fine	100	175
Very Good	95	120

7
RED BOOK VARIETIES

Just as the collecting of coins has evolved over the hobby's lifetime, so has the collecting of Red Books. In the first heyday of American coin collecting in the 19th century, complete date runs of certain popular series were the goal for most collectors, whereas today's hobbyists are attuned to a myriad of mintmarks and varieties. Likewise, Red Book collecting has developed to include a number of varieties.

Originally, *Guide Book* collectors were content to obtain a copy of each edition issued from 1946 to the current date. There was also the possible inclusion in a set of the second printing of the first edition. Gradually, however, the list of collectible Red Books expanded to include varieties such as signed copies, presentation copies, error printings, special editions, and authorized editions. (Special editions and authorized editions are discussed in detail in chapters 5 and 6, respectively.)

Advanced collectors now actively search for these different *Guide Book* varieties. In this chapter, we will first look at presentation copies and signed regular editions. Then we will examine editing copies and error books. Although your collection may not include these varieties, you may wish to expand it to include them in the future. The search for unusual examples of the Red Book is limited only by a collector's ability to notice the unusual.

PRESENTATION COPIES

In recent years, presentation copies have been given to contributors who worked on that edition of the *Guide Book*. A presentation copy is a regular *Guide Book* that has an interleaf bound into the front of the book. On this page is a circular design with an eagle at its top and a partial wreath at its bottom. The words "Presentation Copy For" appear in the middle of the circle, followed by a line. A contributor's name is usually handwritten on the line, directly above the signature of R.S. Yeoman or Kenneth Bressett. The earliest edition for which I have been able to find a presentation copy is the 37th edition (1984). The tradition continues to this day, and in recent years these copies have been accompanied by a special contributors' lapel pin (see chapter 8).

Presentation copies are greatly desired and highly collectible. Every one is unique, since most are inscribed to individual contributors. The number of copies released each year is directly related to the number of contributors that worked on the particular edition (although in some years additional copies were made). For example, the 37th edition (1984) lists 76 contributors plus 31 individuals as recipients of "Special Credit." Therefore, there are only around 107 presentation copies in existence for that edition. And, of course, the volumes only become available if a contributor sells his or her copy. Presentation copies enter the market infrequently. When one does, there is usually spirited bidding for it.

There are also some (although very few) presentation copies in which the inside front cover has been signed (by either Yeoman or Bressett) but the contributor's name has not been written. These copies are far scarcer than those with completed pages and should bring a premium, although valuation is subjective and pricing information is not currently available.

Presentation copies are usually kept in excellent condition. If you find one that has been used and abused or written in, the book will have a much lower value. Keep this in mind before making a purchase. In New condition, a presentation copy signed by Yeoman carries a value of $45 to $55, and one signed by Bressett is valued at $40 to $50. The values of copies showing wear will be reduced by about $20.

SIGNED COPIES

In the early years of the Red Book's publication, Yeoman would often sign books, making them out to collectors who had no association to the edition's development. Today, these books are quite scarce. Although they are worth a premium regardless of the inscription, copies with Yeoman's signature but without the name of a collector are more desirable, unless the collector is one of particular note. The exact value of these books is determined by individual buyers and what they are willing to pay. As usual, condition is a consideration in the value of the book.

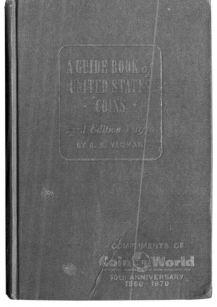

Consider, for example, the *Coin World* authorized edition shown here. As discussed in chapter 6, this edition was released to commemorate the publication's 10th anniversary. This particular copy has been used extensively, as is apparent by the spots and dent on the cover. In addition, there are also several markings through the book's interior. However, the original owner obtained not only the signature of R.S. Yeoman, but also the signatures of a number of coin dealers and notables in the industry, including Mort Reed, J.O.

Amos, Russ Rulau, and Margo Russell. Despite its evidence of wear, this book would bring a nice premium over a mint-condition but unsigned copy. The value of the signed book shown is $50 to $75, whereas it would be valued at $125 if in New condition.

There is at least one complete set of editions signed by Yeoman, which belongs to a Midwest collector. This set includes signed copies of each book from the first edition (1947) to the last edition released before Yeoman's 1988 death, the 42nd edition (1989). A full set is always an admirable collection—but a *signed* full set is truly the Mount Everest of *Guide Book* collections, equivalent to completing a gem set of Morgan dollars.

There also exists at least one copy that Yeoman signed with his real name. This particular third-edition book is inscribed, "To Brother Ernie Hewitt R.S. Yeoman (Dick Yeo)." Unique books such as this one will always inspire spirited bidding when they appear at auction.

EDITING COPIES

Every year, a panel of contributors submits price adjustments and other changes for the Red Book and Blue Book. Originally, contributors would write their comments directly on the pages of a copy from the previous year.

Shortly after its introduction in 1942, however, the publisher began the practice of interleaving onionskin pages into special editing copies of the Blue Book. This allowed contributors to include longer notes for R.S. Yeoman to consider as he prepared the next edition.

By the 19th edition (1962) of the Blue Book, regular editing copies were being produced for the Blue Book. In these books, each page that appeared in the original edition alternated with a blank interleaf page. The extra space provided by the interleaved pages allowed contributors to be much more detailed in their comments. (See the appendix for more on Blue Book editing editions.)

After the *Guide Book* began publication in 1946, editing copies were made of the first and second editions, following the form of the Blue Book editing copies—that is, with blank pages inserted between all the pages of the original book. However, these are the only early editions from which editing copies were made, and the evolution of the Red

Book's editing copies began to lag behind that of the Blue Book's.

After the first two years of Red Book editing copies, changes and comments were simply written in copies of the previous year's book. Shown here are sample editing pages from two contributors. The pages have been removed from their original volumes, perhaps by Yeoman or his staff. One set is marked by Yeoman as being contributed by "Boosel," and contains pricing adjustments and comments by Harry X Boosel. This collector was widely known as "Mr. 1873" because of his specialty in coins of that year, and appropriately enough, all of his penned-in corrections and remarks relate to issues of the year 1873. The other pages are not labeled, and their contributors are unknown. These pages are collectible, but there is not currently an established market value for them because they are so scarce.

In 1964, specially printed editing copies were once again provided to Red Book contributors, and the practice would continue through 1967. The spines of five such copies are illustrated here, along with a standard 1963 Red Book for comparison. The added thickness caused by the extra pages is evident. Note also that two volumes are dated 1964, and there is no 1965 date. A printing error resulted in all 1965 editing copies reading "1964" on their spines, although the correct date was printed on the book's title page. As shown in the photo of the 16th-edition editing copy (right), each page was interleaved with a blank page for editing. The examples in these pictures were never used by contributors, so the added pages are still blank.

No more than 50 editing copies were produced in any year. There is, however, at least one complete set of *Guide Book* editing copies. Books from the first couple of years are particularly rare and valuable, but all editing copies bring very strong prices. One interleaved editing copy of the first edition sold for $2,090 at the 1991 ANA Centennial auction held by Bowers and Merena.[29] In the Charles Davis auction of February 2008, the five interleaved copies offered for sale brought from $325 (for an "as new" 20th edition) to $475 (for a "near new" 18th edition with the error date imprint "1964"). A complete set of five would be valued at around $2,100.

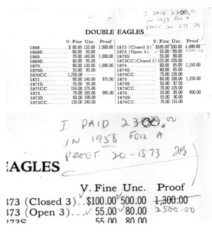

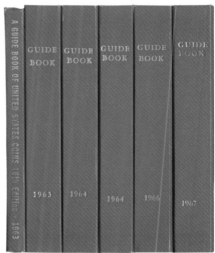

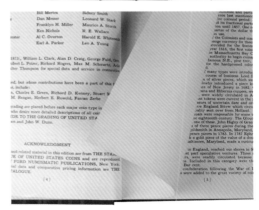

January 11, 1966

Mr. Leo A. Young
3244 Grand Avenue
Oakland 10, California

Dear Leo:

Separately we are sending you an interleaved 19th Edition,
A GUIDE BOOK OF UNITED STATES COINS so you can set down your
revisions opposite the coins in the regular listings. The
procedure is the same as in other years, and we hope you will
again favor us with your expert advice by suggesting changes in
the 20th (1967) edition.

The deadline is February 21, 1966. By mid-March we will have
averaged all figures submitted to us and start setting type for
the new edition. Please send your data earlier if you can. It
will make our work here easier if all panelists do not wait till
the last day to send in price information.

Please submit only prices--not precentage changes, For example,
"raise all 5%" is not practical data, and cannot be used.

Please use the same container to return the book to us. A label
and first class postage are enclosed with the book for your
convenience.

If for any reason you cannot participate, please notify us at once
so we can appoint another panelist in your place.

Thank you for your cooperation.

Very truly yours,

WHITMAN PUBLISHING COMPANY

Dick

R.S. Yeoman
Editor

RSY:sw

COIN BOOKS • STICKER FUN • PUNCHOUTS • PUZZLES • BOOKS • GAMES • CRAYONS • PLAYING CARDS • COLORING BOOKS • GIFT WRAP • STORY BOOKS

R.S. Yeoman sent letters of instruction to the Red Book contributors who received interleaved editing copies. This letter, dated January 11, 1966, was typed on special stationery that celebrates Whitman Publishing's 50th anniversary that year.

ERROR COPIES

Collectors of the *Guide Book* frequently expand their collections to include various misprinted editions. These error editions are often sold and purchased as regular editions, because the seller may not be aware of the error pages. Depending on the type of error, the value of an error edition is approximately one and a half to two times that of a regular edition, or sometimes more. As always, books in better condition garner better prices.

The existence of error books, far from being reason to reproach the makers of the Red Book, is almost a given in the fast-paced world of book publication. As Yeoman noted in 1983, "Our quality control staff is as efficient as any in the industry, and they tell me that every attempt is made to inspect each book and sort out all rejects before packaging. Nonetheless, they estimate that with every printing, perhaps a few dozen 'mistakes' could escape apprehension. . . . Yes, there are mistakes in a very few Red Books out there in that vast land of numismatics." The case of the Red Book is unusual, however, in that copies with errors have attained a kind of celebrity status. A somewhat bemused Yeoman sums it up: "Somehow, as publishers, we are unique: our errors are not embarrassing; they are sought-after gems!"[30]

Collector interest in error Red Books was particularly strong in the 1980s, when collector and dealer Ed Lesniak wrote a series of articles for *Coin World* on these curiosities. "It just might be," Lesniak mused, "that error 'Red Books' have a place in a complete set. They may be sought after by collectors [just] as they look for the 1972/72 Lincoln and 1942/41 Mercury to add to their coin sets." The floods of letters he received in response to his original article provided information on additional error editions, which he then passed along to other collectors. Lesniak alerted readers to errors whether they pervaded an entire print run, such as the flipped photo of the Georgius Triumpho obverse in the 1984 edition, or were one-of-a-kind anomalies. Despite his fascination with error copies, he made a point of observing that the Red Book's makers "have a very fine product and strive for perfection." Nevertheless, he acknowledged, "even with all the safeguards, errors are possible."[31]

Binding Errors

Despite the quality-control measures taken by the Red Book staff, inevitably mistakes occur from time to time in the production of the book. In his *Coin World* articles, error-book collector Ed Lesniak reported a number of Red Books of different editions that had repeated pages, missing pages, or both. One 1984 edition, for example, contains this page sequence: pages 1 through 32; 97 through 128; 65 to 256. Pages 33 through 64 never appear, but pages 97 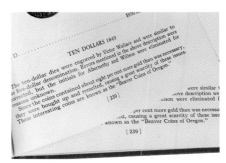 through 128 are duplicated. In another case, Lesniak tells of a reader who owned *two* copies of the same 1973 edition error, in which the page order was 1 through 48; 33 through 48; and 65 through 255. As Lesniak observes, "If two copies of the same error exist, I have to think that there can be additional ones. Look at your copy to see if it is normal or a mate to the above." Possibly the most bizarre case of misbound pages reported in a Red Book occurred in a 15th (1962) edition copy, whose pages followed this dizzying order: 3 through 64; 33 through 64; 97 through 160; 197 through 224; 193 through 225. For some reason, the incidence of error editions reported to Lesniak—and

ENTHUSIASM FOR ERRORS

The "error edition" phenomenon seems to have begun relatively early in the life of the Red Book, and to have come as a surprise to the book's creator. As Q. David Bowers notes in his foreword, when readers approached Yeoman with misprinted Red Books, his instinct was to offer an error-free replacement—which was not what the collector wanted! Yeoman relates this discovery in his essay "The Red Book Story—Chapter One: A Retrospective," from the 1984 Red Book:

> I was a little slow to pick up on the trend, but I became positively aware of the inclination a few years back. The "mint error" syndrome seems to have drifted into the world of publishing as well. Printing and binding discrepancies have taken on a special interest for a growing number of Red Book owners. At first when an occasional convention visitor would come up to me with an obviously imperfect catalog which might have an upside-down or double-stamped cover, laminated pages, missing pages or the like, I would assure the "victim" that Whitman expected to replace the offending volume at no charge. Then I came to realize that each of those enthusiastic folks had no intention of parting with his or her catalog. Rather, they usually asked me to certify in writing adjacent to the manufacturing imperfection that the mistake was in the nature of a genuine "Mint Error," to be attested to with my signature—no less!

Error editions gained fans in high places, as when no less important a personage than Mint director Eva Adams toured the Whitman facilities in 1963. As Kenneth Bressett recalls,

> In this tour of the plant she stopped at the final inspection line and saw one of the Red Books that was cased in upside down (in other words, it had an upside-down cover). We laughed that the Mint was not the only factory to make mistakes. Several weeks later, she asked Dick Yeoman if she could have that upside-down book. Of course it had been scrapped long before that, so he had one specially made for her and sent that to her.

This may have been one of the rarest error editions of all, in that it was a deliberately created one!

Mint director Eva Adams looks over a Red Book press sheet with (from left to right) R.S. Yeoman, two unidentified pressmen, and Whitman sales manager Marshall Thomas.

described by him in these articles—was markedly higher in the states of Ohio and California. Red Book collectors who live in these states may wish to keep a particularly sharp eye out for error editions in their local bookstores!

More recent binding errors include a 1986 (39th) edition that is missing pages 65 to 96. A 1988 (41st) edition boasts the following page sequence: 1 to 32, 97 to 128, 65 to 96, and 127 to 270! Most recent of all is the 1997 error copy whose pages number 1 to 96, 65 to 80, and 113 to 323. Only one error special edition is known, a 1997 edition that is missing some pages in the center of the book. It is held by a Midwest collector, and is currently valued at $350. Among regular editions, error books with binding errors—such as duplicated, missing, or misplaced pages—are currently valued at $50 in New condition.

Error 16th Editions

Probably the best-known Red Book binding error, which occurred in the 16th (1963) edition, was caused by an unusual printing mistake. In this edition page 237 was mistakenly set with a duplicate of page 239, which

Values of Error 16th Editions

Variety	Fine	Very Fine	New
Misprint with duplicate page	$10	$15	$30
With page 237 pasted in by publisher	100	200	300
Individual replacement page 237	—	—	—

also appeared in its proper place (see photo on page 253). When Yeoman learned of the mistake, he had the presses stopped and corrected the edition before allowing it to resume printing. Despite his intervention, however, a small number of the error copies still managed to find their way into the public's hands. Yeoman relates the incident in "The Red Book Story," and his telling is so entertaining it deserves to be quoted at length:

> The blunder we would rather forget started in the makeup room in May 1964 [actually 1962]. That one reminds me of Murphy's Law, "If anything can happen, etc." The printing plates for the 16th edition were made ready on the press, and I was off to the Flambeau River, in the wilds of Northern Wisconsin, to help open the fishing season. My partner and I were stepping into a rowboat when an auto pulled into the clearing . . . [and] a man jumped out, waving a piece of paper and calling my name. . . . There was trouble with the Red Book back at the plant, and I was given no choice but to phone the office immediately. Imagine my dismay, when I called back, to learn that soon after the catalogs started to roll off the press, an inspection showed that page 237 was missing and page 239 was duplicated. A form consisted of 64 pages on each side of the press sheet, thus, 128 book pages were involved in the miscue. Under the circumstances I could only instruct the crew to set the incorrect sheets aside and remake the form. I also asked them to print a supply of single page no. 237 in case repairs to the misprinted sheets could be made. When I returned to duty, three days later, the production schedule was back to normal and catalogs were being bound, cartoned, and shipped. It was then that I learned wrongly-printed sheets had somehow been mixed with the others, bound in completed catalogs, and too late to be retrieved. In order to meet our shipping timetable with enough books, steps were taken to repair some of the remaining errored books, which involved removing the duplicate page by hand and glueing in page 237. Because the missing page was in the little-used Private Gold section, very few complaints ever came our way. But when they did, we either replaced an entire book when requested, or supplied a single insert of page 237 for those taking the alternate choice.

Readers who opted to have the entire book replaced must have kicked themselves in later years when the flawed book became a popular collectible. By the time Yeoman wrote about the event in 1971, collectors had come to embrace this scarcity. He wraps up his story with a whimsical charge:

> So, you seekers and collectors of Red Book errors, that is our confession and your challenge. If you have a 16th edition, turn to page 237; if it isn't there, it's too late for a replacement. But, rejoice, you may have our most embarrassing but unusual of all Red Book errors. No, we don't know how many wrong books got away from us, but surely there are some still waiting to be found. Good hunting!

This error's enduring popularity means that it is hard to find in New condition. Values are largely determined by collectors.

Yeoman had a few hundred copies of page 237 printed and kept them on hand in the event that anyone requested it for replacement. It is unknown exactly how many people asked for the replacement page, although Ken Bressett has estimated that there were only about two dozen requests.[32] As Yeoman noted, requests were probably limited because the error occurred in a part of the book that many people did not have reason to consult; it is likely that few readers noticed the error during the one-year period before the book was supplanted by the next edition. The remaining replacement pages were discarded when the next edition of the Red Book was printed. If any of these extra pages escaped destruction, they are extremely rare, and their value can only be speculative at this time. As of this writing, no books with the replacement page glued in by Whitman have been reported; nor have any of the individual replacement pages. If either did become available, in a properly described auction listing it would undoubtedly set a pricing record among 1963 Red Books!

Inverted Bindings

Some Red Books look like normal editions from the outside, but their pages are inverted within the covers. The pages are usually upside down, with the beginning of the book attached to the back cover. These are extremely popular errors and generally bring two to three times the price of a regular edition. In Charles Davis's February 2008 numismatic literature auction, inverted copies of the 21st, 24th, and 27th editions in "Fine/Near New" condition sold for $55 each. In general, inverted-binding copies from the 20th edition to the present are valued at $35 to $55 in New condition, while earlier editions with inverted bindings carry a value of $50 to $75, likewise in New condition. Damaged books or books that have been written in, on the other hand, are far less desirable.

Many books with inverted bindings are known. The following print runs are known to have produced books in which the pages were inverted within the covers:

19th (1966) edition	30th (1977) edition	44th (1991) edition
20th (1967) edition	31st (1978) edition	45th (1992) edition
21st (1968) edition	33rd (1980) edition	47th (1994) edition
22nd (1969) edition	34th (1981) edition	48th (1995) edition
24th (1971) edition	37th (1984) edition	52nd (1999) edition
27th (1974) edition	38th (1985) edition	56th (2003) edition
28th (1975) edition	42nd (1989) edition	59th (2006) edition
29th (1976) edition	43rd (1990) edition	

This list is by no means complete, because many other editions probably exist—even, possibly, for every year the book has been published. (There is even one known copy of a first-edition Blue Book with inverted pages.) As Ken Bressett said in 1991, "the most common Red Book error is one with the cover put on upside down. I hear about a few of these every year, despite the fact that each book is hand-inspected when it comes off the press."

Copies with inverted bindings can be found everywhere, including at your local coin shop. Examine the contents of each book you come across, since you will not be able to tell until the book is open whether its contents and cover do not align. Browse carefully, and you may be able to purchase a book with an inverted binding for the cost of a normal copy.

In 1996, Whitman began producing a spiralbound, or coil-bound, edition of the Red Book. Production of these spiralbound books has resulted in some extraordinary error editions. One example was brought to my attention by Rich Schemmer, a noted error-coin specialist in Long Island, New York. This 60th (2007) edition was published with its spiral binding on the right side of the book, where the book would normally open, rather than the left. The pages inside are perfect and the book can be easily be read. But this particular copy is worth a premium because of the mistake.

There are other error books from the 60th edition, including another copy in which the spiral binding is on the right side. In this book, however, the interior pages have been inverted in relation to the cover. To read this copy normally, one must hold it with the cover upside down.

These are just two examples of error printings since the advent of spiralbound Red Books. It is likely that others exist.

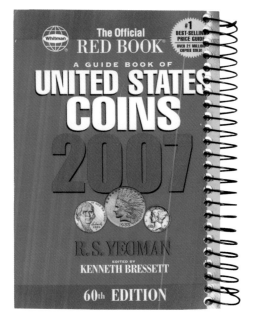

Unnotched Spine

Another error due to a binding mistake is the unusual "unnotched spine." Regular copies of the *Guide Book* include an indentation on both the front and back covers where the cover meets the spine. Books without this indentation are described as having unnotched spines. (For purposes of comparison, the illustrations show a regular Red Book next to the unnotched-spine book.) These copies bring only a small premium, since the error is not dramatic and may even go unnoticed by most collectors. Yet an unnotched spine is a legitimate error, and these books are certainly collectible. Interestingly, the example shown—a 22nd (1969) edition—is a contributor's sample and features a "perfect" (glued) binding rather than the sturdier sewn binding standard among Red Books produced for sale. Perhaps this deviation from the usual binding process resulted in the unnotched spine. The contributor's sample shown here is valued at $100 or more, whereas a regular-edition Red Book with an unnotched spine would carry a value of $20 to $25 in New condition.

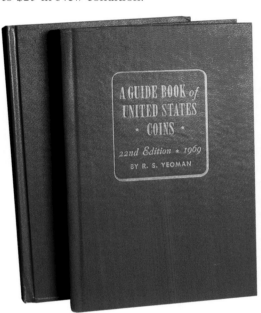

Bound Advance Copy

One of the most unusual editions I have ever seen is an advance copy that was bound and sold as a regular 13th-edition *Guide Book* (see illustration on next page). Advance copies of the Red Book were made without covers and were sent annually to contributors for comments. "Front Guide Book of United States Coins" and "Back Guide Book of United States Coins" are printed, respectively, on the first and last pages of the unbound books. In the past, similar copies of the Blue Book have been made for contributors; one is shown here to illustrate what these advance books usually look like. This error book is distinguishable as an advance copy because the identifying phrases on the first and last pages are visible. Even more intriguing is that these notations are reversed: "Front Guide Book of United States Coins" is printed on the blank page opposite the last page of the index in the book's rear, while the page facing the title page at the front of the book reads "Back Guide Book of United States Coins." This is the only known copy to display this mistake. Its value is $200 to $250; the value of the unbound advance Blue Book is $100.

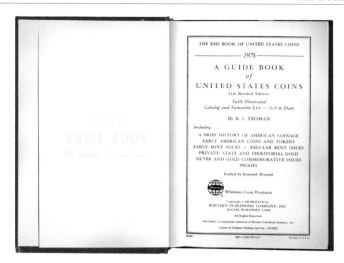

THE RED BOOK OF UNITED STATES COINS

——— *1978* ———

A GUIDE BOOK
of
UNITED STATES COINS
31st Revised Edition

Fully Illustrated
Catalog and Valuation List — 1616 to Date

By R. S. YEOMAN

Including . . . .

A BRIEF HISTORY OF AMERICAN COINAGE
EARLY AMERICAN COINS AND TOKENS
EARLY MINT ISSUES • REGULAR MINT ISSUES
PRIVATE STATE AND TERRITORIAL GOLD
SILVER AND GOLD COMMEMORATIVE ISSUES
PROOFS

Edited by Kenneth Bressett

Whitman Coin Products

Copyright © MCMLXXVII by
WESTERN PUBLISHING COMPANY, INC.
RACINE, WISCONSIN 53404

All Rights Reserved

WHITMAN is a registered trademark of Western Publishing Company, Inc.

Library of Congress Catalog Card No.: 76-9233

**Advance copies of the Red Book usually resemble the unbound Blue
Book shown below, rather than the bound copy shown above.**

Cover-Printing Errors

Another popular error is "doubled-die" cover printings. Although this is a totally incorrect description for the printing error, because of its resemblance to the numismatic phenomenon it has become an easy and acceptable way to describe these books. The cover printing appears doubled because it has been printed two (or more) times. You may have to look closely to see the error because the words are generally printed fairly close together. In the book illustrated, you can easily see an example of this doubling, which appears on the spine as well as the front.

The most extreme cover misprinting I have yet found is on a 27th (1974) edition with a second strike both offset and ungilded. The misstruck, ungilded cover text can be discerned as interruptions in the gilt. This is a very unusual error and not often found. Strangely, the spine was correctly printed, and shows no evidence of the error.

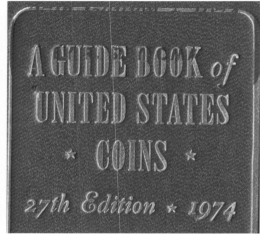

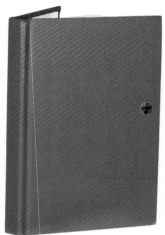

These misprinted covers are not very common, but they are popular collectibles. Generally, they are valued at three times the cost of a current edition. They are usually found in nice condition, although some (such as the 15th edition shown) may display some use.

Two more cover errors were provided by Fred Weinberg of Encino, California. Fred is a dealer in error coinage and was kind enough to provide a number of Red Books for inclusion in this study. In addition to bringing my attention to two inverted editions, Fred had two of the nicest misprinted covers that I had ever seen.

One of these, a 39th (1986) edition, displays off-center printing on both the cover and the spine. This is one of the finest off-center printings that I have ever had the opportunity to observe.

The other is extremely unusual in that the cover was not printed at all. This 33rd (1980) edition is completely blank on the outside, on both the front and the spine. Aside from some early editing copies, which this is not, only four other Red Books have been reported as having covers with no printing whatever: a 19th (1966) edition and a 36th (1983) edition, both reported in the mid-1980s by Ed Lesniak in *Coin World,* and a 26th (1973) and 33rd (1980) edition. These are the only Red Books known to date that completely missed the cover-printing process.

Extreme Errors

There are many other minor errors that are also collectible. For example, a book may be missing a portion of its cover or one of its pages may have been cut incorrectly. There is even one copy known with its red cover mistakenly folded over, forming a seam in the front. These errors are minor, but still interesting and collectible. The limit to what you can collect is set only by what you are able to find and are interested in saving.

There are not, on the other hand, many times that the term "extreme error" can be accurately applied to a *Guide Book* printing. However, mistakes—including big ones—can, and do, happen. One of the most extreme Red Book errors is visible in a copy of the 39th (1986) edition (illustrated), whose cover was attached with the wrong side facing out, then stamped with the title as usual. This resulted in a Red Book with very little red to boast of! The plain cardboard inner surface that in standard books is covered by the endpapers now faces outward, while the layer of red laminate, usually the outermost surface of the cover, is visible only at the book's edges. This highly unusual copy is probably the second most extreme error edition Red Book.

The most extreme *Guide Book* error I have encountered is in a copy of the 1976 edition. The interior of this book was inserted by the bindery into the cover of a different Whitman publication altogether—the seventh edition of Neil Shafer's *Guide Book of Modern United States Currency!* It is interesting to note that only pages 1 through 127—approximately the number of pages that would be in a regular copy of Shafer's book—are included in this odd copy. The last page, 127, is pasted to the cover. This error is so unusual that one of the book's owners went to what were probably considerable lengths to have both Shafer and Yeoman sign it. The rarity of this error in addition to these two signatures guarantees that this book will sell for an extraordinary price if it ever appears at auction.

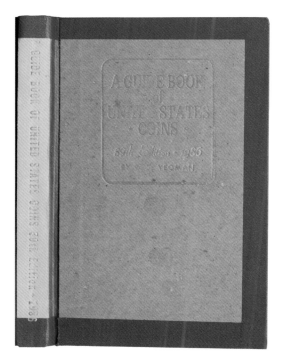
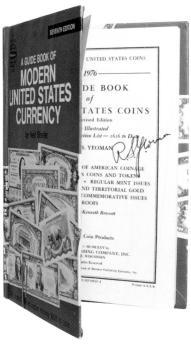

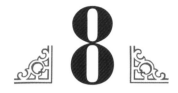

Red Book Collectibles and Curiosities

This chapter will explore collectible items, not books themselves, that are related to the Red Book. The items classed as collectibles were produced for the public and are regularly collected as extensions of the *Guide Book* series. Later in the chapter we will look at items not created for general distribution that may still occasionally find their way into a collector's hands; these we term "curiosities."

Red Book and Blue Book Silver Medals

To celebrate the 40th anniversary of the Red Book in 1986, Whitman Publishing's advertising manager Ed Metzer decided the company would offer collectors a limited-edition medal composed of one ounce of .999 fine silver. Over the next 11 years, Whitman issued commemorative silver rounds for each year's Red Book and Blue Book. Readers ordered these silver rounds by mailing in their payment along with the gold-colored sticker attached to each edition's front cover. Two medals of equal value were offered each year: one from the Red Book and one from the Blue Book. The cover of each year's Red Book illustrated the obverse of the corresponding silver round (with the exception of the 50th anniversary edition). A common reverse design was utilized for all the Red Book and Blue Book rounds. It featured the Whitman logo and the legend "Whitman Coin Products One Troy Oz. .999 Fine Silver Racine, Wisconsin."

To carry out the manufacture and shipping of these rounds, Metzger turned to Bill Spencer of American Coin and Stamp Supply, located in Racine, Wisconsin. A distributor for Whitman since 1972, Spencer reports that all the medal dies were engraved by Landmark Engraving, although the mints differed from year to year. Spencer provided much of the mintage information in the listings that follow.

At left: the reverse type of all the Red Book and Blue Book silver rounds. At right: the plastic case (actual size 3-3/4 by 4-3/4 inches) that came with each Red Book medal.

1986 Silver Medals

The first commemorative Red Book medal replicated the standard Red Book cover as rendered for the 40th edition. The selling price was $9.95, including postage (but not sales tax). The rounds were struck at the North American mint, and 1,000 were made.

The date on the medal corresponded to the book's copyright date rather than the cover date (1987), so the silver round read "40th Anniversary Edition" followed by the date span "1946–1986." Medals in the following years would also be dated according to the copyright date of the edition they accompanied.

A medal was also issued for the Blue Book this year. The date span was "1942–1986," reflecting the first Blue Book's publication in 1942. Its design, like that of its counterpart, mimicked the cover of the book it commemorated.

1987 Silver Medals

The medal released with the 41st edition of the Red Book (cover date 1988) was based on the obverse of the Spanish pillar dollar, a coin also

Some medals from this issue have interruptions in the reeding on the edge.

known as the "piece of eight." Starting with the first edition, this coin had been the first one illustrated in every Red Book. The obverse of the medal offered through the Blue Book was that of the reverse of the same coin. On the Blue Book medal, the coin's actual date was replaced with "1942–1987," marking the 45th anniversary of the Blue Book.

This silver round exists in a variety, according to Spencer. Most of the medals in the series feature reeded edges, but Spencer has revealed that the first 20 of the 1987 Red Book and Blue Book medals to be struck did not feature reeding around the entire rim; instead, a blank or smooth space interrupted the reeding (see illustration). After these 20 were struck, it was decided that the rest should have entirely reeded edges.

The medal's price increased to $10.95. This may have reflected the increased cost of production or the increased cost of silver. The same quantity was struck as in the previous year—1,000 pieces—but these medals were minted at Golden State.

1988 Silver Medals

For their third year of issue, the design chosen for the medal was based on the obverse of the Continental Dollar. As stated on page 30 of the 42nd-edition *Guide Book*, this coin "was the first silver dollar sized coin ever proposed for the United States." (All page references in this section refer to the edition of the Red Book under discussion, unless otherwise noted.) The coin's date of 1776 was replaced with the copyright date of the Red Book, 1988, and the legend "42nd Edition Red Book" was added to the design. The purchase price remained $10.95. Golden State was again the minting company, and the quantity minted remained at 1,000.

However, the Blue Book medal did not follow the pattern of previous issues and duplicate the design of the Continental Dollar's reverse. Instead it honored the Fugio cent. These coins were noted on page 40 of the corresponding edition of the Blue Book as "the first coins issued by authority of the United States."

1989 Silver Medals

The 43rd-edition Red Book (whose cover date was 1990) offered a medal based on the obverse of the 1915 Panama-Pacific Exposition $50 commemorative gold coin. Page 233 of the 1990 *Guide Book* stated that this "was the first fifty dollar sized coin ever issued for the United States." The obverse of the medal added "43rd Edition Red Book" to the central design. Interestingly, for the first time, the date was kept the same as that on the original coin. The medal was illustrated on the *Guide Book's* cover and offered for $10.95.

The Blue Book offered the reverse of the same coin design as the Red Book. Merely the legend was adjusted. It was changed to read, "47th Edition Blue Book 1989." This mirrored the coin offered through this book.

A change of mints took place, with the 1989 silver rounds being minted at the National Refinery. Again, 1,000 were made.

1990 Silver Medals

The design utilized for the 1991 edition Red Book cover and corresponding silver medal was based on the obverse of the 1852 $10 gold Moffat & Company coin (as shown on page 256 of the *Guide Book*). During the California Gold Rush era, Moffat & Company had recognized the need for hard coinage and issued coins that had designs similar to those of the federal government, but with its own company name on Lady Liberty's tiara. In the same vein, Whitman replaced Moffat's name on the tiara with its own. It also changed the legend to "44th Edition Red Book 1990." The cost of the medal remained $10.95. The mint (National Refinery) and quantity struck (1,000) likewise remained the same as the year before; the quantity would go unchanged until the 1993 issues were manufactured.

The Blue Book's 48th-edition commemorative medal displayed the same design as the reverse of the 1852 $10 gold Moffat & Company coin. The legend was changed to read "48th Edition Blue Book 1990."

1991 Silver Medals

For the 45th edition of the Red Book (cover date 1992), the offered medal was based on Charles Barber's design for the obverse of the 1892 to 1916 silver coinage. His design was used for the dime, quarter, and half dollar. (These coins can be seen on pages 123, 137, and 159 of that edition of the *Guide Book*.) This time Whitman Publishing left the legend on Liberty's tiara alone. Instead, it replaced the stars on the obverse with "45th Edition Red Book 1981."

The Blue Book's medal displayed the reverse of the Barber design for the quarter and half dollar, with the legend changed to read "49th Edition Blue Book 1991." The purchase price of each medal was reduced to $9.95.

1992 Silver Medals

The 46th edition of the *Guide Book* honored the 100th anniversary of the Columbian Exposition commemorative half dollar. The first in a long series of U.S. commemorative coins, the Columbian half dollar was issued in 1892 and 1893 for the World's Columbian Exposition. Although it was considered a failure in its day, with two million being melted down by the Mint and almost as many released into general circulation at face value, its status rose considerably over the following century.[33] It was described on page 230 of the 1993 *Guide Book*. The medal displayed the legend "46th Edition Red Book 1992" and was offered for $9.95.

Once again, the Blue Book offered a medal that displayed the same coin's reverse. Its legend changed to read "50th Anniversary Edition Blue Book 1992."

1993 Silver Medals

The silver medal offered with the 47th (1994) edition of the Red Book portrayed the obverse of the 1793 Chain cent, the type known as Flowing Hair. The nation's first large cent and the first coin officially produced by the U.S. mint, the Chain cent was celebrating its 200th anniversary. The publishers could not have chosen a better coin to be represented by medal. The artwork is beautiful, and many collectors will never have a chance to own this rare coin. It can be viewed on page 78 of the 1994 *Guide Book*. For the medal, the coin's original legend was changed to read, "47th Edition Liberty Red Book 1993."

The Blue Book's 51st-edition commemorative silver round displays the Chain cent's reverse design. The coin legend was changed to read "51st Edition Blue Book," and the medal was dated 1993. The purchase price of this year's silver medals was maintained at $9.95. However, fewer were struck: the quantity minted dropped slightly, to 800 pieces. The National Refinery was again the mint employed.

1994 Silver Medals

For the 48th (1995) edition medals, the honored coin was the 1794 half cent. This design, the "Liberty Cap," features a bust of Liberty facing right, with behind her the liberty cap on a pole, as shown on page 73 of the 48th-edition *Guide Book*. The medal's main design was a faithful representation, with a legend that read, "Red Book Liberty 48th Edition 1994."

The 52nd-edition Blue Book offered a medal that displayed the reverse of the 1794 half cent. The legend was changed to read, "Blue Book 52nd Edition 1994." This year, each medal cost $10.95. The price hike reflected the increased cost of silver. Another drop occurred in the quantity produced, with a total of only 700 pieces issued. The medals were again produced by the National Refinery.

1995 Silver Medals

The commemorative coin chosen for the 49th edition of the Red Book was the Heraldic Eagle $10 gold coin (or "eagle"), released from 1797 to 1804. The original coin appeared on page 210 of that edition of the *Guide Book*. The medal's legends read, "Liberty 1995" and "49th Edition Red Book."

The Blue Book medal displayed the reverse of the eagle coin. Its legend was changed to read "53rd Edition Blue Book," and it was dated 1995. Each medal was offered for $10.95.

The 1995 medals were produced by Golden State, the same company that had minted the 1987 and 1988 issues, and which would mint the remainder of the series. The mintage was maintained at 700 pieces.

1996 Silver Medals

The silver round offered through the 50th edition of the Red Book (cover date 1997, publication date 1996) was the first in the series not to be illustrated on the book's cover. The Red Book bore a 50th anniversary emblem, whereas the medal displayed the Roosevelt dime, which was first issued in 1946 to honor the only four-term president. The coin was illustrated on page 131 of the 50th-edition *Guide Book* (and can also be found in almost any pocketful of loose change). The medal read, "Red Book 50th Anniversary Edition" and "In God We Trust." It was dated 1946–1996. These dates were reflective of the history of both the Red Book and the dime's design.

The 54th-edition Blue Book's commemorative medal replicated the Roosevelt dime's reverse, with the dime's legend changed to read "Blue Book 54th Edition." This medal was dated 1997. The purchase price of each silver round increased to $11.95, and the quantity produced sank to 600 pieces.

RED BOOK AND BLUE BOOK SILVER MEDALS

1986

1987

1988

1989

1990

1991

Note: Reverse type of all medals shown on page 262.

RED BOOK AND BLUE BOOK SILVER MEDALS

1992

1993

1994

1995

1996

1997

1997 Silver Medals

The cover design of the 1998-dated Red Book was changed back to the thematic designs of the issues prior to the 50th anniversary edition. (There was, however, a dramatic change to the cover, as illustrated in chapter 4.) The cover again displayed the honored coin. This time, the famous 1848 "CAL." quarter eagle ($2.50 coin) was the basis for the medal's design. Made with metal from the first delivery of gold from the California gold finds, this coin is considered by many to be the nation's first true commemorative coin and could be seen, along with a notation on its pricing history, on page 194 of the 51st-edition *Guide Book*. It had a total mintage of 1,349 pieces and a historic following. For the first and only time, the Red Book cover and the corresponding medal displayed the reverse of the coin being honored. This is because the important notation "CAL." appears on the coin's reverse.

Once again, the Blue Book's commemorative silver round replicated the same coin as the Red Book. Since the *Guide Book* had utilized the reverse this year, the Blue Book's medal portrayed the obverse. The coin legend was changed to read "55th Edition Blue Book 1997."

The purchase price was maintained at $11.95. The order form gave no indication that these would be the last releases in the commemorative medal series. Again, 600 pieces were minted.

Medal Sales Today

The silver medal series concluded with 24 pieces in the set, released over a period of 12 years. Today a lively aftermarket has developed for these rounds, and pieces routinely sell for a strong premium over their silver value. A complete set of all 24 Red Book and Blue Book medals is presently valued at $500 or more.

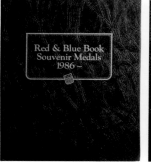 

Internet sales are strong. Online auctions garner quite a bit of bid-ding, especially when the rounds are properly described in the lot name. Frequently, a set of two pieces will sell for $45 or more, especially when accompanied by their original-issue plastic holder. Even individual pieces in a plastic holder with the plug still in place (for the missing medal) will attract strong bids.

Usually, no more than one or two individual pieces are put up for auction each month. To date, there have been no auctions of complete 24-piece sets.

In addition to the annual plastic holders, Whitman Publishing issued a custom-made album for storing the set of medals. It was issued in the early days of the series, and only identifies spaces for rounds produced through 1991. The album itself is rather scarce, and is actively collected when offered. Its present value in New condition is $25 to $35.

OTHER MEDALS AND ELONGATED COINS

In addition to the medals issued in tandem with the Red and Blue Books, Whitman Publishing had other commemorative pieces struck on different occasions. This section describes these issues, in addition to commemorative elongated coins that honored the Red Book.

ANA 100th Anniversary Medal

In 1991, Whitman Publishing issued a special-edition brass-plated aluminum medal for the ANA's hundredth anniversary. The obverse utilized the same design as that on the cover of the special-edition *Guide Book* released for the same event. (See chapter 5 for a picture of this cover.) On the reverse, the dates "1936–1991" were recorded to honor the 56th anniversary of Whitman coin products. This medal was produced with a matte finish.

The 5,000 medals struck were given away as premiums at the 1996 Denver ANA show. Because of the limited production number, the piece is infrequently offered for sale and draws strong bids when properly described. Its present value is $25.

Red Book 50th Anniversary Medals

Special commemorative items were produced for the 50th anniversary of the *Guide Book* in 1996. Not only were there the special-edition Red Books described in previous chapters, and the silver round described earlier; other commemorative medals were also produced.

The obverse of this medal displayed a portrait bust of R.S. Yeoman, with the legend "Red Book 50th Anniversary Edition" around the top and "R.S. Yeoman" underneath. The reverse was a replica of the cover design on the corresponding anniversary Red Book. There were 5,000 pieces struck in brass and given away at the 1996 Denver American Numismatic Association show. Each was presented in a cloth pouch. The medal is somewhat scarce, and the pouch is even scarcer. Currently, the medal is valued at about $15, plus an additional $10 if it includes the original pouch. Silver versions were also produced, but only 100 pieces were struck. These pieces are very scarce and are rarely available for sale.

Anniversary sets of three medals were also minted, but never distributed. According to Bill Spencer, only 50 of these sets were made. Each set contained one 1-ounce silver round, one overstruck silver dollar (Morgan or Peace), and one gold-plated round. The reverse of the gold-plated round featured the same Red Book 50th anniversary logo used for the brass medals, while the reverse of the two silver pieces displayed the Whitman logo. The three were housed in a red (of course) display card stamped in gold with the set number. Whitman Publishing decided not to publicly distribute these sets, so they are one of the best-kept secrets of Red Book collectibles. The current value of the set, with display card, is $150.

The Red Book 50th anniversary medal set shown above contains a medal struck over a Peace dollar. Some sets contained overstruck Morgan dollars.

The brass version of the Red Book 50th anniversary medal, shown with pouch.

Red Book 50th Anniversary Elongated Coins

The 50th anniversary of the Red Book also saw another commemorative—one that seems not to have been produced in any other year. At the Racine Numismatic Society coin show of March 2, 1997, the society commemorated the Red Book's landmark anniversary by rolling out five coins with a special imprint. The imprint replicated the *Guide Book* cover design and gave the name, date, and location of the event. The coins rolled out were the Wheat cent, steel cent, Memorial cent, Buffalo nickel, and Jefferson nickel. The elongated Memorial cents were distributed free to those who attended the coin show, while complete sets of all five pieces were sold for $5. An estimated 1,000 Memorial cents and 200 five-piece sets were rolled out. The current value for these elongated coins is $10 to $15.

60th Anniversary Limited-Edition Medal

Offered at coin shows and through the Whitman Publishing Web site in 2006, this limited-edition medal celebrated 60 years of Red Book publication. The medal's obverse displayed busts of editors R.S. Yeoman and Kenneth Bressett; the reverse proclaimed the celebration of 60 years in publication. The medal cost $29.95 when purchased alone, but was also offered for the reduced price of $19.95 when purchased as a package with the 2007 Limited Edition *Guide Book*. Each medal was released in an individually numbered ANACS slab and slipcase. The medal was struck in nickel silver (which is also called "German silver" and does not actually contain any silver) and was limited to 500 pieces. At an appreciation ceremony at the zANA World's Fair of Money in Denver (August 2006), Whitman publisher Dennis Tucker presented a unique strike in .900 fine gold to longtime Red Book editor Kenneth Bressett, who also received from artist Charles Daughtrey the original artwork of the portrait used to create the medal.

This medal is rarely available on the secondary market. The issue has sold out, and Internet auction sites do not offer the medal with any frequency. Since spring of 2007 I have seen only one offered on eBay, and at that time the medal was still available through the Whitman Web site. None have been offered since that time. Current value for the medal is $50.

RED BOOK EPHEMERA

R.S. Yeoman Biographical Pamphlet

In 1978, *Numismatic News* produced a giveaway item that is now scarce: an eight-page pamphlet measuring 5-3/8 by 7-3/4 inches, with a cover replicating that of the 1978 *Guide Book*. The booklet contained a biographical essay on R.S. Yeoman and his work in the coin hobby, entitled "Mr. Red Book," illustrated with sepia-tone vintage photographs.

Current value estimates for this pamphlet are in the $10 to $30 range. At this time, none are known to have R.S. Yeoman's signature. A copy with his autograph would sell for a considerable premium over the regular price.

Red Book 50th Anniversary Mini-Folder

A miniature coin folder made to resemble the first-edition *Guide Book* was produced to commemorate the occasion of the book's 50th anniversary. The folder was 4-5/8 inches by 3-1/2 inches, with an exterior that resembled the cover of the first edition and an interior that resembled Whitman's famous coin folders. It included a spot to hold a Roosevelt dime from 1946, the year of the first *Guide Book*, and another to hold a Roosevelt dime from 1996, the year of the *Guide Book*'s 50th anniversary.

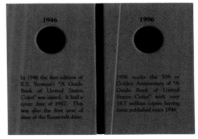

These mini-folders were distributed at the August 1996 ANA convention in Denver, Colorado. Some included the coins. It is not known how many were produced, but the population shrank almost at once due to a mishap: after the convention the remaining folders were shipped back to Whitman headquarters, but they were lost en route. Thus, the only surviving folders are those that were distributed at the convention. For that reason, the mini-folders are considered very scarce, particularly those in mint condition (such as the one shown here). The current estimated value of the mini-folder, complete with coins, is $50. In a properly described auction it would probably sell for more.

Promotional Products

Perhaps the scarcest Red Book collectibles, if indeed any at all survive, are the "brilliantly printed window streamers" that Whitman included in cases of Red Books shipped to dealers in the 1960s. As described in the June 1962 *Merchandiser*, "these window streamers announce the fact that you [dealers] have Red Books available and indicate some of the major revisions in this edition." Although it is unlikely that any of these advertising banners still exist, a collector lucky enough to unearth one would own a truly unusual piece of Red Book history.

Decades later, a similar marketing tool—the point-of-purchase poster—would be sent to booksellers to promote the Red Book. According to Whitman publisher Dennis Tucker, these colorful posters have been distributed annually since 2005, in quantities of about 20,000 per year. They measure 18 by 24 inches and are folded horizontally and vertically for shipment. So far none have been reported on the secondary market. As with any advertising ephemera, they doubtless will gain collectible status in coming years.

Another Red Book collectible that has yet to be acknowledged is the vintage advertisements for the book, which appeared in coin publications such as *The Numismatist*. As can be seen from the ones reproduced throughout this book, these pieces of ephemera often have great character and charm, showing the changing styles in commercial art throughout the long life of the Red Book—and providing illuminating glimpses as to how the book has been promoted through the years!

RED BOOK CURIOSITIES

In this section we will look at Red Book–related objects that, although often fascinating, were not produced for general circulation and are not, strictly speaking, collectible. Some of these are unique objects, such as the Braille Red Book; others were created strictly for use within Whitman Publishing, and their presence outside those precincts is a mystery. To be blunt, you should not hope or expect to find these pieces available for sale. They are included here as a kind of museum display to educate and entertain the Red Book lover. Enjoy your tour!

Unique Red Books

As earlier sections of this book have indicated, one-of-a-kind Red Books were sometimes created, often as a joke between Q. David Bowers and Kenneth Bressett. (See Bowers's foreword and chapter 2 for more on the unique grey, fur-bound, and advertising copies.) At one time, Bressett has recounted, Bowers even challenged him to produce a Red Book bound in plaid! One highly unusual Red Book variation, however, was created in a different spirit.

A *Merchandiser* from 1970 relates the story. Davyd Pepito, a 17-year-old coin collector in California, was in need of a *Guide Book* in Braille. "Being blind and unable to read printed Red Books," he wrote to the Covina Coin Club, "I have tried since I was 13 to find a Braille one." The nonprofit organization Uncap International took on the challenge, after receiving permission from Whitman, and Pepito received his Braille Red Book—in installments. "I now have half the book," he is quoted as saying. "You see, for every one page of print, it takes four pages of Braille. So this one print volume is taking four of Braille." In fact, the final transcription would span nine Braille volumes and take three months to complete. This unique 1969 edition Red Book is now in a private collection. In August 2008 it was displayed at the Whitman Coin and Collectibles Atlanta Expo, in conjunction with a fundraising effort to benefit the National Federation of the Blind.

Test Copies

Publishers often create test versions of upcoming books to see how a particular binding or cover design will look. Often these are dummy books, without any internal printing. These experimental books are produced individually or in very small quantities, and are usually never seen by members of the public, as their only function is to aid in the design process. Occasionally, however, one of these rarities will find its way out into the world—and, if luck is smiling, into a collector's hands.

Three of the four test copies shown here were prepared for the Red Book's 50th anniversary edition. This landmark event was marked by a special cover design on the standard Red Book and the introduction of a new spiralbound softcover edition, as discussed in chapter 4. One of the test copies shown here, however, will immediately stand out because it is a paperback—which should not exist! The cover design of this test copy is identical to that of the actual spiralbound issue of that edition, featuring the 50th anniversary emblem. According to Kenneth Bressett, only six of these paperbacks were produced, and they were made to test the perfect (that is, glued) binding equipment.

Of the original printing of six copies, only two are known today: one is in Bressett's collection, and the other is also in a private collection. Apparently no one knows what happened to the other four copies, and they may well have been discarded or destroyed. On the other hand, one may someday show up in a garage sale. As Ken Bressett notes, this book is nearly as rare as a 1913 Liberty Head nickel! Its estimated value is $750 to $1,000.

The remaining two 50th-anniversary mockups shown here were made to test possible cover designs for the hardback edition. Although neither design was utilized, they offer an intriguing peek at what the golden anniversary Red Book *could* have looked like.

Both covers are oversized—6 inches by 9 inches as opposed to the regular hardback dimensions of 5-1/4 inches by 7-3/4 inches. One of the covers under consideration was

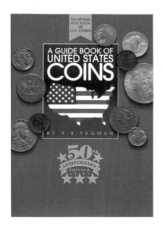
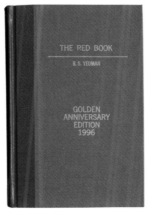

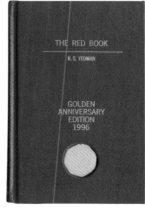

dressed in red cloth and had a red leatherette binding. The front reads "The Red Book" at the top, under which "R.S. Yeoman" appears, separated by a single line. Further down is the legend "Golden Anniversary Edition 1996." The spine reads, *"A Guide Book of United States Coins* 50th Edition 1996." It is certainly interesting that the year is stated as 1996 in both places. After all, although the copyright date was in fact 1996, the anniversary edition date was 1997!

The other hardcover test copy for the 1997 edition features a full cover of red leatherette. The wording on the cover and spine—including the incorrect date—is the same. This book, however, features a space punched into the heavy cover that, presumably, would have contained a special commemorative medal had it been chosen to represent the anniversary. Faint indentations in the cardboard backing of a Liberty Bell design offer a tantalizing glimpse of what that medal might have looked like.

Although both designs were excellent, the publisher went with a third version (shown in chapter 5). This decision may have been made based on what the publisher perceived to be the preferred book size: the standard 5-1/4 inches by 7-3/4 inches. In fact, these test copies are only slightly smaller than the leather Limited Editions that would be released starting just a few years later. In my opinion, either of these test copies would have made a great book. However, the final rendition made one big improvement: the correct year was printed. Each of these test copies is estimated to be worth $750 to $1,000.

The final test copy shown here is from the first year of leather Limited Editions (cover date 2005). In many respects it looks just as the finished books would—even down to the gilt edging on the pages and the ribbon page marker. However, as can be seen here, although the cover bears the imprint of the title, no gilding or ink has been used. Moreover, the leather cover is a brighter shade of red than was ultimately used for production. The pages of this test copy are blank, like those of its fellows. This unique test copy resides in the Whitman Publishing archives. It too is estimated to have a value of $750 to $1,000.

Printing Plates

Among the more unusual *Guide Book*–related items are the printing plates that were used for the pictures throughout the book. In fall of 2004 an eBay seller offered more than 200 of these plates for sale. According to the seller, the plates had been thrown away during one of the changes of ownership undergone by Whitman Publishing, and he had retrieved them before they were disposed of by the refuse collectors.

These pieces are all unique, since there was only one plate prepared for each type coin. The sale information stated that Whitman used the plates in Racine, Wisconsin, in the 1950s and 1960s. The larger and more popular pieces, such as the Morgan dollars, Peace dollars, and $20 gold pieces, realized the highest prices. They sold for between $30 and $40. The others sold for between $12 to $25, depending upon the desirability of the particular design. Shown here are the plates for the Saint-Gaudens MCMVII (1907) double eagle, High Relief, and the 1859 Indian Head cent with Laurel Wreath reverse.

The opportunity to obtain so large a collection of plates may never come again. However, many of these plates may become available again individually in the future.

Contributor Lapel Pins

Starting with the 2007 edition, Whitman Publishing has presented each year's panel of Red Book contributors (and Whitman Publishing staff) with commemorative lapel pins. These are made in relatively small quantities, determined by the number of contributors each year. Each is one inch in diameter, made of metal enameled in red and white. The design varies somewhat, as seen in the illustrations, but the central emblem of a book is always present. Each bears the legend "Official Red Book Contributor™" and the cover date of the Red Book edition. Only one of these pins has ever appeared for sale; their recipients are not very likely to wish to part with them—but there still exists the possibility that in years to come a sharp-eyed collector may obtain one. The lapel pins are distributed along with the year's contributor presentation copies, accompanied by a letter of thanks on Whitman letterhead.

RELATED COLLECTIBLES

In this section you will find memorabilia and other collectible items that are less directly connected to the Red Book. These include publications like the *Whitman Numismatic Journal* and the *Merchandiser*; Whitman coin boards; and even more obscure memorabilia. (See also the listings for Blue Book silver medals earlier in this chapter, and the appendix for more on Blue Book collecting.) This is just a sampling of the items that collectors may wish to obtain to enhance their Red Book collections.

Whitman Periodicals

When Kenneth Bressett began editing the Red Book in 1965, he also took on the task of editing a new Whitman publication: the *Whitman Numismatic Journal*. Published from January 1964 to December 1968, this monthly periodical was created to increase market interest and supplement the annual Red Book. R.S. Yeoman's regular column "U.S. Coin Value Guide Line" offered more timely information on coin values, for example, than could be provided in a yearly publication. Although diminutive at only 64 pages and 5 by 7-1/2 inches (just under the size of a Red Book), the *Journal* was filled with articles by such distinguished numismatic names such as Q. David Bowers, Eric Newman, Walter Breen, Robert Obojski, and J.E. Charlton, as well as Lawrence Block, today an award-winning author in the field of crime fiction.[34] The *Journal* is scarce today, and sets that come up for auction on Internet sites such as eBay often see a flurry of bids—especially if they are accompanied by their original slipcases.

Special cardboard slipcases were created for the *Whitman Numismatic Journal*, which was published from 1964 through 1968; today these cases are extremely scarce.

Even more of a challenge for the collector to find are back issues of the *Merchandiser* newsletter Whitman sent to its retailers. As noted in chapter 2, this newsletter was published as the *Whitman Coin Supply Merchandiser* from 1960 to 1966, as the *Stamp and Coin Supply Merchandiser* from 1969 to 1971, and then again as the *Coin Supply Merchandiser* from 1972 through the end of 1974. At only four pages per issue, and measuring 8-1/2 by 11 inches, the *Merchandiser* was a low-cost but informative means of updating booksellers and hobby dealers about the latest developments in its books and products. Rare vintage photographs and columns by R.S. Yeoman add to the appeal of this hard-to-find item. Because it is so scarce, dollar values cannot be determined.

Coin Boards

Produced from 1935 to 1940, these boards were the first in the Whitman line of coin displays. (See chapter 2 for more discussion of coin boards.) They were succeeded by modern, tri-fold coin folders, and in 1960 by coin albums.

At left, a vintage Whitman coin board; at right, Whitman's Tribute Edition of the Buffalo nickel coin board, released in 2008.

The boards were called "penny boards," but were actually issued in four different denominations—cent, nickel, dime, and quarter—and encompassed eight different series—the Indian Head cent, the Lincoln cent, the Liberty nickel, the Buffalo nickel, the Barber dime, the "Mercury" dime, the Barber quarter, and the Standing Liberty quarter. Uniquely, the Barber quarter series utilized two different boards. Due to the span of the set's release and size of the coins, this series did not fit on one board. The board shown here dates from 1938 and was sized for display in a standard 11-by-14-inch frame.

On these coin boards, each coin slot included a notation with the coin's date and mintage. These mintages were rounded off, and collectors will notice that some of these numbers are very different from the actual mintage figures. The slot for the 1896-S quarter, for example, stated that the mintage was 200,000, when there were actually only 188,039 coins produced. Other stated mintages were lower than the actuality. The 1897-S quarter was actually struck 542,229 times, but the coin board noted only 500,000. The estimates may seem fairly close—but consider that the 1897-S mintage was rounded off by more than the total production of the 1913-S!

In recent years, these original coin boards have become very popular with collectors. After all, they offer a great way to attractively display popular coin collections. The explosion of Internet auctions has only helped to increase their recognition and availability. The standard reference on these collectibles is David W. Lange's *Coin Collecting Boards of the 1930s and 1940s*.

In 2008, Whitman released a commemorative Tribute Edition of the Buffalo nickel coin board, and a two-piece set of the 1909–1958 Lincoln cent boards. These are nostalgic but also perfectly functional replicas of the originals.

Commemorative Mini-Folders

In 1990, to commemorate the 50th anniversary of the launch of their coin folders, Whitman Publishing offered a special-edition mini-folder. Its size when closed is a diminutive 3 by 3-3/4 inches; it opens to a width of 9-3/16 inches, not counting the paper flap. The first interior page reads, "Our First Year," and has spaces for the 1940, 1940-D, and 1940-S wheat cents. Page two of the folder reads, "Our 25th Anniversary," and has one space for a 1965 cent. (No mintmarks were used in 1965.) The last page reads, "Our 50th Anniversary," and includes space for the 1990 and 1990-D cents. A flap covering the last page contains text relating the occasion for the collectible and briefly summarizing the history of Whitman coin folders.

These folders were given away at the 1990 ANA Convention in Portland, Oregon. No exact records of the number produced were kept, but it is estimated that 5,000 were made. Most people did not properly care for this little souvenir, and few were preserved in New condition. Today, nice pieces sell for between $15 and $20.

Appendix

COLLECTIBLE
BLUE BOOKS

The Blue Book is not as popular among collectors as the Red Book, so information on this series is less readily available. Collector Rich Mantia notes that Blue Books "are given less respect because they have had traditionally less content and are thinner overall, along with [having] self-covered paper bindings for many issues."[35] Nevertheless, old editions of the *Handbook* offer many of the same attractions as their scarlet sisters: information on changes in the coin market, developments in numismatic research, and insight into the growth and development of coin collecting. They can also be had for a more modest investment, since according to the 2009 Red Book, editions after the 12th are likely to cost the collector only a few dollars, even in Very Fine or better condition.

Collectors should be aware that the dating system for the *Handbook* was not always consistent. Although the second edition initiated the convention of dating the volume one year ahead of copyright date, after publication skipped one year (1944) a hiccup took place, and the fifth and sixth editions (published in 1945 and 1946, respectively) bore no identifying date. The delay between the eighth and ninth editions (published in 1949 and 1951, respectively) adds to the confusion. The table here is provided to clarify the relationship between edition number, stated date, and copyright date for the early Blue Books.

Starting with the 40th edition (1983 cover date), Blue Books were released only in softcover format until the 61st edition. At this time the publishers reintroduced the hardcover format for the *Handbook* while continuing production of the softcover. The hardcover book has been an excellent addition, and I personally believe it to be an improvement over the softcover version. (Naturally, however, I will continue collecting both editions in order to complete my set!)

Blue Book Edition-Year Correspondence

Edition Number	Edition Date	Copyright Date
1st	1942	1942
2nd	1943	1942
3rd	1944	1943
4th	none	1945
5th	none	1946
6th	1948	1947
7th	1949	1948
8th	1950	1949
9th	1952	1951
10th	1953	1952

IMPORTANT BLUE BOOK EDITIONS

The First Edition (1942)

The first *Handbook* was published in 1942 and, unlike its successors, its cover date matched its copyright date. Also unlike all subsequent editions, the first edition featured rounded corners on its cover and pages. It also had a plain (unprinted) spine, which was maintained until the 21st edition (1964). Copies of the first edition are frequently available for purchase. In average condition, examples are priced around $50; near-new copies, with full gilt on their cover, are available for between $100 and $150. These values will most likely increase greatly in the years to come.

There is one known copy of the first edition with R.S. Yeoman's signature on the first insert page. It was sold in 2002 for $175. There is also believed to be at least one copy of the first edition that was printed with its contents bound upside down. Although the condition of this book is unknown, if it were to appear at auction it would bring a healthy price, possibly even three times the value of a regular edition.

The Second Edition (1943)

Whitman released the second edition later in the same year as the first edition. It, too, had a copyright date of 1942, but this time the cover date was 1943. It had a great number of improvements, such as many new photos, including the 1859 Indian Head cent without shield on reverse and the copper-nickel variety. (Interestingly, for the latter, a 1906 cent was shown, but the type was produced from 1860 to 1864, so there should have been two photographs.) Another major change was in the price listings. The valuations of many key dates increased by 50 to 100 percent. Also, the corners on the cover were squared off, unlike the first edition's rounded corners.

Copies of the second edition are valued at approximately $25 in nice condition and $50 to $75 in near-new condition with full gilt. There are surely books in existence that contain Yeoman's signature, and these would probably fetch between $50 and $100, depending upon their condition. Editorial copies would also be worth a nice premium.

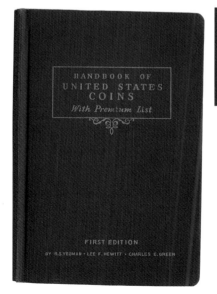

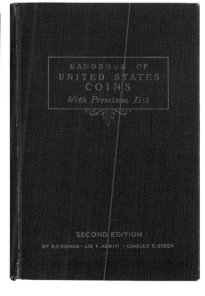

The Third Edition (1944)

The third edition of the *Handbook*, published in 1943 with a cover date of 1944, offers several interesting varieties. Books for this year were issued with covers in several different shades of blue. These ranged from light, like the robin's-egg blue copy shown here, to dark. If you are up for the challenge of finding them, it would be fascinating to see how many different shades the third-edition covers came in!

The Fourth Edition (No Date)

The fourth edition of the *Handbook* was published in 1945, two years after the third edition. Perhaps because of the hiatus, it had no cover date. The fifth edition would reset the series' dating conventions, with a cover date of 1947 and a copyright date of 1946. From this point on, the Blue Book would match the Red Book in bearing a cover date one year ahead of publication.

The fourth-edition *Handbook* was produced in several versions. One is the standard edition, which many collectors consider necessary to a complete set. However, the two varieties are more popular because they are fairly unusual.

For reasons we can only speculate, some fourth-edition Blue Books feature covers that were recycled from the third edition and overstamped "Fourth Edition." The "Collectible Red and Blue Books" essay in the 2009 Red Book observes that these Blue Books (along with the similar overstamped ninth-edition issues) may be "the only 'overdate' books in American numismatic publishing"! It is possible that this was a means of using up extra covers from the previous year's edition; or, as the *Guide Book* posits, the older covers may have been used to correct a binding error. The gilt wears off these covers more readily than for the others, and this reuse of the covers may be the cause. These copies, however, are quite popular.

The other variant of the fourth edition is particularly unusual in that it features a black cover. This was the only edition of the *Handbook* whose cover was a color other than blue. The black Blue Book is very scarce, particularly in Very Fine condition. The copy shown is in near mint to mint condition, with just the faintest rub of the gilt on the upper-left corner of the title.

The Ninth Edition (1952)

The ninth edition was released in 1951 with a cover date of 1952. As they had for the fourth edition, the publishers utilized the previous year's leftover covers. They were overprinted with the words "Ninth Edition." This variation is very scarce and one of the most difficult Blue Books to obtain in nice condition. As a result, even copies of poor quality are very collectible. Any available copies usually sell immediately to knowledgeable collectors.

The 12th Edition (1955)

The early years of the Blue Book were a treasure trove of varieties as Whitman experimented with variations in style and material for the covers. One version of the 12th edition was produced with a regular cover, as shown. However, the publisher also released another version of this edition. The cover was a much darker blue color and textured with a pebble grain. This experimental cover was an improvement on the regular surface in that it did not absorb stains as readily and its shiny finish was easier to clean. There were, however, other problems. The example shown is in mint, never-opened condition, yet it is brittle and chipped. These signs of wear are especially noticeable at the lower left corner near the spine.

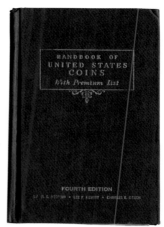

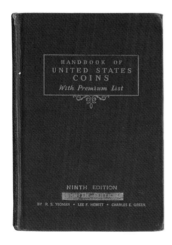
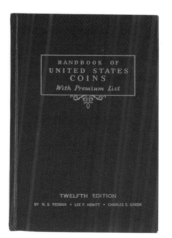
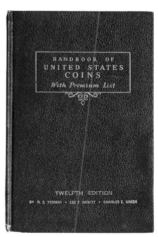

The 19th Edition (1962)

There is a noteworthy error in the 19th edition. The listing of contributors is incorrectly labeled with the notation "Contributors to the Eighteenth Edition." Although this is quite interesting, there is no added value for books with this mistake because all copies were printed this way.

The 45th Edition (1988)

The 45th edition (with a cover date of 1988) was printed with an interesting error. The spine of this book reads, "Handbook of United Stated Coins—45th Edition 1988." The mistake is so slight that the editors should be forgiven for it, but it is definitely supposed to read "States" rather than "Stated." Although the error was eventually caught, production continued without the correction being made because most of the books had already been printed and shipped.

Therefore, there are no special error covers for the 45th edition because every cover from the year was printed with the same mistake. Copies described as having an "unusual error" have been sold for large premiums—but there is nothing unusual about this error, and the book does not have any added value.

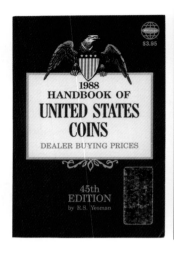

BLUE BOOK VARIETIES AND COLLECTIBLES

There are collectibles and curiosities associated with the Blue Book just as there are for the Red Book. Chapter 8 describes the silver medal rounds that commemorated the Blue Book, but rarer Blue Book collectibles are described in this appendix. (See also chapter 7 for an example of a Blue Book advance copy, another possible collectible.) Editing copies and error editions are always fun to keep an eye out for, and you may also want to consider putting together a set of signed Blue Books. This is at least as challenging as collecting signed copies of the *Guide Book*, particularly because of the many variations of some editions. As shown by this brief study, collecting the *Handbook* can be as interesting as collecting the *Guide Book*, and there are many interesting items to be unearthed during your search.

Editing Copies

Editing copies are usually worth a premium over the value of a regular edition, whether they take the form of interleaved copies or marked-up standard editions. (See chapter 7 for more discussion of editing copies.) Used editing copies, in which a contributor's notes are preserved, allow us to trace revisions that were made during the preparation of each edition. Consider the first of these shown here. From its cover, it appears to be a regular first edition (although in very nice condition). However, opening the book to the flyleaf shows the notation "Priced by Chas. E. Green 8/17/43" in Yeoman's handwriting. In this editing copy, Green made a considerable number of notations, including price changes to the half dollars, silver dollars, commemorative coins, and, particularly, gold coins. The notes he made allow us a glimpse into the past.

Three of the editing copies shown here are seventh-edition books marked up with revisions to be used in the eighth edition. In these we can see the notes Yeoman made as he received each one. In one copy he noted, "Stuart Mosher 4/25/49 checked 5/2/49." A second book includes the notation "David Bullowa 4/25/49," while a third reads "E.A. Parker San Francisco Received 4/30/49 checked 5/2/49."

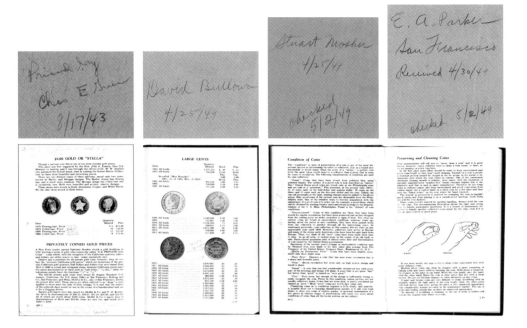

Each of these three contributors concentrated on his area of specialty. Parker repriced many gold coins and Mosher edited the narratives. (Strangely, in spite of Mosher's contributions, he was never listed as a contributor to the *Handbook*.) Bullowa corrected copy everywhere—even noting that there were several incorrect photographs. He realized, for example, that the wrong reverse was shown for the 1825 large cent. Bullowa also pointed out that an illustration paired an 1876 obverse with a With Rays reverse that was only used in 1853! The dedication of Yeoman's contributors is clear from the edits preserved in these copies. As one contributor has stated, Yeoman was gifted in that he was able to find the best people available to contribute to the *Handbook* and the *Guide Book*.

Another editing copy of note is from the 11th edition. This book and a sixth edition of 1948 are the only ones known without any printing on the cover. It also appears to be a test of the printing, prior to approval for production. There are very few notes in the book, and they are mostly concerned with typos. A simple handwriting comparison (between this book and one of the seventh-edition editing copies described) leads me to believe that these notes were recorded by contributor David Bullowa. Editing copies like these also show that, no matter how much care was taken in the preparation, sometimes mistakes survived the editorial process: one note in the 11th-edition editing copy concerns the 1950-S Roosevelt dime, which was mistakenly dated 1050-S. Although the editor noted the correction, the book as published still shows the incorrect date.

Error Editions

Although the errors mentioned earlier in this appendix are not considered error editions because all copies were printed with the mistakes, there have been several error editions produced. Interestingly, there are fewer *Handbook* error editions than *Guide Book* error editions (discussed in chapter 7). Additionally, the errors are rather minor. This may be because fewer books were printed of each edition. Regardless, some mistakes have slipped through production.

The first error illustrated here occurred during the production of the 25th anniversary edition Blue Book (cover date 1968). Some copies feature wrinkles in the cover material (see illustration). This error is as minor as it sounds.

The next example of an error edition *Handbook* is also minor. As can be seen, some copies of the 32nd edition (1975) were produced with miscut pages. The error extends from pages 7 through 10. There is not a hefty premium on books with this error; estimated value in today's market is approximately $10.

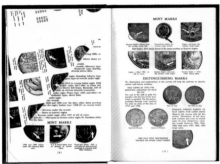

At least one error copy of the softcover 60th edition (2003) exists. This too is a minor error: the plastic cover laminate snagged in production, so that it has ridden up in wrinkles at the bottom of the book. Probably as a result, the ink on the front lower cover shows streaking. Its value is estimated at $10 to $15.

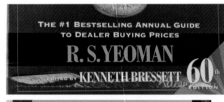

Dennis Tucker has reported a hardcover 2005 Blue Book in which the bar code on the inside front cover was placed incorrectly. Instead of being right side up on the lower left of the inside cover, it is upside down on the upper right of the first endpaper. Tucker also notes that some advance proof copies of the softcover 2007 Blue Book were delivered to Whitman headquarters with misprinted covers, so that the date overlapped the word "Coins" in the title (see illustration). Whitman ordered the printer to destroy all the books with this error cover, and the only copy known to have survived is held in the Whitman Publishing archives in Atlanta. Although it is unlikely that any more will surface, this book is, as Tucker says, "an intriguing example of what *might* be out there waiting for discovery by the keen-eyed collector!"

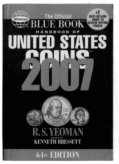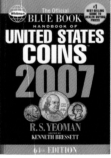

The error on the cover of this 2007-dated *Handbook* is evident when the book is viewed next to a correctly printed copy (right).

Blue Book Collectibles

The most significant collectible items related to the Blue Book are the silver rounds discussed in chapter 8, but at least one other interesting item warrants mention. The *Handbook of United States Type Coins*, a 32-page booklet, was first published in 1943. This short guide, produced by Yeoman with the assistance of A.S. Porter Jr., was inserted as a part of the Whitman coin folder for type coins. It contained no coin values (wholesale or otherwise), but provided descriptions and black-and-white photographs of regular-issue U.S. coins and varieties, from half cents through dollars, along with capsule histories of their production. The original 1943 pamphlet featured a self cover, and it was slightly smaller than the 1948 version, shown here. The 1948 printing was only slightly changed: it was given a blue cover, and featured updated content that included the newly issued Roosevelt dime and Franklin half dollar. These booklets were no longer included in the type coin folder but were sold separately because of popular interest in the subject. Two versions are known, according to Kenneth Bressett, who points out that they can be distinguished by the advertisement on the inside back cover. The earlier version gives a price of 75¢ for the *Hand Book* (*sic*) and $1.50 for the *Guide Book*; the later printing, from circa 1961, shows prices of $1.00 and $1.75, respectively.

The booklet shown here is from the later printing. It is roughly the size of the *Handbook*, at 5-3/4 by 7-1/2 inches. The first version, from 1943, was slightly smaller. The booklet illustrated is in mint condition and estimated to be worth $25 to $35.

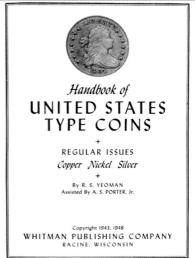

NOTES

1. David T. Alexander, "The 'Red Book' of U.S. Coins," *COINage* 41, no. 4 (April 2005): 68.
2. Quoted in Ed Reiter, "The Numismatist of the Century," December 27, 1999. This article originally appeared in *COINage* magazine but is now available on the PCGS Web site at http://www.pcgs.com/articles/article1783.chtml (accessed July 2, 2008).
3. The interested reader may consult the following articles in the *E-Sylum*, the electronic journal of the Numismatic Bibliomania Society: "Was There a B. Max Mehl–William von Bergen Alliance?" *E-Sylum* 10, no. 21 (May 20, 2007); "More on von Bergen and Max Mehl," *E-Sylum* 10, no. 22 (June 3, 2007); and "On the Business and Death of William von Bergen," *E-Sylum* 10, no. 23 (June 10, 2007). All are accessible through the archives at http://www.coinbooks.org/club_nbs_esylum_v10.html.
4. Quoted in Reiter, "The Numismatist of the Century."
5. Quoted in Reiter, "The Numismatist of the Century."
6. Alexander, "The 'Red Book' of U.S. Coins," 69.
7. R.S. Yeoman, "Introduction," in *Perspectives in Numismatics*, ed. Saul B. Needleman (Chicago Coin Club, 1986). Text available online at http://www.chicagocoinclub.org/projects/PiN/introduction.html.
8. Bowers, "Inside the Red Book," part three, *The Numismatist* 110, no. 1 (January 1997): 57.
9. Yeoman, "Introduction," in *Perspectives in Numismatics*.
10. David W. Lange, *Coin Collecting Boards of the 1930s and 1940s: A Complete History, Catalog and Value Guide* (Pennyboard Press, 2007), 7.
11. R.S. Yeoman, "The Red Book Story—Chapter One: A Retrospective," in *A Guide Book of United States Coins*, 37th edition (Racine, WI: Western Publishing, 1983), 247.
12. Yeoman, "Introduction," in *Perspectives in Numismatics*.
13. Yeoman, "The Red Book Story," 248.
14. Quoted in David Crenshaw, "The Renowned Red Book," *The Numismatist* 118, no. 6 (June 2005): 45.
15. The fourth and fifth editions are the only Blue Books that do not identify themselves by date on the title page. (More recent editions carry the date on the cover.) See the appendix for details.
16. Q. David Bowers posits that this system was used so that the Red Book "would not become obsolete quickly." See his article "Checking out the 'Red Book,'" *The Numismatist* 106, no. 11 (November 1993): 1558.
17. Bowers, "Inside the Red Book," part one, *The Numismatist* 109, no. 11 (November 1996): 1338.
18. Bowers, "Inside the Red Book," part one, 1337.
19. Susan Headley, "The U.S. Coins Red Book: A Good Source of Coin Values and Prices?" About.com review of *A Guide Book of United States Coins*, 61st edition, http://coins.about.com/od/coinvalues/fr/redbook.htm (accessed July 2, 2008).
20. Mike Thorne, "New Red Book Out," *Coins*, November 2005, 54–55.
21. Ed Lesniak, "Collect 'Red Books' for Enjoyment First," *Coin World*, June 19, 1985.
22. Ed Lesniak, "Leave Those Check Marks and Names Alone: Markings in 'Red Book' Add to Volume's Enjoyment," *Coin World*, July 23, 1986.

23. Arlyn G. Sieber, *Pioneer Publisher: The Story of Krause Publications' First 50 Years* (Krause, 2008), 122.

24. Jan A. Nedelka, Amazon.com reader review of *A Guide Book of United States Coins*, 58th edition, October 10, 2004, http://www.amazon.com/review/R2H98SNX F99Q15/ref=cm_cr_rdp_perm.

25. Avid Reader, Amazon.com reader review of *A Guide Book of United States Coins*, 59th edition, March 30, 2006, http://www.amazon.com/review/R2PWVBL0U22OFK/ ref=cm_cr_rdp_perm.

26. Thorne, "New Red Book Out."

27. Crenshaw, "The Renowned Red Book," 47.

28. Crenshaw, "The Renowned Red Book," 48.

29. Crenshaw, "The Renowned Red Book," 46.

30. Yeoman, "The Red Book Story."

31. Ed Lesniak, "Readers Continue to Report Error 'Red Books,'" *Coin World*, April 17, 1985.

32. Crenshaw, "The Renowned Red Book," 46.

33. Michael Moran, *Striking Change: The Great Artistic Collaboration of Theodore Roosevelt and Augustus Saint-Gaudens* (Atlanta: Whitman Publishing, 2008), 113.

34. In his web log of March 18, 2004, Block recalled, "In 1964–5 I had my only honest job since college, working as a writer/editor in the coin supply division of Whitman Publishing, in Racine, Wisconsin" (http://www.lawrenceblock.com/content_ blog.htm; accessed July 2, 2008). Block was one of the associate editors of the *Journal* and worked on numerous coin books, including *Swiss Shooting Talers and Medals*, which he cowrote with Delbert Ray Krause.

35. *E-Sylum* 11, no. 18 (May 4, 2008). http://www.coinbooks.org/club_nbs_esylum_ v11n18.html.

SELECTED BIBLIOGRAPHY

Valuable resources on the history of the *Guide Book of United States Coins* are past editions of the book itself, as well as its reviews in back issues of *The Numismatist*. A selection of other useful references is provided below.

Adelson, Howard L. *The American Numismatic Society: 1858–1958*. New York: American Numismatic Society, 1958.

Alexander, David T. "The 'Red Book' of U.S. Coins." *COINage* 41, no. 4 (April 2005): 68–74.

"Annual Red Book Survey Made." *The Numismatist* 76, no. 6 (June 1963): 800.

Bowers, Q. David. "Inside the Red Book." Pts. 1–5. *The Numismatist* 109, no. 11 (November 1996): 1337–1339; 109, no. 12 (December 1996): 1459–1461; 110, no. 1 (January 1997): 57–59; 110, no. 2 (February 1997): 162–163; 110, no. 3 (March 1997): 281–283.

———. "Your Numismatic Library." Chapter 31 in *The Expert's Guide to Collecting and Investing in Rare Coins*. Atlanta: Whitman Publishing, 2005.

Brake, Cindy. "Opportunities Abound for Numismatic Book Searches." *Coin World* online edition, December 31, 2007. http://www.coinworld.com/news/011408/BW_0114.asp.

Crenshaw, David. "The Renowned Red Book." *The Numismatist* 118, no. 6 (June 2005): 44–48.

Funding Universe. "Western Publishing Group, Inc.: Company History." http://www.fundinguniverse.com/company-histories/Western-Publishing-Group-Inc-Company-History.html.

Harper, David C. "New Leather-Bound Red Book a Great Idea." *Numismatic News*, December 7, 2004.

Lange, David W. *Coin Collecting Boards of the 1930s and 1940s: A Complete History, Catalog and Value Guide*. N.p.: Pennyboard Press, 2007.

Lesniak, Ed. "Collect 'Red Books' for Enjoyment First." *Coin World*, June 19, 1985.

———. "Collectors Seek Knowledge About 'Red Book.'" *Coin World*, July 2, 1986.

———. "Leave Those Check Marks and Names Alone." *Coin World*, July 23, 1986.

———. "New Error 'Red Books' Fill Dealer's Shelves." *Coin World*, December 26, 1984.

———. "Readers Continue to Report Error 'Red Books.'" *Coin World*, April 17, 1985.

———. "Readers' Letters Reveal 'Red Book' Errors." *Coin World*, June 13, 1984.

Marcus, Leonard S. *Golden Legacy: How Golden Books Won Children's Hearts, Changed Publishing Forever, and Became an American Icon Along the Way*. New York: Golden Books, 2007.

Murray, Bill. "Red Book Still an Informative Guide." *Coin World*, October 21, 1987, p. 68.

Numismatic News. "Mr. Red Book." Iola, WI: Numismatic News, n.d., ca. 1978.

Rapsus, Ginger. "The Red Book Story." *The Numismatist* 101, no. 9 (September 1988): 1561–1565.

"The Red Book: Yesterday and Today." In *A Guide Book of United States Coins*, 1st edition commemorative reissue, by R.S. Yeoman, annex pages 16–25. Atlanta: Whitman Publishing, 2006.

Sieber, Arlyn G. *Pioneer Publisher: The Story of Krause Publications' First 50 Years.* Krause Publications, 2001.

Starck, Jeff. "In the 'Red': At 58, *Guide Book* Still Popular, Collectible." *Coin World*, August 31, 2004.

Thorne, Mike. "Coin Collecting in 1952: Those Were the Good Old Days!" *COINage* 38, no. 8 (August 2002): 78–82.

———. "New Red Book Out: 2006 Edition a Good Buy." *Coins*, November 2005, 54–55.

"Whitman Revamps Annual 'Red Book' for 2006 Edition." *Coin World*, July 18, 2005.

Yeoman, R.S. "The Red Book Story—Chapter One: A Retrospective." In *A Guide Book of United States Coins*, 37th edition, 247–252. Racine, WI: Western Publishing, 1983.

Yeoman, R.S., and Paul M. Green. "Red Book Keeps Place on Hobby's Best-Seller List." *Numismatic News*, March 24, 1987.

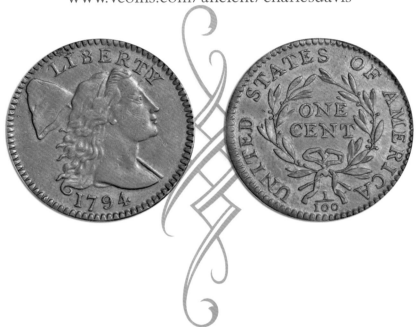

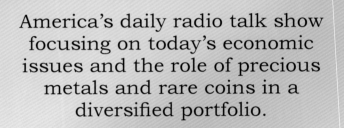